Africa and Israel:
Relations in Perspective

Studies in International Politics

Leonard Davis Institute for International Relations
The Hebrew University, Jerusalem

Africa and Israel: Relations in Perspective, Olusola Ojo

The Illusion of Deterrence: The Roosevelt Presidency and the Origins of the Pacific War, Abraham Ben-Zvi

Europe's Middle East Dilemma: The Quest for a Unified Stance, Ilan Greilsammer and Joseph Weiler

Dynamics of Dependence: U.S.-Israeli Relations, Gabriel Sheffer, ed.

Jordan's Palestinian Challenge, 1948–1983: A Political History, Clinton Bailey

STUDIES IN INTERNATIONAL POLITICS
LEONARD DAVIS INSTITUTE FOR INTERNATIONAL RELATIONS
THE HEBREW UNIVERSITY, JERUSALEM

Africa and Israel:
Relations in Perspective

Olusola Ojo

Westview Press
BOULDER & LONDON

Studies in International Politics, Leonard Davis Institute for International Relations, The Hebrew University, Jerusalem

Published in 1988 in the United States of America by Westview Press, Inc., 5500 Central Avenue, Boulder, Colorado 80301, and in the United Kingdom by Westview Press, Inc., 13 Brunswick Centre, London WC1N 1AF, England

Library of Congress Catalog Card Number: 88-28215
ISBN: 0-8133-7582-7

Printed and bound in the United States of America

∞ The paper used in this publication meets the requirements of the American National Standard for Permanence of Paper for Printed Library Materials Z39.48-1984.

10   9   8   7   6   5   4   3   2   1

Contents

List of Tables. ix
List of Abbreviations. xi
Preface. xiii

1   INTRODUCTION.   1

2   FOUNDATION AND GROWTH OF
    RELATIONS, 1958–1969.   7
    The Israeli Initiative   8
    Technical Assistance Programs. 18
    Military Assistance. 20
    Economic Relations 22
    Relations at the Multilateral Level. 24

3   THE OCTOBER 1973 WAR
    AND AFRO-ISRAELI RELATIONS. 33

4   THE ERA OF NON-FORMAL
    RELATIONS, 1973–1978 55
    Multilateral Relations 58
    Bilateral Relations. 69

5   THE PERIOD OF GRADUAL
    RAPPROCHEMENT, 1979–1985. 85
    Africa's Reactions to Camp David
        and the Peace Treaty. 86
    The Beginnings of Change 91
    Expansion of Afro-Israeli Relations 93

6 ISRAEL AND SOUTH AFRICA 111
     Historical Links 111
     The Early Years. 114
     The Era of Quiet Normalization of Relations 117
     The October 1973 War. 121
     Economic Relations . . . . : 125
     Military Cooperation 128

7 NIGERIA AND ISRAEL. 139
     The Nigerian Civil War 144
     The October 1973 War. 148
     The Egyptian-Israeli Camp David Accords 152

8 CONCLUSIONS. 163
     Policy Options and Prospects. 164

Index 171

Tables

2.1 Afro-Israeli diplomatic representation, 1970................. 17
2.2 Cooperation agreements between African states and Israel..... 19
2.3 Months spent by Israeli experts abroad by continent and
field of activity, 1968–1970............................... 20
2.4 African trainees in Israel in 1969........................... 21
2.5 Loans from Israel to Africa, 1958–1966...................... 22
2.6 Africa's trade with Israel, 1960–1969....................... 23

3.1 Africa's break of diplomatic relations with Israel.............. 35
3.2 Africa's trade with Israel, 1969–1972....................... 37
3.3 Selected African countries' trade with Israel, 1970–1973....... 37

4.1 Voting record of selected African states on selected resolutions
on the Middle East, 30th session of UN General Assembly,
1975.. 64
4.2 Voting record of selected African states on selected resolutions
on the Middle East, 31st session of UN General Assembly,
1976.. 70
4.3 Voting record of selected African states on selected resolutions
on the Middle East, 32nd session of UN General Assembly,
1977.. 71
4.4 Israeli electronic exports to selected African countries,
1977–1978... 76
4.5 Israel's trade with Africa, 1973–1978....................... 79

5.1 Africa's trade with Israel, 1979–1982....................... 104

6.1 Israel's trade with South Africa, 1967–1973................. 119
6.2 Israel's trade with South Africa, 1973–1984................. 127

7.1 Nigeria's trade with Israel, 1973–1984..................... 153

Abbreviations

AG	Action Group
AHG	Assembly of Heads of State and Government (OAU)
ANC	African National Congress
BADEA	Arab Bank for African Development
CAR	Central African Republic
ECA	Economic Commission for Africa (UN)
EEC	European Economic Community
ELF	Eritrean Liberation Front
FAO	Food and Agricultural Organization (UN)
FLNA	National Front for the Liberation of Angola
FRELIMO	Front for the Liberation of Mozambique
FROLINAT	National Front for the Liberation of Chad
IAI	Israel Aircraft Industries
ILO	International Labor Organization (UN)
IMF	International Monetary Fund
ISCOR	Iron and Steel Corporation (South Africa)
ITU	International Telecommunication Union
MPLA	Popular Movement for the Liberation of Angola
NATO	North Atlantic Treaty Organization
NCNC	National Council of Nigerian Citizens
NIEO	New International Economic Order
NPC	Northern People's Party
NPN	National Party of Nigeria
NPP	Nigerian People's Party
OAU	Organization of African Unity
OPEC	Organization of Oil Producing and Exporting Countries
PFLP	Popular Front for the Liberation of Palestine
PLO	Palestine Liberation Organization
SWAPO	South West Africa People's Organization
UNDP	United Nations Development Program
UNESCO	United Nations Educational, Scientific, and Cultural Organization

UNIFIL	United Nations Interim Force in Lebanon
UNITA	Union for the Total Liberation of Angola
UPGA	United Progressive Grand Alliance
UPN	Unity Party of Nigeria
WHO	World Health Organization (UN)

Preface

Academic interest in Africa's relations with Israel has considerably declined since the African states' almost total break of diplomatic relations with Israel in 1973. Yet despite the diplomatic rupture, political, economic, and other forms of transnational relations between Africa and Israel have continued to exist and, in many cases, to grow. Five African states—Cameroun, Côte d'Ivoire, Liberia, Togo, and Zaire—have since reestablished diplomatic ties, bringing to eight the number of black African states having diplomatic relations with Israel. Israel maintains "interest offices" in more countries.

This study is an examination of Africa's relations with Israel since about 1960. Its organization follows the basic chronology of the relationship itself, with each of the first four chapters after the introduction devoted to an analysis of the various themes of the relationship. The next two chapters are case studies on Israel's relations with South Africa and Nigeria, respectively. The concluding chapter is both an overview of past and contemporary relations and an examination of the controversial issue of the resumption of ties with Israel.

Many people and institutions have directly and indirectly contributed to this book. I would particularly like to thank the University of Ife, Ile-Ife, for granting me sabbatical leave to complete the project and the Hebrew University of Jerusalem's Harry S Truman Institute for the Advancement of Peace for providing a base and support for the research. I am grateful to Professor Harold Schiffrin, Dr. Edy Kaufman, Ms. Dalia Shemer, Ms. Cecil Panzer, and the entire administrative and library staff of the Truman Institute, Dr. Gabriel Sheffer of the Leonard Davis Institute for International Relations, and Professor Marion Mushkat of the Political Science Department of Tel Aviv University for their encouragement and other forms of assistance during my stay in Israel. I would also like to express my appreciation to Dr. Naomi Chazan and Ambassador H. Aynor of the Truman Institute and Dr. Leopold Laufer of the Leonard Davis Institute for their friendship and their willingness to exchange ideas and information on the subject, and for Naomi's and Leopold's painstaking criticism of the draft. I would also like to thank Dov Sibony for his research assistance while at the Truman Institute.

I am also grateful to the officials of the Israeli and Nigerian foreign affairs ministries and other African officials at the OAU and UN who generously shared their views on the subject and sometimes provided information which otherwise would have been unavailable to me. Many of the interviews and discussions were conducted off-the-record. My special thanks also go to Captain Sagi of Zim Israel Navigation Company, Jacob Levav and Yaakov Shur of Solel Boneh Company, Yehuda Paz of the Histadrut's Afro-Asian Institute in Tel Aviv, Yaacov Vidislavski of the Settlement Study Center, Rehovot, and to Mrs. Mary Sennerman and Fannette Modek of the Mount Carmel International Training Center for Community Services in Haifa. Responsibility for the views expressed in this book, nonetheless, remains entirely mine.

I owe a debt of gratitude to my family for their support and encouragement and for coping with my long absence from home in the course of my research for this book.

Olusola Ojo
University of Ife

ONE

Introduction

It is sometimes assumed that formal diplomatic relations are a precondition for the establishment, maintenance, and growth of other bilateral ties between states. The severing of such diplomatic relations is often taken as heralding the simultaneous curtailment, or even abandonment, of other bilateral links. Consequently many casual observers of Afro-Israeli relations have assumed that the massive break of diplomatic ties between most of Africa and Israel in 1973 ended all contacts between the two.

However, although all but three (four until 1976) black African states severed diplomatic ties with Israel, economic relations did not suffer from Israel's political setback in Africa. In fact, commercial and economic links have expanded rapidly. Trade has doubled and in some cases even tripled and quadrupled, particularly as regards the larger or more economically viable states like Cameroun, Côte d'Ivoire, Gabon, Ghana, Kenya, and Nigeria. With the exception of Angola, Benin, Congo, and Guinea (before the 1980s), which have pursued "radical" foreign policies; of Chad, because of the breakdown of internal political order as a result of the civil war; and of Mali and Niger, which are very close to the Arab states for Islamic considerations, Israel has continued economic relations with other African states as well. These were at a lower volume than with the first group of states mentioned, but because of economic rather than political reasons.

This lack of correlation between economic and political relations was not entirely new, although it became particularly pronounced with the absence of diplomatic relations. Even in the days of formal diplomatic contacts, Israeli economic and other non-formal ties did not entirely reflect the state of political relations. This was the case with the black African members of the "Casablanca group of states" after the

1

1961 Casablanca resolution that denounced Israel. Nor did the level of Israel's non-formal contacts decline with the gradual deterioration of political relations between 1970 and 1973. In fact, Israel's exports to Africa not only increased by almost 100 percent between 1967 and 1972, but Israel also started for the first time to record a favorable balance in its trade with Africa precisely when the state of political relations began to be unstable.

With the exit of the diplomats, Israel quietly seized on the extensive non-formal ties it had developed with Africa in the preceding one and one-half decades to develop its economic relations with the continent. The fact that these were one aspect of their contacts that had been mutually beneficial facilitated the development. The positive results of Israeli aid projects had contributed to African goodwill toward Israel and, perhaps more significantly, to a reputation for effective work and quality manufactured products. Besides, severing diplomatic ties need not entail any material loss, which would not have been the case if economic contacts had been severed. Moreover, it was possible to quietly continue to improve private economic relations without the publicity and consequent embarrassment that may be attendant on political and diplomatic ties.

The break of diplomatic ties per se did not lead to a total political blackout of Israel in Africa. Indeed, since 1973 discrete political contacts have been maintained and military assistance, arms sales, and technical cooperation have continued with some countries. The Egyptian-Israeli peace treaty provided an opportunity to formalize these contacts and a basis for a mutual review of relations. The changed political environment, and the worsening economic situation in Africa from the late 1970s, facilitated this reassessment.

Unlike in the early 1970s, when considerations of "African unity," the need for Third World solidarity, and Israel's identification with the West—and particularly the United States—had a negative effect on Israel's image in Africa, the political environment of the late 1970s and 1980s was decidedly different. Africa is now more divided than in the early 1970s, and unlike then, the "Israeli factor" is conspicuously absent as a cause. Ideological differences have become more pronounced, and indeed more important, than the fact of "continental unity" as a determinant of Africa's foreign relations. Chad, Western Sahara, and the history of the Organization of African Unity (OAU) in the last few years provide evidence of this. Closely related to the growing importance of ideological differences is the fact that, unlike in the early 1970s, close ties with the West, and with the United States in particular, are no longer viewed as a negative political factor in Africa. Indeed, the worsening economic situation of the African states, exacerbated by drought and famine on a scale hitherto unknown, has led to a determined effort by many African leaders to cultivate the goodwill and sympathy of the West. And, because of the powerful Jewish lobby in the United States, Israel is perceived by many African states as being in a good position to intercede with the American administration for more generous aid.

Moreover, by the late 1970s the warm relations between Africa and the Arab world, which developed out of the political support Africa had provided in 1973 by breaking diplomatic ties with Israel, had become very cool. Africa's refusal to toe the line with respect to Egypt's peace agreement with Israel led to further mutual disenchantment. Israel, on the other hand, was eager to capitalize on the peace treaty to work its way back to Africa. However, there were no sustained Israeli diplomatic moves to that effect until 1981. These efforts have not resulted in any dramatic diplomatic breakthroughs for Israel. Still, although the hope that the peace treaty would lead to a general renewal of formal ties has remained largely unfulfilled, as only Cameroun, Côte d'Ivoire, Liberia, Togo, and Zaire have done so, relations have nonetheless shown marked improvement.

A number of explanations can be offered for the present state of Afro-Israeli relations. First, there has been a significant change in the political stance of African states toward the Middle East. Africa's initial involvement was influenced by Egypt's membership in the African system, but emphasis has decidedly shifted to concern for the plight of the Palestinians. Even before the Camp David Accords, OAU resolutions tended to lay as much stress on the need for Israel to withdraw from Egyptian territory and other Arab territories captured in 1967 as on the need for the recognition and implementation of the "inalienable rights of the Palestinian people." The overwhelming Arab opposition to the Camp David Accords and the peace treaty, partly for what the Arabs regard as the inadequacies of the agreements with regard to Palestinian rights, has meant a continuation of the African position. Furthermore, the OAU has made the problem of political and territorial concessions to the Palestinians the crux of the Arab-Israeli conflict. Despite the treaty and the establishment of formal relations between Egypt and Israel, Egypt has continued to encourage that attitude.

Second, Africa's dependence on Arab aid has often been advanced as a deterrent to its renewed diplomatic contact with Israel. The Arab figure of over seven billion dollars in aid to black Africa since 1973 is often cited as an indication of the massive use of Arab petrodollars in the service of the Palestinian cause in Africa. Overt threats to deprive Africa of that aid should it review its Middle East policy are therefore seen to have kept Africa in line.

However, such an argument suffers important limitations. It seems an oversimplified analysis of Africa's foreign relations. While one cannot dismiss the claim that the possibility of receiving Arab aid will be a constant factor in the formulation of some African states' Middle East policy, Arab aid as well as its impact have been grossly exaggerated. The figures are very much open to dispute; and what is considered Arab aid has not amounted to much more than mere commitment for many states. The acute lag between Arab aid commitment and disbursement brings the alleged primacy of Arab aid as the determinant of Afro-Israeli relations into serious question. Indeed, many of the recipients of Arab aid have received no more than a few million dollars for a handful of projects.[1]

The aid linkage explanation also grossly underrates the autonomy of African states. There are quite a few African states, like Côte d'Ivoire and Nigeria, which are not beneficiaries of Arab aid but which nonetheless have maintained the diplomatic boycott of Israel (Côte d'Ivoire only until 1986).[2] It should also be noted that, prior to 1982, Zaire was, at least on paper, the third largest recipient of Arab aid in Africa—yet the loss of Arab assistance did not deter it from resuming relations with Israel. Arab aid as a monofactoral explanation is therefore not very convincing.

Third, Israeli-South African links have become a complicating factor in Afro-Israeli relations. Significant African opinion regards these links as seriously harming the cause of African liberation. The ousted Nigerian president, Shagari, made this clear:

> We acted as Africans because of Israel's continued cooperation with racist South Africa. Israel has further intensified this cooperation with South Africa and we, as Africans, have continued to be horrified by this attitude. So it is not just the question of Israel's quarrel with the Arabs, it has another quarrel with Africa as well. We just cannot ignore Israel's continued strong and growing friendship with an enemy.[3]

The same sentiments were echoed by the former Nigerian head of state.

In a wide-ranging review of the country's foreign policy in December 1984, General Buhari justified Africa's continued diplomatic isolation of Israel:

> The overwhelming evidence of Israeli military, nuclear and economic collaboration with the apartheid regime in South Africa is good ground to believe that the underlying reason for which Nigeria severed diplomatic relations with Israel in the first instance is still relevant. It is inconceivable that a people who have themselves been victims of racial horror and genocide can turn round to provide instruments of death and repression to a regime dedicated to the destructive principle of racial superiority. . . . If Israel wishes to have full diplomatic relations with Nigeria restored, she must review her present collaboration with South Africa.[4]

Finally, some African states favor the status quo and do not believe they are worse off for it. These countries have continued to maintain economic and commercial ties with Israel and to send students for training in Israeli institutions despite the absence of formal diplomatic relations. Moreover, they have not been blacklisted by Arab aid agencies.

This study is an examination of the complexities of Afro-Israeli relations. Its organization follows the basic chronology of the relationship, with the next four chapters devoted to each of the four phases of that relationship. Chapters 2 and 3 examine relations from about 1958, when Israel launched its diplomatic initiative in Africa, to 1973, when most African states severed their diplomatic ties. The next two chapters investigate post-1973 ties. Chapters 6 and 7 are case studies, the former examining Israeli-South African relations as these have constituted one of the major complicating factors in contemporary Afro-Israeli relations. Chapter 7 is a study of Israel's ties with the largest and most important African country, namely, Nigeria, and reflects the degree of complexity in Afro-Israeli ties. The Arab-Israeli conflict has become politically internalized within African countries; thus for Nigeria, as for many African states, the state of bilateral relations with Israel is no longer primarily determined by what happens in the Middle East but by internal political factors. The concluding chapter examines the issue of the resumption of ties with Israel.

NOTES

1. For a breakdown of total Arab aid between 1975 and 1982 by countries, see Arab Bank for African Development (BADEA), *Annual Report*, 1985, p. 84.

2. Although there is a published Arab figure of $54.5 million in aid to Côte d'Ivoire between 1975 and 1982, President Houphouët-Boigny stated categorically in October 1983 that his country had not received a dollar in Arab aid. See *Jeune Afrique*, 12 October 1983, p. 57.

3. *Africa Now*, November 1984, p. 58.

4. *West Africa*, 17 December 1984, pp. 2565–2566.

TWO

Foundation and Growth of Relations, 1958-1969

Despite the long-standing Zionist interest in the continent,[1] there was virtually no Israeli presence in Africa until the late 1950s. Until 1985 there was a significant Black Jewish population in Ethiopia, and the former Ethiopian monarch took his historical links with biblical King Solomon very seriously. (Indeed, the Ethiopian monarchy traced its royal legitimacy to the union of the Queen of Sheba and King Solomon.) Moreover, two African countries had also participated in the United Nations action that led to the creation of the State of Israel (Liberia voted for, and Ethiopia abstained on, the resolution that gave birth to the state). There was also a strong personal friendship with, and affection for, Israel by the late President William Tubman of Liberia.[2] But overall, the low Israeli profile was hardly surprising. Israeli diplomacy in the first decade of the state's existence was preoccupied with the superpowers and Europe. Israel's immediate needs, in view of its uncompromisingly hostile regional environment, were security and economic survival. The attainment of these twin objectives was perceived by Israeli leaders to depend on the degree of support from the major powers. Besides, Israel was effectively cut off from Africa by the Egyptian naval blockade of the Straits of Tiran. As a result, Africa, which in any case was still largely a colonial dependency, and the Third World generally, figured marginally in the foreign policy of Israel.

This chapter investigates the factors that led to both a change in Israel's attitude toward Africa and a favorable African response. It further examines the growth of Afro-Israeli relations in the first decade of Africa's independence.

7

THE ISRAELI INITIATIVE

The exclusion of Israel from the Afro-Asian Conference in Bandung in 1955 and from the Second International Socialist Conference in New Delhi in 1956 as a result of Arab pressure shocked the Israelis. Not only was it excluded from Bandung, it was also branded as a bridgehead of Western colonialism. Unwanted by its immediate neighbors, effectively isolated from its own subregion in Asia, being a target of vitriolic condemnations by the Soviet bloc countries, and sometimes even unsure of the support of the United States, Israel did not want to be further isolated in Africa. The need to get out of the diplomatic isolation into which Arab diplomacy had driven her forced Israel to evaluate her policy (or non-policy) toward Africa in particular, and the Third World in general.[3]

However, as Samuel Decalo observes: "Israel's quest for an international mission had to await the normalisation of the power-status in the Middle East and the recession of the Arab threat, both apparent in the years following the Sinai campaign."[4] The Sinai campaign provided the needed opportunities to open up to Africa. For the first time, Israel had direct access to the Red Sea and the Indian Ocean through the Gulf of Aqaba: the gate to the south for communication with Africa was thus opened. That in itself heightened the importance of Africa in the perception of Israeli leaders. She needed the friendly disposition of East African states to secure free navigation in the Red Sea.[5] In other words, relations with Africa became politically and strategically important.

Besides, Africa's friendship could be important not just in counteracting Arab pressure, but also in gaining support for Israel's position in the Middle East. Israeli foreign policy elites even believed that not only would African support thwart Arab efforts to isolate her in international forums, but the sheer weight of diplomatic opinion could actually encourage the Arabs to settle peacefully with her. As Leopold Laufer noted: "In pre-1967 days, it was fashionable in Israel to speculate that 'the road to Cairo may lead through Africa,' that is, that the African leaders friendly to both Israel and the Arabs might convince Egypt and, through Egypt, all the Arabs, to opt for co-existence."[6]

The motive was not only political, it had economic components as well. Israel was finding it increasingly difficult to compete in the European Common Market, where despite certain arrangements she still faced problems of tariffs, quotas, etc. She could not trade with her neighbors and she was only able to count on the American market to a limited extent and only for a limited list of products. Close contacts with Africa, therefore, could bring economic advantages. Trade with Africa could ensure a valuable and expanding market for Israeli exports as well as a means of securing raw materials for her industries. It could thus frustrate the Arab boycott policy, which attempted to isolate Israel economically.[7]

The prospects were particularly good. The process of decolonization was accelerating. And as the Israeli newspaper *Ha'aretz* observed: "The Africans are not powerful . . . but their voices are heard in the world and their votes in international institutions are equal in value to those of more powerful nations."[8]

More significantly, the black African states had no "traditional positions" on the Middle East conflict. Neither did they hold any animosities toward the Jews or Israel. Rather it was the Arabs who had a not very favorable image in many parts of Africa, particularly in Central and Eastern Africa, as a result of the Arab slave expeditions in the region until the imposition of colonial rule. The scale and ruthlessness of the Arab slave trade ensured that the memory would not easily be wiped out. As late as the mid-nineteenth century, between 40,000 and 50,000 African slaves passed through Zanzibar annually. Sultans Said and Barghash perfected the capture and sale of slaves to a smoothly efficient commercial transaction and their "long-gowned agents, holding high the Sultan's red flags, ruthlessly roamed the African forest in pursuit of ever-thinning numbers of natives who kept fleeing further inland."[9] The violent overthrow of Arab hegemony on the island of Zanzibar in 1964, less than a month after the termination of British colonial rule over the island, vividly demonstrated the extent of African resentment of the Arabs in contemporary times.[10]

Conversely, many Africans were sympathetic to the plight of the Jews. Maurice Yameogo, the former president of Upper Volta (now Burkina Faso), claimed that everyone

> knows that together with the Africans, the Jews constitute what the vanity and egoism of certain people call the inferior races, the accursed races, the contemptible, the despised. It is just therefore, that the pariahs of the world should regain the land which was the cradle and grave of their fathers and prove that man is equal to man.[11]

The contacts that had been made by Israelis with African leaders through the socialist and labor movements provided an opportunity for, and a base from which to launch, the new Israeli policy in Africa. It was, for example, at the First Session of the Asian Socialist Conference that Moshe Sharett, then Israel's foreign minister, met a number of participating trade union leaders from Ghana (then the Gold Coast). Fruitful future relationships with Ghana developed from that contact.[12]

Israeli diplomatic initiatives were launched in 1956, with the setting up of the first consulate general in Ethiopia (although she had maintained an honorary consul in Liberia since the early 1950s). Soon after, another consulate was established in Accra, Ghana. This was upgraded to an embassy a year later upon Ghana's independence in March 1957. In September of the same year another embassy was set up in Liberia.

Israel also began to host a stream of African visitors, many of whom were to take the reins of their countries' governments upon independence. The early visitors included trade unionists from Ghana, Nigeria, Northern Rhodesia (Zambia), and Upper Volta, a ministerial delegation from Western Nigeria, and youth and trade union leaders from East Africa and Guinea.[13]

The first All-African Peoples Conference held in Ghana in 1958 provided the first real opportunity for Israel to establish contact with many future African leaders. Foreign Minister Golda Meir, who was on an official visit to Ghana, met in a special session with the participants. Several private meetings were also held.[14]

Such contacts often led to requests for Israeli assistance, and these requests were quickly met. In fact, Israel believed that an effective way of winning the friendship of the new African states was by identifying with their social and economic development through the offer of technical assistance. The striking similarities between certain conditions in Africa and Israel, as well as Israel's experience in tackling these very problems, made it easier for Israel to respond positively to African requests. For example, Israel suffers from many of the natural shortcomings which plague Africa: "a hot climate, a tendency to soil erosion, drought, and an unequal distribution of rain throughout the year. There is also a diversity of agricultural cultures, some belonging to cold climates and others to tropical ones."[15]

There is also a psychological dimension to Israel's assistance to Africa and other developing countries. Since its creation, Israel has been a recipient of foreign assistance. The country, therefore, derives great satisfaction from participating in assistance programs to other countries as well.

There were, in addition, strong ideological and humanitarian underpinnings. Golda Meir, the main force behind active Israeli involvement in Africa in the late 1950s and early 1960s, was impressed by the human dimension of African problems. Her West African tour of February and March 1958 exposed her to the "African condition." She saw many parallels between the situation in Africa and that in Israel during her early years there, and she believed Israel should assist. She saw this as a personal and moral challenge, in keeping with her own socialist approach. Assistance to Africa and the Third World became an obligation.[16] When submitting her ministry's 1961/62 budget to the Knesset (the Israeli Parliament), for example, she devoted the equivalent of 165 newspaper column lines to Africa, 86 to Asia, and 22 to Latin America.[17] Again, in her 1963 address to the Knesset she stressed that "Israel has always assumed, is assuming and will continue in the future to assume, an active role in every operation and every objective meant to consummate the restoration of human and national dignity to once-downtrodden peoples in Africa and in every place on earth."[18]

It is not being suggested that humanitarian considerations alone explain Israel's assistance to Africa. Political, economic, and humanitarian factors combined to create the Israeli phenomenon in Africa in the 1950s and early 1960s. As an Israeli foreign ministry publication explains, the "aim is, very generally, to achieve a proper blend, first of altruistic aspirations—the wish to help, and second, of considerations of our own legitimate advantage—gaining friends, furthering political information, and advancing economic objectives."[19]

The Israeli willingness was complemented by African receptiveness. Many African leaders were fascinated by the "Israeli miracle." Israel's self-transformation into an industrial state and the way it turned its desert into flourishing, productive agricultural land in a very short time was an inspiration to African leaders who were eager to fulfill the high economic expectations of independence. They believed the Israeli model could help transform their rural subsistence economies into industrial ones. President Houphouët-Boigny of Côte d'Ivoire expressed the sentiments of most of his contemporaries:

> This dispersed people which has suffered so much throughout the ages has foregathered once again in the ancient land which it found devastated, neglected, infested with mosquitos and a breeding-ground for every conceivable disease. Without losing heart in the face of implacable nature and more than hostile

neighbours, Israel took up its task courageously, and, after less than ten years, it can be considered a modern state. We must follow its path.[20]

Similar sentiments were expressed by Dr. J.G. Kiano, Kenya's Minister of Commerce and Industry:

Israel is both an inspiration and a challenge to us. She is an inspiration because we have a manifest proof that the many problems facing us faced Israel also at the declaration of her independence and now they are being dealt with effectively and most rapidly. Israel is a challenge because we who hold the reins of our government must do likewise. Our political freedom must be buttressed by economic prosperity.[21]

Furthermore, the experience of Israel in welding a mosaic of immigrant groups into a modern nation seemed to many African leaders a promising precedent for their own attempt to forge national consciousness among the ethnic and tribal conglomerates that make up the African states. The late President Jomo Kenyatta affirmed: "You [Israelis] have built a nation with Jews coming from all the corners of the world; we want to build a unified Kenya composed of a multitude of tribes joined together through *Harambee* [working together]."[22]

The Africans were also fascinated by such Israeli institutions as Gadna, Nahal, and the kibbutz. Gadna is a voluntary organization for teenagers drawn from secondary schools, youth groups, and immigrant villages. It primarily trains youngsters for pioneering and defense, and it fosters the study of specialized military and technical trades. Its volunteers have built roads, aided immigrants, and fortified frontier villages. Nahal, on the other hand, is an integral part of the army. It was formed after the establishment of the State of Israel for Gadna graduates who intended to join old settlements or establish new ones. At the time, defense and land reclamation were the country's priorities, and Nahal was formed to allow young people to fulfill the terms of their military service while training in modern agriculture and settling new communal settlements. These institutions attracted the attention of African leaders who were faced with the difficult task of combining vocational training with rural development and containing the influx of school dropouts to the towns, as well as instilling the value of manual and agrarian labor in young people.[23]

Besides, Israel appealed ideologically to most of the first generation of post-independence black African leaders. Many of them espoused some form of socialism and wanted to develop along socialist lines; but they did not want to align, or be thought to be aligned, with Soviet-bloc countries in those days when Cold War tensions were still very high. Hence many of them took pains to point to the distinctive character of their own brand of socialism, which they often referred to as African socialism. Israel's combination of a strong private and public economy, a well-developed cooperative sector including a collective economy with various levels of cooperation, and a powerful trade union appealed to both African leaders and intellectuals. Many of them saw in Israeli institutions such as the kibbutz, the moshav, and the cooperatives the right model for their own development. President Dacko of the Central African Republic (CAR) praised Israel for achieving a solution that could only be derived from the Soviet Union, but "without the big shoe."[24] Israel was seen as an exemplary but small country that could not impose any neocolonial domination on the African states.

The personal experiences and the positive image of Israel gained by the first stream of African visitors stimulated subsequent African interest. For example, after a six-week seminar for leaders of the International Union of Socialist Youth held in Israel in 1959, there were requests from African leaders for Israel to establish prototypes of some of the Israeli institutions seen by the participants. A Gadna delegation visited Ghana, Liberia, and Nigeria soon after the seminar. On one of his visits, John Tettegah, the secretary-general of Ghana's Trade Union Congress, asserted that Israel had given him "more in eight days than I could obtain from two years in a British university."[25]

In addition, Israeli assistance was believed to be relatively cheaper than similar aid from the West. The Ophthalmological Center in Monrovia, which the Israelis set up at a cost of $40,000—as against $300,000 earlier estimated by American experts—was a classic example.[26] What was equally important, Israeli aid was very fast and easy to get, unlike aid from other sources. It sometimes took less than three days between the request for, and the arrival of, experts. And the greater willingness of the Israelis to let the Africans dictate the nature of the assistance facilitated a hospitable reception. Moreover, the attitudes of the first generation of Israeli aid workers in Africa were very impressive. They were sensitive to African feelings, always willing to improvise and, unlike most Europeans with whom Africans have had contacts, the Israelis were always willing to engage in manual labor, and to work and live in rural areas.[27] Stuart Schaar observes: "Where other donors have been hesitant to venture, Israel has often been willing to try out new things and to run the risk of blundering, in a way reminiscent of the hit-or-miss schemes that were experimented with in its own early days of the settlement in Palestine."[28]

There were, of course, other factors which contributed to the development of Afro-Israeli relations in the early years. The role played by France, especially in francophone Africa, cannot be under-estimated. Many of the French leaders had been either former pupils or parliamentary colleagues (some were ministers in the government) of Leon Blum, a founding member of the Socialist Party in France and one of the country's first post-World War II prime ministers. Leon Blum was a staunch Zionist, and he used his very close friendships with such leaders as Houphouët-Boigny, Leopold Senghor, Modibo Keita, and Dacko, among others, to stimulate these leaders' interest in Israel.[29]

The rivalry for continental leadership between President Kwame Nkrumah of Ghana and President Abdel Nasser of Egypt also helped Israel. Nkrumah played an important role in linking African national-ists with Israeli officials. He was encouraged by the Ghanaian pan-Africanist George Padmore, "who felt profound sympathy for the Jews, and who had little use for Nasser, whom he considered to be a tool of the Russians."[30]

Although religious considerations were not dominant in the foreign policies of black African states throughout the 1960s, most African Christians were, nevertheless, attracted to Israel. They were familiar with stories of biblical Israel; indeed, many of them, ignorant of the fact that Judaism rather than Christianity is Israel's state reli-gion, regarded the creation of Israel as a fulfillment of biblical proph-ecy. From an account by an Israeli of an experience with a Ghanaian delegation led by the future foreign minister of Ghana, Kojo Botsio:

> As soon as they arrived [at the Jordan River] they took off their gaily-coloured Kente cloths and dipped merrily in the holy wa-ters of the river they had known about all their lives. Now they were standing where Christ had stood—chanting hymns. Love of the Bible and veneration for Jerusalem and the Holy Land among African Christians was to be one of the main elements of easy mutual understanding.[31]

The Arab states were, expectedly, opposed to Afro-Israeli ties. But their sometimes unsophisticated tactics in dissuading Africans from developing ties with Israel produced negative effects, as they only pushed many African states further into the Israeli orbit. Their efforts were largely uncoordinated, and the extension of their own inter-Arab rivalry into Africa sometimes took precedence over their goal of expelling Israel from the continent. Their inability and unwillingness to provide an alternative to Israeli assistance in African countries, as well as their attempts to intimidate and blackmail a number of states, merely reinforced traditional African resentment of Arabs in many countries. President Tombalbaye of Chad bitterly accused the Arabs of fomenting instability in his country because of his ties with Israel.[32] He stressed that he would strongly resist any attempt to embroil Chad in the Arab-Israeli conflict or to turn Chad into "a tool of any country which is interested in exploiting this dispute for its own interests." In Nigeria the "undiplomatic" actions of Arab embassies and those of the wives of Arab ambassadors in Lagos during Golda Meir's visit in 1964 received strong condemnation by the Nigerian government and press.[33]

Many African states contain Islamic majorities or "minorities of sufficient strength and numbers to exert strong pressures on the political system."[34] But the Arab attempt to exploit this Islamic affinity produced very limited results. They often presented the Arab-Israeli conflict to African Muslims as a religious dispute between Muslims and non-Muslims. It is pertinent to recall that Islam sees the world as being divided into two hostile camps—the World of Peace (where Islam prevails) and the World of War (the world of the infidels). The territories that fall outside the Islamic realm, by the very fact of their being under non-Muslim rule, cannot have peace. And since all good Muslims are under the *sharia* (Islamic law) obligation to wage a *jihad* (holy war) against "infidels," the Arabs hoped that the African Muslim populations would force their governments to repudiate ties with Israel. Zionists were accused of perverting the Koran, and Israel of distributing fake copies of the Koran. The Sixth World Islamic Conference of December 1964 resolved that Islamic preaching throughout the world would include indoctrination on the "dangers of Israel."[35] But black African leaders, including those who were Muslim, were essentially secular. Besides, in countries that were not homogeneously Muslim, the leaders knew the dangers that were inherent in allowing religious disagreement to intrude into national politics. It was therefore imperative—that is, in the interest both of these leaders themselves and of national integration—to keep religion and the Arab-Israeli conflict out of their internal politics.

The sensitivities of leaders to Islamic pressures, however, curtailed the extent to which some countries were prepared to develop friendly ties with Israel. A good example was Nigeria. Because of the opposition of some northern Muslim-cum-political leaders to Israel, the federal government did not open an embassy in Israel, although Israel maintained an embassy in Lagos and gave financial and technical assistance to both the federal government and the southern regions.

The Arab demand for the annihilation of Israel was also repugnant to African states. As members of the UN, which they looked to for the resolution of many of their own problems, such demands ran counter to their obligations under the UN Charter. As late as 1969, for example, the delegate of Zaire, in opposing a pro-Arab draft resolution at the General Assembly, reiterated his country's rejection of a resolution which implied the disappearance of a sovereign member of the UN. The Liberian delegate added that the draft resolution was destructive of the principles "on which the UN was founded."[36]

Israel was usually among the first countries to establish diplomatic relations with the newly independent African states. Her diplomatic representation grew at a phenomenal rate: six representatives in 1960, twenty-three in 1961, and thirty-two in 1972. In fact, Israel was represented in all non-Arab League OAU states. This was also complemented by African missions in Israel, although because of budgetary constraints the number of African missions in Israel was smaller. In 1969 there were fourteen of these; more significantly, however, most of them were in Jerusalem and not in Tel Aviv (see Table 2.1).

The close relationship between Africa and Israel was also reflected in the many high-level official visits in both directions. In 1958 Foreign Minister Meir visited Côte d'Ivoire, Ghana, Liberia, Niger, and Senegal. She made four additional visits to Africa during the next five years. In 1962 Israeli President Itzhak Ben-Zvi visited the CAR, the Congo, Liberia, Senegal, and Zaire, and in 1966 Prime Minister Levi Eshkol paid official visits to Côte d'Ivoire, Kenya, Liberia, Madagascar, Senegal, Uganda, and Zaire. The list of African visitors was even more impressive. Between 1958 and 1965, the heads of state of the CAR, Chad, the Congo, Côte d'Ivoire, Dahomey, Gabon, Gambia, Liberia, Madagascar, Mali, Uganda, and Upper Volta visited Israel. There were many more ministerial delegations.

TABLE 2.1

AFRO-ISRAELI DIPLOMATIC REPRESENTATION, 1970

African State	Israeli Representation	African Representation
Botswana	acc	. .
Burundi	acc	. .
Cameroun	emb	. .
Central African Republic	emb	emb, Jerusalem
Chad	emb	. .
Congo	emb	ca, Jerusalem
Côte d'Ivoire	emb	emb, Jerusalem
Dahomey	emb	acc
Equatorial Guinea	acc	. .
Ethiopia	emb	cons, Jerusalem
Gabon	emb	emb, Jerusalem
Gambia	acc	. .
Ghana	emb	emb, Tel Aviv
Guinea*	emb	. .
Kenya	emb	acc
Lesotho	acc	. .
Liberia*	emb	emb, Jerusalem
Madagascar	emb	ca, Jerusalem
Malawi	emb	acc
Mali	emb	. .
Mauritius	acc	. .
Niger	emb	acc
Nigeria	emb	. .
Rwanda	emb	. .
Senegal	emb	. .
Sierra Leone	emb	. .
Swaziland	emb	. .
Tanzania	emb	. .
Togo	emb	. .
Uganda	emb	. .
Upper Volta	emb	emb, Jerusalem
Zaire	emb	emb, Jerusalem
Zambia	emb	. .

Source: African Department of the Ministry of Foreign Affairs, Jerusalem, 1984.

*Guinea broke diplomatic relations in 1967; Liberia moved her embassy from Tel Aviv to Jerusalem in 1969.

acc=accredited; ca=chargé d'affaires; cons=consulate general; emb=embassy; . . =no representation.

These visits often resulted in the signing of cooperation agreements. By 1968, twenty-two African states had signed such agreements with Israel (see Table 2.2).

TECHNICAL ASSISTANCE PROGRAMS

No other aspect of Afro-Israeli relations in the 1960s is as well publicized as Israel's technical assistance programs. From a modest beginning in 1958, with a budgetary allocation of only $94,700, Israel's assistance soon grew to become the dominant feature of Afro-Israeli relations—involving all black African states and covering wide areas of activities. Within a few years, not less than twenty-four official or quasi-official Israeli institutions were involved in the program.[37]

Because of budgetary constraints Israel's assistance did not usually involve capital-intensive projects, but was concentrated on projects that required knowledge and expertise in areas where Israel had made great strides herself. These included agriculture, youth organization, community development, vocational training, health and medicine, construction, management, and public service.

The assistance essentially took two forms: sending Israeli experts for specific projects or to carry out on-the-spot training; and training of Africans in Israeli institutions. Between 1958 and 1970 a total of 3,948 Israeli experts were sent abroad; 2,483, or 63 percent of them, served in Africa (see also Table 2.3). Usually these experts were sent on short missions. However, because Israel's image in Africa was thought to be very much tied to the reputation of these experts, only well-qualified people were sent out. A number of other Israeli experts served in Africa under the auspices of the UN and its agencies. In 1969 alone thirty-eight experts were sent in such a capacity, with fourteen as part of the delegation from the United Nations Development Program (UNDP), nine with the Food and Agricultural Organization (FAO), eight with the International Labor Organization (ILO), six with the World Health Organization (WHO), and one serving with UNESCO.[38]

Between 1958 and 1972, 9,182 Africans were trained in Israeli institutions under cooperation agreements. Most of the trainees participated in short-term courses. Except for courses at the Hadassah-Hebrew University Medical School in medicine, which took seven years, and nursing, which took three or four years, most of the courses lasted three to four months (see Table 2.4).

TABLE 2.2

COOPERATION AGREEMENTS BETWEEN
AFRICAN STATES AND ISRAEL

Country	Date of Signature
Mali	11/24/60
Upper Volta	6/11/61
Madagascar	8/27/61
Dahomey	9/28/61
Côte d'Ivoire	5/2/62
Gabon	5/15/62
Ghana	5/25/62
Central African Republic	6/13/62
Liberia	6/25/62
Rwanda	10/23/62
Cameroun	10/24/62
Gambia	12/16/62
Burundi	12/20/62
Niger	1/11/63
Tanzania	1/29/63
Uganda	2/4/63
Togo	4/12/64
Chad	10/7/64
Zaire	1964
Sierra Leone	8/22/65
Kenya	2/25/66
Malawi	5/31/68

Source: Ministry of Foreign Affairs, *Israel's Program of International Cooperation* (Jerusalem: Division of International Cooperation, 1970), p. 60.

Scarcity of resources often limited Israel's ability to give capital assistance to African states. Nonetheless, a few loans and grants were made. Beginning with a $20 million credit agreement with Ghana in July 1958, most of Israel's loans and grants were extended in support of either projects to which Israel had assigned technicians and experts or companies jointly owned by Israel and particular African states. For example, in July 1964 Malawi received hospital equipment, medical staff, and a nurses training program in Israel. Kenya also received equipment and staff for a rural social workers school. One of the largest grants

TABLE 2.3

MONTHS SPENT BY ISRAELI EXPERTS ABROAD
BY CONTINENT AND FIELD OF ACTIVITY, 1968–1970

Field of Activity	Africa	Asia	Latin Amer. & Caribbean	Med. Area & Others	Total
Agriculture	1,090	579	1,053	214	2,939
Youth Organization	1,862	32	165	–	2,059
Health & Medicine	573	1	8	12	594
Education	364	1	14	3	407
Industry & Construction	142	93	46	8	289
Public Service	612	42	114	–	768
Social Works & Community Development	101	6	–	43	150
Coop. Activities	97	18	61	–	176
Science & Technology	100	29	38	13	180
Miscellaneous	253	99	183	188	723
Total Man/Month	5,190	923	1,680	482	8,275
Percentage	63	11	20	6	100

Source: Hershlag, *Israel-Africa Cooperation*, p. 59.

($250,000) went to Upper Volta toward equipment for and the construction of facilities for the multi-purpose Agricultural Center near Bobo-Dioulasso.[39] Many Israeli-supported agricultural projects received free seeds, while some received tractors and other equipment. Although the number and amount of Israel's loans were small, their terms were, nonetheless, relatively liberal. Recipients were allowed to use large parts of the loans for local costs of procurement from third parties. For a list of loans given by Israel to African states between 1958 and 1966, see Table 2.5.

MILITARY ASSISTANCE

Israel was also involved in a fairly extensive military assistance program to African states. Many African leaders were impressed by the record of the Israeli army both as an instrument for integrating the heterogeneous Israeli society and as a professional fighting force. Although facts are difficult to obtain, Israel is known to have been involved in the train-

TABLE 2.4

AFRICAN TRAINEES IN ISRAEL IN 1969
(by profession)

Professional Field	Total Number	Months of Study	Average Stay of Trainees in Months
Agriculture	113	350.5	3.1
Cooperation	120	268	2.2
Community Development	67	342.5	5.1
Academic Studies	35	159	4.5
Health and Medicine	39	418.5	10.7
Mgt. & Public Service	34	193	5.7
Youth Services	47	128.5	2.7
Vocational Training	8	41	5.1
Miscellaneous	12	25.5	2.1
Total	475	1,926.5	4.1

Source: Ministry of Foreign Affairs, *Israel's Programme of International Cooperation* (Jerusalem: Division of International Cooperation, 1970), p. 59.

ing of police and military personnel. Some of these activities may have started before the independence of some of the states. For instance, pilots from Ghana and Uganda started receiving training in Israel as early as 1962. Indeed, Israel was responsible for the training of the first units of paratroopers in Africa. The first group of Tanzanian officers returned from Israel only two days before independence, and the first pilots from Ethiopia, Ghana, and Uganda were trained in Israel, as were the first groups of Nigerian civilian air force ground personnel. The first naval school in Ghana was also set up by Israel. A large number of Ethiopian officer and border commando units were trained by Israelis. Conventional police training was also given to small groups of police officers from all over Africa. Israel also sold small arms to African countries.[40] Israel was reported to have sold arms to both Kenya and Uganda between 1964 and 1967, including 120mm mortars and some aircraft to Uganda. In Uganda, some of these arms were accepted as partial payment for imports.[41]

By 1966 the Israeli military presence in some African countries was quite substantial. In Ethiopia the staff of Israel's military mission was estimated to be about one hundred, second only to that of the United States. Most of the men were involved in training the army and a few

TABLE 2.5

LOANS FROM ISRAEL TO AFRICA, 1958–1966
(in $U.S. m)

Country	Amount	Year
Ghana	$20.0	1958
Guinea	2.0	1965
Côte d'Ivoire	1.5	1963
Kenya	2.8	1965
Liberia	13.0	1959
Madagascar	20.0	1964
Mali	70.0	1966
Nigeria	8.4	1960
Sierra Leone	3.6	1963
Tanzania	58.0	1963–1965

Source: Mohamed O. Beshir, *Israel and Africa* (Khartoum: Khartoum University Press, 1974), p. 23.

served with the air force. Some were also involved in training border patrol commandos. In Uganda, the Israeli military mission was the most important foreign mission in the country in 1965. Ugandan military and police officers, including members of the Ugandan intelligence service, were trained by the Israelis both in Uganda and Israel.[42] In Sierra Leone the picture was similar: by 1964 Israel had taken over the training of the entire officer corps of the Sierra Leonean Army.[43]

ECONOMIC RELATIONS

The development of Afro-Israeli relations was also reflected in the steady growth of trade between the two, particularly after 1962. Africa's exports to Israel, which were calculated at $14.54 million in 1962, had by the end of the 1960s risen to $25.33 million. Imports also rose from $8.72 million in 1962 to $26.06 million in 1969 (see Table 2.6). The items exchanged consisted mainly of clothing, pharmaceuticals, agricultural machinery, electronic products, and office supplies from Israel; and, from the other side, the export of primary products including industrial diamonds from West and Central Africa, uranium from Gabon and Zaire, beef from East Africa, and carbonates from Kenya. Others included timber from the Congo, Côte d'Ivoire, and Gabon; food commodities, such as oil seeds, from Ethiopia; coffee from Côte d'Ivoire, Kenya, Tanzania, and Uganda; cocoa from Ghana and Nigeria; and peanuts from Malawi.

Trade was reinforced through the establishment of commercially operating joint companies, the extension of trade credits, and medium-term loans partly tied to Israeli procurement. Israeli exports were also promoted by Israeli personnel engaged in technical assistance programs in Africa.[44] Vigorous trade promotion efforts were made by Israel, especially after 1966. A number of commercial attachés were added to embassy staff. By 1969 there was a noticeable change in the pattern of trade: for the first time, Israel recorded a favorable balance of trade with African countries.

However, the level of trade was generally low. Throughout the 1960s, African exports to Israel peaked at $25.72 million—or only 2.4 percent of Israel's imports for that year, while African imports of Israeli goods did not exceed $26.1 million or 3.6 percent of Israel's total exports. This resulted principally from the non-complementarity between the African and Israeli markets. There was, for instance, almost no demand in Africa for Israel's two leading exports—citrus and polished diamonds; neither could much of Africa's primary

TABLE 2.6

AFRICA'S TRADE WITH ISRAEL, 1960–1969
(in $U.S. m)

Year	Exports	Imports
1960	$20.78	$15.54
1961	15.70	10.83
1962	14.54	8.72
1963	17.36	9.02
1964	22.11	10.60
1965	23.24	18.90
1966	22.24	17.24
1967	24.04	20.44
1968	25.72	22.47
1969	25.33	26.06

Source: Central Bureau of Statistics, *Statistical Abstracts of Israel*, 1963–1972.

exports—agricultural raw materials—be absorbed by Israel's predominantly light and medium industries without prior processing elsewhere.
In fact, Israel's principal imports—equipment inputs for industry, oil,
and grains—were not available in Africa.

Nevertheless, the absolute figures alone do not give the complete
picture. Until 1969 the trade balance was in Africa's favor; and however
small the figures may appear, black Africa's trade with Israel was a significant proportion of particular African countries' overall trade, or of
trade in certain commodities. For example, Israel was Gabón's third best
customer with respect to wood purchases in 1961, and Côte d'Ivoire's third
largest for uncut diamonds. Overall, Israel was Zaire's eighth largest customer in 1961, and fifth largest in 1962. And from almost nothing in the
mid-1950s, Israel had, by 1961, become East Africa's sixth most important
customer.

RELATIONS AT THE MULTILATERAL LEVEL

Close Afro-Israeli relations were demonstratively evident in African and
international forums where the black Africans often gave Israel solid
diplomatic support. At pan-African conferences, the black Africans
frustrated Arab attempts to inject the Arab-Israeli conflict into African
politics. Beginning with the First Conference of Independent African
States in Accra in 1958, the Arabs tried to get the Middle East conflict on
the agenda of all pan-African conferences. But despite the numerical
superiority of Arab states at the 1958 conference (five out of eight participants were Arab), black African states resisted the Arab moves to have
Israel condemned by the conference; the conference communiqué
merely called for "a just solution"[45] of the conflict. The pattern
remained the same in all governmental conferences through the founding of the OAU in 1963.

The only exception was the 1961 Casablanca Conference, which
branded Israel as a neo-colonialist bridgehead in Africa and which attributed the entire Middle East conflict to Israel's denial of the legitimate rights of the Palestinians. It should be stressed, however, that the
conference resolution did not at the time represent the consensus of
African opinion. First, of the countries represented at Casablanca, only
three were black African. Second, a similar resolution sponsored by
Arab states at the Belgrade Non-Aligned Conference a few months after

Casablanca was vehemently opposed by African leaders, including President Nkrumah who was a signatory to Casablanca.[46] And third, Nkrumah was even reported not to have approved of the Casablanca resolution, although this was subsequently denied.[47] The states that assembled at Casablanca had different objectives, and it appears that the endorsement by the three African states was a mere quid pro quo to get their own positions endorsed. The fact that the close ties between these states and Israel were not affected by the resolution suggests that their leaders were able to convince Israel not to attach any significance to it.

Whatever little pressure the Arabs were able to exert in the late 1950s and early 1960s became neutralized by the sheer number of the newly independent African states that were opposed to the Arab position on the Middle East conflict. Despite the efforts of President Nasser and other Arab leaders, the OAU bluntly refused to discuss or make any reference to the Middle East conflict from 1963 until after the June 1967 war. The black African leaders regarded the Arab-Israeli conflict as an issue external to Africa and therefore one in which involvement could divert their collective attention from their own major concerns, namely, decolonization, national integration, and economic development. Even in 1967 the issue inevitably came up not so much because of a change in the attitude of the Africans, but mainly because that year's OAU summit followed closely on the UN General Assembly's emergency debates on the war. Although Guinea broke diplomatic relations with Israel because of the war, an attempt by her and Somalia to get the OAU council of ministers to meet in emergency session to discuss the war failed. And despite all the passions aroused by the war and the UN debates, the African leaders refused to have the issue formally debated. They merely adopted a declaration which expressed concern at the Middle East situation and sympathy for Egypt. Arab calls for militancy were rejected as the summit underlined its desire to work within the framework of the UN to secure withdrawal of Israeli forces.

In February 1968 the OAU ministerial council passed a controversial, strongly anti-Israel resolution which claimed that Egypt was "the victim of Zionist aggression" and demanded the "immediate and unconditional withdrawal" of Israeli troops. However, a number of states, including Côte d'Ivoire, Dahomey, Ghana, Madagascar, Niger, Togo, and Upper Volta objected to the passage of the resolution.[48] At the next summit the resolution was reversed: the OAU returned to its previous position and rejected condemnation of Israel. It reaffirmed support for

Egypt, but did not demand unconditional Israeli withdrawal. Instead, it called for Israeli withdrawal of its forces "in accordance with the Security Council [Resolution] 242."

The situation was much the same at the UN. Not only did the black Africans often refrain from voting against Israeli positions, they played a very active role in the sponsorship of resolutions favorable to Israel. They often urged both the Arab states and Israel to be flexible in the interest of a just settlement, to the consternation of the Arabs. President Nkrumah set the tone of the African position in 1960 when he stressed, in a speech at the UN, that the Middle East conflict could only be resolved by the recognition of "the political realities" in the region—a speech the Saudi Arabian delegate described as "an imperialist defence line conveniently employed to their advantage."[49] Many African states were co-sponsors of pro-Israeli draft resolutions in 1961 and 1962 which called for direct negotiations between the Arabs and Israelis. In fact, twelve of the twenty-one sponsors of such a resolution in 1962 were African.[50] Israel reciprocated the African gesture by stiffening its position on apartheid in South Africa.[51]

Goodwill toward Israel in Africa was reflected in both speeches and voting behavior of black African states at the emergency session of the General Assembly held in the wake of the June 1967 war. In their speeches, while the African delegates spoke against the acquisition of territory by force, they emphasized "reasonable, peaceful and just solutions" to the conflict. Most of them did not support any of the Albanian, Cuban, and Soviet draft resolutions which were condemnatory of Israel. The Yugoslav-sponsored non-aligned draft received only modest African support (twelve states supported it, eight were opposed, ten abstained). Many of those who voted in its favor did so not because they were happy with all of its provisions, but because they agreed with some of them. Many of them did not want to be seen voting against a resolution which denounced territorial acquisition by military force. The Nigerian delegate, for instance, said shortly before the voting that although he would vote for the resolution, he regretted that it had not been possible to formulate a resolution that "might go as far towards bringing tranquility into the situation as we consider essential to eventual peace in the Middle East."[52]

A breakdown of the 266 votes cast by black African states on all resolutions and amendments submitted by Albania, Cuba, the Soviet Union, and Yugoslavia yields: 46 in favor (essentially pro-Arab votes), 110 against (essentially pro-Israel), and 110 abstentions. Thus, Africa's votes were 17.2 percent pro-Arab, 41.4 percent pro-Israel, and 41.4 percent abstentions.[53] In fact, most African states supported a pro-Israeli Latin American draft which linked Israeli withdrawal of troops with Arab abandonment of the state of belligerency with Israel.

With African support, Israeli officials began, for the first time, to be elected to key UN positions. Previous attempts had been blocked by the Arabs. In 1962 an Israeli was elected to the executive board of the WHO. In 1963 another Israeli was elected vice-president of the Fourth Committee of the General Assembly, and Israel was elected to the executive board of UNICEF in the same year. The Africans also foiled Arab attempts in 1962 to unseat Israeli observer delegates to the Fifth Session of the UN Economic Commission for Africa (ECA) in Leopold-ville (as Kinshasa was then called) and to the Colloquium on Socialism in Dakar, Senegal.

Throughout the 1960s, then, Israel enjoyed good political and diplomatic relations with black African states. Although the volume of trade was low, this was due more to structural economic problems than to any political obstacle. The Africans successfully resisted pressure which Arab states mounted either bilaterally or through multilateral organizations such as the OAU, the UN, and the non-aligned movement.

NOTES

1. In 1898, Theodor Herzl, the visionary of the Jewish State and founder of the Zionist Movement, wrote:

> There is still one other question arising out of the disaster of the nations which remains unsolved to this day, whose profound tragedy only a Jew can comprehend. That is the African question. Just call to mind all those terrible episodes of the slave trade, of human beings who merely because they were black were stolen like cattle, taken prisoner, captured and sold. Their children grew up in strange lands, the object of contempt and hostility because their complexions were different. I am not ashamed to say—that once I have witnessed the redemption of Israel, my people, I wish to assist in the redemption of the Africans.

Cited in Ministry of Foreign Affairs Information Department, *Israel-Africa: A Study of Cooperation* (Jerusalem, n.d.).

2. Ehud Avriel, "Israel's Beginnings in Africa," in Michael Curtis and Susan A. Gitelson (eds.), *Israel and the Third World* (New Brunswick, N.J.: Transaction Books, 1976), p. 70.

3. For a detailed exposition of Israel's foreign policy, see Samuel Decalo, "Israel's Foreign Policy and the Third World," *Orbis*, vol. 11, no. 3 (Fall 1967), pp. 724–745; Michael Brecher, *The Foreign Policy System of Israel: Setting, Images, Process* (London: Oxford University Press, 1972); idem, *Decisions in Israel's Foreign Policy* (London, OUP, 1974); Shimeon Amir, *Israel's Development of Cooperation with Africa, Asia and Latin America* (New York: Praeger, 1974).

4. Samuel Decalo, "Messianic Influences in Israeli Foreign Policy," University of Rhode Island, *Occasional Papers in Political Science*, no. 2, 1967, p. 4.

5. See Arthur Jay Klinghoffer, "Israel in Africa: The Strategy of Aid," *Africa Report*, vol. 17, no. 2 (April 1972), pp. 12–14.

6. Leopold Laufer, *Israel and the Developing Countries: New Approaches to Cooperation* (New York: Twentieth Century Fund, 1967).

7. See Z.Y. Hershlag, *Israel-Africa Cooperation: Final Report (Research Project on Israel-Africa Cooperation)* (Tel Aviv University, 1973), p. 12.

8. *Ha'aretz*, 19 August 1962, cited in Decalo, "Israel's Foreign Policy," p. 737.

9. See Olusola Ojo, *Afro-Arab Relations* (London: Rex Collings, forthcoming), pp. 2–4; Opoku Agyeman, "Pan-Africanism Versus Pan-Arabism: A Dual Asymmetrical Model of Political Relations," *Middle East Review*, vol. 16, no. 4 (Summer 1984), pp. 2–16.

10. See Joel Lieber, "The Arabs and Black Africa," *Midstream*, vol. 12, no. 2 (1966); John Okelli, *Revolution in Zanzibar* (Nairobi: East Africa Publishing House, 1967).

11. Ministry of Foreign Affairs, *Israel-Africa*. Former President Senghor of Senegal put it differently: "We black Africans understand both the Arabs and the Israelis, because together with us they form a triad of suffering people. The Jews were persecuted for 2000 years, the Arabs for three centuries and the Blacks since the Renaissance." Interview by Tullia Zevi in *Africa Report*, vol. 17, no. 7 (July-August 1972), p. 11.

12. Discussions with Ambassador Hanan Aynor, former ambassador to several African countries and former director of the African Department, Ministry of Foreign Affairs, Jerusalem, November 1984. See also Decalo, "Israel's Foreign Policy," p. 730.

13. Ibid.

14. Ibid.; see also Ehud Avriel, "Some Minute Circumstances" (memoir), *Jerusalem Quarterly,* 14 (Winter 1980), p. 38.

15. D.V. Segre, "The Philosophy and Practice of Israel's International Cooperation," in Curtis and Gitelson (eds.), *Israel in the Third World,* p. 17; Laufer, *Israel and the Developing Countries,* p. 27.

16. Discussions with H. Aynor; see also Decalo, "Messianic Influences."

17. *Davar,* 21 March 1961, cited in Edy Kaufman, "Israel's Foreign Policy Implementation in Latin America," in Curtis and Gitelson (eds.), *Israel and the Third World,* p. 121.

18. *Israeli Digest,* March 1963, quoted in Decalo, "Messianic Influences," p. 8.

19. Ministry of Foreign Affairs, *Israel's Programme of International Cooperation in Developing Countries* (Jerusalem: Information Division, October 1972), p. 3.

20. Ministry of Foreign Affairs, *Israel-Africa.*

21. Ibid.

22. Laufer, *Israel and the Developing Countries,* p. 214.

23. See Stuart H. Schaar, "Patterns of Israeli Aid and Trade in East Africa: Part II," *American Universities Field Staff (AUFS),* East Africa Series, vol. 7, no. 2 (1968), p. 2.

24. Mordechai E. Krenin, *Israel and Africa: A Study in Technical Cooperation* (New York: Praeger, 1964), p. 4.

25. *Jerusalem Post,* 23 July 1957, cited in Decalo, "Messianic Influences," p. 5.

26. Cited in Jehudi Kanarek, *Israeli Technical Assistance to African Countries* (Geneva: Africa Institute, 1969), p. 2.

27. Laufer, *Israel and the Developing Countries,* p. 27; Krenin, *Israel and Africa,* p. 9.

28. Stuart H. Schaar, "Patterns of Israeli Aid and Trade in East Africa: Part I," *AUFS,* East Africa Series, vol. 7, no. 1 (1968), p. 4.

29. Discussions with H. Aynor, 6 November 1984. See also Barnet Litvinoff (ed.), *The Letters and Papers of Chaim Weizmann* (New Brunswick, N.J.: Transaction Books, 1978, 1979).

30. Benjamin Rivlin and Jacques Formerand, "Changing Third World Perspectives and Policies Toward Israel," in Curtis and Gitelson (eds.), *Israel and the Third World,* pp. 335–336.

31. Avriel, "Some Minute Circumstances," p. 29.

32. See Olusola Ojo, "The Arab Factor in the Chadian Conflict," in

Dunstan Wai et al. (eds.), *Africa and the Arab Middle East: Relations in Perspective*, forthcoming.

33. For details and similar Arab tactics, see Ojo, *Afro-Arab Relations*, pp. 61, 68–69; A.B. Akinyemi, *Foreign Policy and Federalism: The Nigerian Experience* (Ibadan: University of Ibadan Press, 1974), p. 103; Laufer, *Israel and the Developing Countries*, p. 204.

34. Ibrahim Abu-Lughod, "Africa and the Islamic World," in J. Paden and E. Soja (eds.) *The African Experience*, vol. 1 (Evanston: Northwestern University Press, 1970), p. 549.

35. *Africa Report*, vol. 10, no. 2 (February 1965), pp. 50–51.

36. *United Nations General Assembly Official Records* (hereafter *UNGAOR*), 24th Session of the Special Political Committee, 686th Meeting, 5 December 1961.

37. For the list of agencies, see Moshe Decter, *To Serve, To Teach, To Leave: The Story of Israel's Development Assistance Program in Black Africa* (New York: American Jewish Congress, 1977), p. 11.

38. Ministry of Foreign Affairs, *Israel's Programme of International Cooperation in Developing Countries* (Jerusalem, 1970), p. 58.

39. Laufer, *Israel and the Developing Countries*, p. 138; discussions with H. Aynor.

40. See Abel Jacob, "Israel's Military Aid to Africa, 1960–1966," *Journal of Modern African Studies*, vol. 9, no. 2 (1971), pp. 165–187; Farouk A. Sawkari, "The Cost and Gains of Israeli Influence in Africa," *African Quarterly*, vol. 14, nos. 1–2 (1974), pp. 5–19; Schaar, "Patterns of Israeli Aid," Part II, pp. 6–7; Laufer, *Israel and the Developing Countries*, p. 171.

41. *New York Times*, 25 November 1967, cited in Schaar, "Patterns of Israeli Aid," Part II, p. 7.

42. Ibid.

43. Jacob, "Israel's Military Aid," p. 179.

44. Laufer, *Israel and the Developing Countries*, p. 206.

45. See *West Africa*, 19 April 1958, p. 362.

46. *Middle East Records, 1961* (Jerusalem: Shiloah Centre for Middle Eastern and African Studies, Tel Aviv University, 1961), p. 192.

47. Emmanuel Lottem, "The Israeli Press—Israel's Relations with Africa," *International Problems*, vol. 14, nos. 3–4 (Fall 1975), p. 10.

48. *Africa Research Bulletin* (Exeter), Political Series (hereafter *ARB*), February 1968, p. 972.

49. See *UNGAOR*, 15th year, 869th plenary meeting, 28 September 1960, p. 67; ibid., 879th meeting, 30 September 1960, pp. 267–275.

50. UN doc. A/SPC/L.90, 10 December 1962.

51. See Chapter 5.
52. 1448th plenary meeting, 4 July 1967.
53. See Fouad Ajami and Martin A. Sours, "Israel and Sub-Saharan Africa: A Study of Interaction," *African Studies Review,* vol. 13, no. 3 (December 1970), p. 412.

THREE

The October 1973 War and Afro-Israeli Relations

The year 1973 marked a decisive turning point in Afro-Israeli relations. Relations which had been carefully cultivated by both sides in the 1960s seemed to have come to an abrupt halt with the severance of diplomatic ties by all but four African countries during and shortly after the October 1973 Arab-Israeli war (see Table 3.1). The break in diplomatic relations was unique in terms of its "suddenness" and the sheer number of the countries involved. However, keen observers of Afro-Israeli relations could even in 1973 have noted growing strains in the relations between the two, both at the bilateral and multilateral levels. In fact, the period between the late 1960s and 1973 was one of mutual disenchantment, and the break in diplomatic relations in 1973 was merely a culmination of a process which had been going on, albeit slowly, since the 1967 war. This chapter discusses Afro-Israeli relations in the years preceding the 1973 rupture of relations and examines the various national, continental, and international factors that caused the break.

Israel's stunning success in the 1967 war damaged her image as an underdog in Africa. With the capture and occupation of the whole of Sinai, the West Bank, Gaza, and the Golan Heights, Israel ceased to appear to many Africans as a tiny country that was just struggling to survive the hostility of millions of Arabs. Many Africans now saw in Israel a military colossus that occupied her neighbors' territories. The erosion of her image as an underdog was accompanied by a corresponding loss of the sympathy that such an image normally evokes. Soon many began to see Israel as "bellicose, aggressive, annexationist and expansionist."[1] By 1970 the Israeli authorities had become increasingly disturbed by this new image held by "many African countries like those elsewhere in the world."[2]

By the late 1960s the "special appeal of Israel" in black Africa had begun to wear off. The hope that the "Israeli miracle" of development would be repeated in Africa through Israeli technical assistance programs had proven exaggerated. Many of the projects did not bring the spectacular results the African leaders had anticipated. Projects in communal farming, agrarian modernization, and youth mobilization—the Gadna and Nahal-type projects—foundered partly because of the traditional social and cultural outlook of the African people and partly because of the fundamentally different political environments in Africa and Israel.[3] Besides, by acceding to almost every request for assistance, Israel undoubtedly overextended herself. This was particularly counterproductive as Israel had very limited capital to back up many of the projects which it helped to initiate. And since there were no clear-cut criteria for selecting projects other than that requests be made by governments, Israel found itself involved in many projects of doubtful viability, or with political overtones, with consequent damaging results. Lack of adequate supervision and follow-up on the part of Israeli authorities of their projects in Africa also contributed to the failure of some of them.[4] And in any case, the Israeli technical assistance program had peaked in 1966. By the 1970s its scope and magnitude were in decline. This was partly due to the economic difficulties caused by the war and partly due to the fact that few technical experts were available for foreign assignments, as they were needed in the development programs initiated in the newly occupied areas. Israel responded to these problems by becoming more selective about the countries it assisted. In the early 1970s efforts were concentrated mainly on such countries as Cameroun, the Congo, Côte d'Ivoire, Ethiopia, Lesotho, Liberia, Madagascar, Tanzania, Togo, Uganda, Zaire, and Zambia.

Israel's interest in Africa generally declined, and this was reflected in the relative decline in the level of assistance. As Oded observes, by the early 1970s Africa had dropped to a lower rung on the Israeli scale of political priorities.[5] As a result of the increasing political difficulties she was facing in some African countries in 1972, Israel returned to a policy of maintaining her presence selectively and concentrated on a much more scaled-down program which also reflected the "new" and more realistic expectations of the African leaders. In 1972 alone 254 experts were sent to Africa and 402 African trainees went to Israel. Nevertheless, the toning-down of expectations by the Africans in itself reflected the relative decline in the value which they ascribed to Israeli assistance. Countries such as Tanzania and Rwanda had begun to withdraw from Israeli projects.[6]

The period also coincided with an increase in foreign assistance from a variety of other sources that were not sympathetic to Israel's interest in Africa—namely, Arab countries and the Soviet bloc. These countries

TABLE 3.1

AFRICA'S BREAK OF DIPLOMATIC RELATIONS WITH ISRAEL

Country	Date of Break
Guinea	6/6/67
Uganda	3/30/72
Chad	11/28/72
Congo	12/31/72
Niger	1/5/73
Mali	5/1/73
Burundi	5/16/73
Togo	9/21/73
Zaire	10/4/73
Rwanda	10/8/73
Benin	10/9/73
Upper Volta	10/10/73
Cameroun	10/13/73
Equatorial Guinea	10/14/73
Tanzania	10/19/73
Madagascar	10/20/73
Central African Republic	10/21/73
Ethiopia	10/23/73
Nigeria	10/25/73
Gambia	10/26/73
Zambia	10/26/73
Sierra Leone	10/27/73
Ghana	10/28/73
Senegal	10/28/73
Gabon	10/29/73
Botswana	11/1/73
Liberia	11/2/73
Kenya	11/8/73
Côte d'Ivoire	11/12/73
Mauritius	7/76

could provide large capital grants and/or entire industrial complexes as opposed to the mere training and expertise which Israel offered. This further undermined the relative importance of Israeli assistance. The noticeable exclusion of Israel from the itineraries of African leaders' overseas trips from the late 1960s[7] was another indication. The only notable visits to Israel between 1968 and 1973 were made by leaders of Lesotho, Malawi (1968), and Swaziland (1969) and by Idi Amin in 1971.

Israel's image in Africa also suffered as she became more industrialized and consumer-oriented. First, those African leaders who were concerned with revolutionary social change became disillusioned with her.[8] And secondly, this resulted in a greater drive by Israel for markets in Africa. From the late 1960s Israel's concern in Africa shifted primarily to trade. She expanded her commercial activities through Solel Boneh, Vered, and other parastatal companies. And as "Israel began to act more like other developed countries, which were competing intently for external markets, its initial attraction began to wear off."[9] Israeli commercial activities came under criticism in some countries. During this period Israel's imports from Africa continued to decline, while her exports continued to grow (see Table 3.2). However, as the figures indicate, the level of trade remained low, even with Israel's principal African trading partners (see Table 3.3). This was because of the structural factors noted in Chapter 1.

There was no other place where Israel's increasingly difficult position in Africa became more evident than in multilateral forums such as the OAU, the UN, and the non-aligned conferences. The continued stalemate in the Middle East, and particularly the continued occupation of Arab, especially Egyptian, territories, kept the conflict in the forefront of OAU politics. Once the issue came up at the OAU summit in 1967, it became difficult for pro-Israeli states within the organization to prevent its inclusion in subsequent meetings. However, Arab attempts to get the OAU to adopt a strongly anti-Israeli stance were initially unsuccessful. In fact, there was no specific item concerning the Middle East on the OAU agenda until the September 1970 summit. The issue was usually introduced as "the continuing occupation of part of the territories of the UAR by foreign forces." And the resolution that emerged from the discussions only expressed concern over "the occupation of a part of a sister-state" and demanded the implementation of UN Security Council Resolution 242 in its totality, not "conditionally or partially."[10] Attempts by the Guinean secretary-general of the OAU, Diallo Telli, to

TABLE 3.2

AFRICA'S TRADE WITH ISRAEL, 1969–1972
(in $U.S. m)

Year	Exports	Imports
1969	$25.33	$26.06
1970	19.94	30.88
1971	16.72	38.02
1972	20.36	37.37

Source: Central Bureau of Statistics, *Statistical Abstract of Israel*, 1971, 1973.

TABLE 3.3

SELECTED AFRICAN COUNTRIES'
TRADE WITH ISRAEL, 1970–1973
(in U.S. $1,000)

Country	Exports to Israel				Imports from Israel			
	1970	1971	1972	1973	1970	1971	1972	1973
Congo	1,715	192	638	58	64	–	–	107
Côte d'Ivoire	926	413	752	1,904	1,162	1,258	1,427	4,925
Ethiopia	1,998	2,202	2,365	4,359	4,363	3,577	3,956	4,007
Gabon	1,640	836	2,008	1,896	1	166	37	281
Ghana	594	842	470	200	2,145	3,104	2,299	2,417
Kenya	1,182	979	1,209	1,667	3,653	4,183	2,797	3,026
Nigeria	40	30	18	10	3,583	4,949	6,146	5,631
Tanzania	130	198	354	369	1,903	1,400	1,319	1,267
Uganda	2,316	1,321	283	–	5,613	7,958	3,095	–
Zaire	304	107	361	–	2,959	2,132	851	1,234

Source: Central Bureau of Statistics, *Foreign Trade Statistics Quarterly*, 1970–1974.

get the organization to take a more active anti-Israeli posture often earned him a rebuke for exceeding his legitimate role as administrative secretary-general. However, the continued occupation of Arab territories by Israel was making it more difficult for African states to resist Arab pressure for tougher action. There is clearly a measure of African self-interest in opposing the principle of annexation of territory by force. African leaders considered South Africa's invasion and occupation of part of the territories of the Front-Line States as a distinct possibility. Besides, many African states faced potential threats of territorial irredentism from their neighbors despite the OAU charter's firm commitment to upholding the territorial integrity of member states. In a speech at the Makerere Institute of Diplomacy on 30 August 1968, Dr. Obote of Uganda expressed the fears of African leaders:

> We cannot rule out the possibility of the Union of South Africa either alone or together with Rhodesia invading or overrunning Zambia. The first thing that Uganda would do if such a situation arises, will be to call for a withdrawal of the invading troops from Zambian territory. We do not see any difference between possible invasion and occupation of Zambian territory by hostile troops, or part of Uganda being invaded by foreign troops, on the one hand, and, on the other, the Israeli occupation of Arab territories.[11]

President Senghor of Senegal put it more dramatically: "Being an African, I understand the Egyptian position. Africa ends at the Sinai peninsula. Territorial integrity has become a myth in our continent and both we and the Semites live on myths."[12]

It is therefore not surprising that Arab propaganda played on this African sensitivity, and all OAU resolutions continually emphasized the need for Israeli withdrawal. It is also pertinent that statements made by most African states on breaking relations with Israel in 1973 claimed that the action was being taken because of Israel's refusal to withdraw from Arab territories: "The Gambians are not alone in saying that the break is relative only to Israel's occupation of Arab lands, for many West African leaders still have great admiration for this new nation which has shown such energy and technical brilliance."[13] The statement by Ghana, one of Israel's closest allies, was typical:

> The government of Ghana cannot remain insensitive to African feelings and objectives regarding the security and territorial integrity of member States of the OAU. The government of Ghana has therefore concluded that continued diplomatic relations with Israel, which is in violation of the territory of an OAU member state, is undesirable. Accordingly, until such a time that Israel withdraws from Arab lands, diplomatic relations between Ghana and Israel shall remain severed.[14]

Nevertheless, the OAU did not get actively involved with the Middle East conflict. Because of the increasingly tenuous position of African leaders in the face of mounting Arab pressures, many African leaders did not want to be forced into a situation where they would have to choose between Israel and the Arabs. The deadlocked UN Jarring Peace Mission provided them with an opportunity for a diplomatic initiative. Although the OAU summit that year adopted a strongly-worded resolution critical of Israel, it set up a committee of ten heads of state to find a means of reactivating the Jarring Mission. The committee appointed a subcommittee of four heads of state—Presidents Senghor of Senegal, Gowon of Nigeria, Ahdijo of Cameroun, and Mobutu of Zaire—to visit Egypt and Israel.

The four leaders visited Egypt and Israel in November 1971 and prepared a memorandum which was more even-handed than the 1971 summit resolution. They recommended the resumption of the Jarring talks "within the terms of Resolution 242 (1967)," an interim agreement for the reopening of the Suez Canal, and free navigation in the Straits of Tiran. They also emphasized the need for "secure and recognized boundaries" which they said "should be determined in a peace agreement."[15] Both Israel and Egypt accepted the report, and for once it seemed the African states were going to succeed where the great powers had failed. But before the euphoria subsided, there emerged irreconcilable interpretations of some clauses in the OAU's recommendations by both parties, and serious dissension within the OAU itself over the committee's report.[16] The division within the ranks of the Africans became obvious during the UN debates on the Middle East which had been deferred until December 1971 to give the OAU committee time to complete its task. A majority of the Africans failed to support proposals along the lines of the OAU report, which were contained in a draft resolution submitted by Barbados and Ghana, that among other recommendations, called for UN support of the "OAU proposal." Most of them, in fact, supported, and indeed cosponsored, a pro-Arab draft which the Ivorian delegate said would deny "the constructive work accomplished by the Committee of African Heads of State."[17] It is also pertinent to note that six of the twenty-two African states that cosponsored the resolution had their heads of state as members of the OAU committee.

The debates at the UN clearly underlined the hardening of attitudes against Israel by a growing number of African states. There was widespread suspicion that Israel was unwilling to consider pulling out of the territories occupied as a result of the 1967 war. According to President Senghor, the problem was the refusal of Israel to confirm "the statement it made to us that it does not intend to annex a part of Egyptian territory. Until it confirms this publicly, negotiations cannot be resumed."[18] The Africans were very upset by the failure of the mission, which they blamed on Israel. *West Africa* noted the damaging effect of this failure on Israel's position in Africa:

> As far as the OAU is concerned, the balance seems to have tilted against Israel at the time of the failure of the 1971–2 OAU peace mission, in which several leaders not ill-disposed to Israel . . . were persuaded that the Arabs were being more reasonable about peace initiatives becase of Israel's refusal to reactivate the UN mission of Dr. Jarring.[19]

In 1972 Chad, Congo, and Uganda severed their diplomatic ties with Israel, and the weakened position of Israel in Africa was evident in the anti-Israel resolution passed at the OAU Rabat summit that year. The resolution was adopted after the president of Mauritania and chairman of the OAU committee had reported that the OAU's Middle East initiative failed because of "Israeli intransigence." He went on to add that Israel "strongly rejected any peace settlement and was even more strongly opposed to anything that might lead to the withdrawal of its forces from occupied territories."[20] The resolution, which was made by Côte d'Ivoire, one of Israel's strongest allies, deplored Israel's "negative and obstructive attitude" and praised Egypt's "positive attitude and its continuous efforts for the restoration of peace in the region." It called on Israel to publicly declare its adherence to the principle of non-annexation of territories through the use of force and requested all states "to refrain from supplying Israel with any weapons, military equipment or moral support likely to enable it to strengthen its military potential and to perpetuate its occupation of Arab and African territories." The trend was unbroken during the 1972 General Assembly session. All attempts to weaken the contents of the anti-Israel draft resolution presented, by having a separate vote on the most anti-Israel clause (paragraph 8), failed. The resolution called for Israeli withdrawal, and asked Israel to declare its acceptance of the principle of non-annexation of territory by force. Moreover, it supported the Palestinian right to self-determination and asked all states to refrain from giving aid to Israel and from any action that might imply recognition of the Israeli position. Only Côte d'Ivoire, Lesotho, and Liberia supported Israel in voting for the proposal to have a separate vote on the anti-Israel paragraph. All the others—except Dahomey, Central African Republic, Gabon, Ghana, Madagascar, Malawi, Swaziland, and Zaire, who were either absent or abstained—opposed the proposal.

In 1973 African support for Israel continued to decline. Between January and May Burundi, Mali, and Niger joined in breaking diplomatic ties with Israel. The Arabs stepped up their pressure on the Africans. Gaddafi, backed by Tunisia, called for the transfer of the OAU secretariat from Addis Ababa on account of Ethiopia's ties with Israel. He also called for a boycott of the tenth-anniversary celebrations of the OAU if African states failed to break ties with Israel. The summit, however, met after an acrimonious ministerial meeting. Although President Ahdijo, who had always supported the Arabs within the organization, warned that the Palestinian people would gain nothing from the attempt to provoke a "useless crisis" within the OAU,[21] the summit nonetheless adopted a resolution which claimed that continued Israeli "aggression" was a "danger which threatens the security, territorial integrity and unity of our continent." It further warned that the OAU might take "at the African level, individually or collectively, political and economic measures against it if it refuses to evacuate the territories of the state victims of [its] aggression."

The non-aligned summit which met in Algiers in August 1973 provided another forum for the Arab states to continue their diplomatic onslaught against Israel. Because of their larger number and the automatic support given them by the Muslim and "radical" Third World states, the restraints which were still injected into the OAU debates and resolutions were significantly absent at the summit, which strongly condemned both Zionism and Israel. It was specific on the action that should be taken immediately against Israel—complete political, diplomatic, economic, and technical isolation. Togo broke ties with Israel immediately after the conference, and Zaire shortly afterwards.

President Eyadema of Togo was said to have come under Arab pressure to make such a move while he was at the non-aligned summit.[22]

Relations between some African countries were also affected during this period as a result of bilateral problems and/or increased Arab military pressure. Uganda, the second country to break diplomatic ties with Israel in 1972, is a clear example. Although ousted President Obote had accused Israel of complicity in the coup that brought Idi Amin to power in 1971, Amin soon developed a fear of Israelis: "Those who helped to make me can help to break me."[23] But he could not contemplate any severance of ties as long as the civil war in southern Sudan was still being fought. Amin had ethnic affinities with the southern Sudanese, whom the Israelis were also helping. The ending of the war in February 1972 removed the Sudanese as a restraining factor. Besides, Israel soon found out that she could not meet the excessive and politically explosive demands of Amin for finance, weapons, and logistics to enable him to launch an expedition against Tanzania. First he wanted to annex the port of Tonga as an outlet to the sea; and second, to teach Nyerere a lesson for harboring the ousted Obote. When Israel failed to meet his demands, he turned to the Arabs, particularly Libya, Kuwait, and Saudi Arabia for money, and to Libya for arms. These Arab countries found in Idi Amin not only an enthusiast in expelling Israel and inviting the PLO, but also a willing accomplice in an effort to impose Islam on an overwhelmingly non-Muslim population. The break with Israel was followed by $18 million[24] in aid from Libya and Saudi Arabia and a $15 million loan from the Saudis. It is also claimed that Amin was promised about $16 million for his personal use, "to be channelled through the Kampala branch of the Libyan Commercial Bank, as well as better publicized military assistance."[25]

Chad was another example. By late 1972 Chad, which was under severe pressure from an Arab-supported rebellion and was suffering a drought, was on the verge of bankruptcy. Israel was not forthcoming with funds; France, which had been sustaining Chad militarily and financially, indicated it would not continue its economic and military assistance as in the past. President Tombalbaye, faced with a Libyan promise to end its support for the rebels and to offer substantial financial rewards, found no difficulty in breaking with Israel. Chad's break with Israel in November 1972 and its invitation to the PLO to open an office in N'djamena was followed by promises of massive Arab funds.[26] Although Arab support for the Frolinat rebels did not end with Chad's break with Israel, as Tombalbaye later found out, some gesture of support in the immediate aftermath of the break led to his premature claim in January 1973 that Frolinat no longer existed.[27]

Ethiopia was another country in which Arab states, especially Iraq, Libya, South Yemen, and Syria, supported armed Eritrean rebellion against the government of Haile Selassie, ostensibly because of the latter's close ties with Israel. In May 1973 Gaddafi precipitated a diplomatic crisis when he demanded that African leaders boycott the tenth-anniversary celebrations of the OAU scheduled to be held in the Ethiopian capital and a shift of the OAU secretariat to Cairo. President Sadat was reported to have offered to use his influence in the Arab world to halt support for the Eritreans if the emperor renounced his ties with Israel. The Ethiopian prime minister was said to have been persuaded, although the emperor refused.[28]

There was also a marked Arab diplomatic offensive in Africa in the early 1970s. This was carried on at various levels. First, there was an increased participation of North African Arabs in the OAU, as evidenced by, among other things, the improved attendance of Arab heads of state at the OAU meetings. The chairmanship of the organization was held by President Ould Daddah of Mauritania in 1971 and King Hassan of Morocco between 1972 and May 1973 (he also hosted the 1972 summit). Second, Arab states increased their diplomatic representation in Africa. In 1967 there were seventy-eight Arab missions in twenty African countries; by 1972 this number had increased to one hundred missions in twenty-six African countries. Egypt was particularly active. In 1968 the Egyptian minister of labor gave instructions that Arab labor representations should be established in Africa, "especially in African countries in which Israeli labor activities have increased considerably."[29] In April 1968 Egypt announced its decision to establish diplomatic missions in eight African states. In 1970 she sent special envoys to Guinea, Mali, Nigeria, and Senegal to explain her position on the Middle East.[30] By 1972 the Egyptian diplomatic network in Africa was nearly as wide as that of Israel.

Third, Arab diplomacy became subtle and more effective. They spoke less of their hostility to the State of Israel but emphasized those issues to which Africa was very sensitive—acquisition of territory by force, Israel's links with South Africa, and continental solidarity. There was a greater coordination of Arab information (propaganda), strategy, and policy, especially in the OAU and other international forums.

This they were able to do because of the greater internal Arab unity achieved after the 1967 war. The war had forced Nasser to withdraw

Egyptian forces from Yemen and to reach an accommodation with Saudi Arabia. The immediate prewar period itself had witnessed the emergence of an alliance of the confrontation states—Egypt, Jordan, and Syria. The occupation of large chunks of their territories by Israel as a result of the war, and their desire to regain them, kept the alliance intact. Besides, the Syrian and Egyptian need for support from the conservative oil-rich states forced them to cease hostile propaganda and subversive activities against them. In a sense, therefore, the Arab world was united more than ever in its enmity against Israel.

In addition, the loss of part of their territories by Egypt, Jordan, and Syria transformed the level of these countries' interest in, and commitment to, the struggle against Israel. Hitherto, their involvement had been informed by their pan-Arab support for the Palestinians. But after 1967, in addition to this pan-Arab support, each of the states had a "primary" national reason to commit its resources to the conflict with Israel, especially in the diplomatic arena.

And fourth, there were more frequent visits by Arab leaders to African states for the purpose of explaining their position. Algeria, Egypt, Libya, and Saudi Arabia were particularly active. The involvement of Libya and Saudi Arabia was in itself new. The revolution that ousted King Idriss from power in 1969 saw the emergence of Gaddafi, a fanatical opponent of Israel. Both Libya and Saudi Arabia used a combination of oil wealth and blackmail (Libya in Chad) to change the attitudes of some African leaders. Between 1970 and 1973 eight black African heads of state visited Tripoli seeking aid. Niger supposedly received $70 million in loans from Libya[31] and an additional $10 million from Saudi Arabia. Senegal received $800,000 in gifts during King Feisal's visit and an offer of $50 million in development finance from Libya.[32] President Mobutu admitted that there was a "direct [link] between the break in relations between certain African nations and Israel and Libyan aid."[33]

In November 1972 King Feisal visited Chad, Niger, Senegal, and Uganda. These visits resulted in promises of substantial financial aid. Although Israel's technical assistance was still being given to some of these states, the promises of huge financial and developmental assistance by Arab countries far outweighed the benefits of two or three Israeli experts in the calculations of some of these leaders. Niger seized the opportunity of Feisal's presence in Niamey to demand Israeli withdrawal from occupied Arab territories and to express support for the just cause of the Palestinians.[34] It is, perhaps, not just a mere coincidence that

Chad and Niger broke ties with Israel a few days after Feisal's visit.

The early 1970s marked the beginning of militant Islam, and the Arabs exploited it. The active diplomatic involvement of Gaddafi and King Feisal brought Islam to the forefront of Afro-Arab relations. It is noteworthy that, except for Uganda, the countries visited by Feisal in 1972 were predominantly Muslim, and even Uganda had a Muslim military dictator. During the visit of President Diori of Niger to Gaddafi in 1971, both leaders spoke of strengthening relations "within the framework of Muslim brotherhood and African unity."[35] There was a sharp increase in the number of Islamic ministerial and other conferences, and these conferences concerned themselves mainly with the Arab-Israeli conflict. In 1970 alone two conferences of Islamic foreign ministers were held, and from 1972 the holding of such a conference became an annual event. These and other Islamic conferences became a forum for exerting pressure on African states to sever their links with Israel. The participation of African states in these conferences and also at a higher ministerial level drew some of the states closer to the Arab position.

It is also important that Egypt's image in Africa improved with Sadat's coming to power. He evoked less apprehension in Africa than his predecessor; and his moderate and calm leadership, in contrast to Gaddafi's, also won him some admirers.

The period from the late 1960s also saw a growing radicalization of some African leaders. This radicalization was born out of frustration with the declining aid of Western countries, Africa's worsening terms of trade, the refusal of the West to effect a breakthrough in Southern Africa, and, to some extent, the need by some African leaders to take a radical foreign policy posture in order to please domestic constituents. Many African states began to diversify their political and diplomatic contacts. Botswana, Liberia, and Niger established relations with the Soviet Union, Chad received Soviet aid for the first time, and the heads of state of Ethiopia and Madagascar visited Moscow. In 1970 East Germany established diplomatic relations with the Central African Republic, Congo, and Guinea (reestablishment) and in 1971–72 with Equatorial Guinea, Chad, Togo, Cameroun, Dahomey, and Liberia. China established relations with Equatorial Guinea and Ethiopia in 1970, with Burundi, Cameroun, Nigeria, Senegal, Sierra Leone, and Togo in 1971, and with Chad, Dahomey, Gabon, Ghana, Madagascar, Mauritius, Rwanda, and Zaire in 1972. All these contacts opened up Africa to Chinese and Soviet-bloc propaganda on behalf of the Arab states and the PLO.

The increasingly pro-American stance of Israeli foreign policy readily played into Arab propagandist hands. The perception of Israel as a "neutral" country waned, and she became associated with the West. In 1972, for instance, the Congo government, in breaking relations with Israel, asserted: "Israel is our enemy like the government of Washington, Pretoria, Salisbury and Lisbon."[36]

In addition, Israeli immigration policies seemed to exhibit some similarities with those of South Africa and Rhodesia. South Africa and Rhodesia expended great efforts in attracting white immigrants, as Israel did in encouraging Jews of the Diaspora to settle in Israel. However, the Jews of Ethiopia were not encouraged until after August 1975,[37] although Ethiopian Christians had no problem receiving visas. As Ali Mazrui pointed out, "the racial elements in such immigration policies could not escape the notice of the more radical of the black nationalists in Africa and the United States."[38]

Israel's growing links with South Africa also undermined her diplomatic position in Africa. Arab propaganda had always pointed to these links without effect. But with increasing visibility of these links as reflected in growing trade, the opening of a South African consulate in Israel in 1972, the increasing official contacts, and intensified Arab propaganda which often tended to magnify these links, "what once would have been considered forgivable errors of policy began to register as part of a pattern of outrageous and gross anti-African conduct."[39] The South African government's own assessment that Israel's position was similar to its own did not help Israel's image in Africa. President Boumedienne of Algeria stressed at the OAU the illogicality of Africa's policy of adopting "one attitude toward racism in South Africa and a different one toward Zionism in North Africa." The African leaders had become convinced of Israeli-South African links, so that when in June 1971 Israel made an offer of 10,000 pounds sterling in humanitarian aid to the OAU liberation funds, the offer was rejected.

Moreover, the Arabs began to make their support for the liberation of Southern Africa conditional on Africa's support for their own cause in the Middle East. Sadat made this very clear at the OAU; it was again stressed by the Saudis on the eve of Feisal's departure for Africa in 1972. A government statement expressed the hope that "the Arab countries and the entire continent of Africa would work together after the liberation of Palestine for freeing the occupied African territories one after another, including Rhodesia."[40]

The closure of the Suez Canal, as a result of the June 1967 war, had an adverse economic impact on the East African states. In 1966, 32 percent of the dry cargo business of these countries passed through Suez. Between 1967 and 1971 the closure of the Canal was estimated to have cost the East African states some $125 million a year in losses of export trade.[41] It led to a considerable rise in freight rates for shipping cargoes to these states, as cargo had to come around through the Cape of Good Hope. The execution of some major projects was consequently affected. Israel was blamed for the continued closure; as early as May 1968 a Nigerian newspaper reported a hardening of sentiments against Israel in East Africa.[42] There were pressures on the non-aligned governments to use their influence within the OAU and the non-aligned movement to get Israel to agree to the reopening of the Canal. It is no wonder that the OAU Middle East Mission of 1971 devoted much effort to the issue of reopening the Canal.

Another aspect of the Suez closure which was offensive to the Africans was the fact that South Africa benefited from it. In October 1970 the Ugandan delegate to the UN complained that the closure of the Canal had made East African states "involuntary partners in the enrichment of South Africa."[43]

Israel also made the mistake of backing "unpopular losers." She supported the Anya Nya rebellion in southern Sudan, and in Nigeria pressures mounted on the federal government to break off relations with Israel during and after the civil war in reaction to Israel's support for secessionist Biafra. The Arabs wasted no time in exploiting all this. An Egyptian release stated:

> We find that Israel always helped the separatist movements on the continent such as the support of the secessionists of Biafra in Nigeria and Katanga in the Congo. Today Israel undoubtedly realizes the situation to which its foolish policy led it with the growing number of African countries that severed diplomatic relations with it.[44]

Algeria reminded General Gowon of Nigeria, when he delayed breaking off relations with Israel during the 1973 war, of the contrasting roles the Arabs and Israelis played during the Nigerian civil war:

> As everybody knows—because the events are still very fresh in the memory—when that country recently suffered the painful and cruel ordeal of the secessionist attempt in Biafra,

the Arab countries, including Algeria, were among the best friends and the strongest supporters of Nigeria, while Israel was among the enemies of Nigeria's unity and integrity. The paradox is so obvious that it is worth mentioning today.[45]

The issue was also emphasized at a November 1973 meeting of the African Heads of Missions in London and the OAU representative in Europe. The meeting claimed that African leaders were "gravely concerned by Israeli support for secessionist movements in Africa."[46] It has also been suggested that Franco-Israeli estrangement as a result of the 1967 war weakened the Israeli diplomatic position in Africa; that it generated confusion among some francophone countries in Africa which still followed France's lead in foreign policy.[47]

The movement in the early 1970s for greater Third World solidarity, which was needed to extract concessions from the developed North for a new international economic order, also undermined Israel's position in Africa. This movement was manifest in the OAU itself, where a minimum consensus on the Arab-Israeli conflict was needed for the much-talked-about African solidarity. During this period there were increased visits between African and Arab members of the OAU, and the increase in diplomatic relations among the states was testimony to this growing concern for unity. However, as long as African states declined to give full support to Egypt, the Arab-Israeli conflict acted as an obstacle to unity. This made some African states impatient with Israel. In 1973 there was a sense of urgency in Africa for a common African approach to a number of international issues. At the tenth-anniversary summit of the OAU in May the Africans, contrary to expectations, were able to adopt a continental approach to negotiations with the European community. And as part of the trade-off, the OAU moved closer to the Arab position on Israel by accepting that Israel's occupation of Egyptian lands constituted an act of aggression threatening the security and unity of the continent.[48]

However, despite all these setbacks, Israel still hoped it could hold the line in Africa. Foreign Minister Abba Eban told Israeli ambassadors to the Third World in Jerusalem in August 1973 that those African states "which severed ties with us gained very little by doing so; and we have reason to believe they are questioning the wisdom of having cut diplomatic ties with us."[49] Requests for Israeli assistance continued to pour in. In late February 1973 the foreign minister of Gabon was in Israel, where it was announced that Gabon and Israel would work out plans for the development of relations. Even in late September the prime minister of Upper Volta sent a personal note to Prime Minister Meir expressing his government's "deep and genuine desire to maintain and strengthen the friendly relations existing between the two countries ever since Upper Volta became an independent state."[50] Israel also asked her strong African allies to use their influence to stem the tide of anti-Israeli diplomatic action on the continent. After Niger severed ties in January 1973, President Houphouët-Boigny was requested to urge his fellow members of the Entente Council (Dahomey, Togo, and Upper Volta) not to follow Niger's example.

But the outbreak of another round of hostilities in October 1973 changed all that. The war brought all those factors which had been latent since the early 1970s to the forefront, and the process begun with Uganda's break of relations in 1972 came to a head. Nine states broke ties with Israel during the war and eleven others shortly afterwards. By mid-November 1973 all black African states, with the exception of Lesotho, Malawi, Swaziland, and Mauritius, had severed their ties with Israel. As a West African diplomat put it: "For one thing, there was an active war on last month. This brought the whole matter to another level. Verbal support for Egypt, an African country, was not enough—the situation required an act against Israel."[51]

The responsibility for the war was placed squarely in Israel's lap, despite the fact that, unlike 1967, the first shots were fired by the Egyptians. General Gowon of Nigeria explained: "If Israel had accepted the UN resolution on the Middle East, the current war would have been averted."[52] An editorial in the Côte d'Ivoire daily on 16 October 1973 was even more specific: "The Jewish State . . . in being intransigent, in refusing the mission of the 'Wise Men' and in refusing to make a declaration on non-annexation, has the responsibility for the present outbreak of hostilities."[53]

The crossing to the west bank of the Suez—into African soil proper—by the Israeli army undoubtedly aroused African anger. This was a reason given by many states for breaking relations.[54] Neither did the failure of Israel to respect the 22 October UN ceasefire agreement make things easier for a few countries that still wanted to hold onto their ties with Israel. Gowon accused Israel of breaking "faith with Nigeria." A Nigerian government statement said that "Israel, by its violation of the UN ceasefire and occupation of more Egyptian territory, had shown itself unworthy of diplomatic relations."[55]

The war also heightened the sense of psychological threat to the "security" of the continent. The Arabs had alleged that South Africa had actually been active in the war on the side of Israel. While this was difficult to verify, Portugal allowed the United States to resupply Israel from the Azores at a time when American traditional allies in Europe refused the use of their bases. This did not go unnoticed in Africa, and it gave some credibility to the Arab claim of Tel Aviv's collaboration with the colonial and minority regimes in Africa.

Some African states, nevertheless, tried to resist the pressure to sever diplomatic ties. Ethiopia, Côte d'Ivoire, Kenya, Liberia, Madagascar, Nigeria, and Senegal were reluctant to join other African states in breaking relations. President Senghor, on arrival in Paris from a trip to Britain on 10 October, criticized countries which had broken off diplomatic relations with Israel. He said that he did not consider such an action an effective way of restoring peace in the Middle East.[57] On 20 October Kenyatta said Kenya was definitely not going to be involved in "the conflict of other peoples."[58] But once there was a flood of states breaking ties, it became very difficult for these states not to join, as they detested the opprobrium of being isolated in African diplomacy. The position of Gowon, as chairman of the OAU, was particularly sensitive. He could not afford to remain outside the OAU stream without weakening the authority and influence of the organization itself. For Kenya, Côte d'Ivoire, and Zambia, severance of diplomatic ties with Israel became expedient once traditional allies such as Ethiopia had done so; the defection of all the other francophone states additionally weakened Côte d'Ivoire's resolve. As a Liberian diplomat admitted: "If others had stood with us, we could have withstood the pressures. We couldn't do it alone."[59]

Finally, it is also probable that some African countries took a hard calculating look at the consequences of an Arab economic retaliation against them if they refused to break with Israel, and the financial rewards of complete identification with the Arabs. Although Ali Mazrui and many African leaders have denied any connection between the Arab oil embargo, Arab surplus petrodollars, and Africa's break with Israel,[60] the "long stick and carrot" tactics that had characterized Arab, particularly Libyan and Saudi, diplomacy in Africa since 1971, could not have gone unnoticed by many of the poor and small African countries, or by those whose regimes were being threatened by Arab-supported armed rebellion. It is also true, as LeVine and Luke observed, that before eighteen African countries announced their break with Israel, the Arabs had indicated a unilateral increase of 70 percent in the price of oil—a threat carried out on 16 October.[61] Sixteen African states severed ties after the Arabs had announced the imposition of an oil embargo against Israel's Western friends. "There was no subtlety in the Arab threat. It was clearly and openly expressed not only to the Africans but to everyone else."[61] In any case, the bitter controversies between the black Africans and the Arabs in the months that followed the African show of exceptional solidarity with the Arabs did not divorce the two issues.

NOTES

1. See, for example, the official Rwandan government statement, Rwanda, *Carrefour d'Afrique*, no. 014, 15–21, October 1973, p. 2.

2. See Efrem Sigel, "Israel and Africa," *Africa Report*, vol. 15, no. 2 (1970), p. 6.

3. See H. S. Aynor, *Notes from Africa* (New York: Praeger, 1969).

4. For details, see Naomi Chazan, "Some Thoughts on the Reestablishment of an Israeli Aid Programme in Africa," Israel-African Studies Association, Conference on the Middle East and Africa, May 31, 1977, p. 4; Z.Y. Hershlag, *Israel-Africa Cooperation: Final Report* (Tel Aviv University, 1973).

5. Arye Oded, "Africa, Israel and the Arabs: On the Restoration of Israeli-African Diplomatic Relations," *Jerusalem Journal of International Relations*, vol. 6, no. 3 (1982–83), p. 52. See also Ethan A. Nadelmann, "Israel and Black Africa: A Rapprochement?" *Journal of Modern African Studies*, vol. 19, no. 2 (1981); Susan A. Gitelson, "Israel's African Setback in Perspective," in Michael Curtis and Susan A. Gitelson (eds.), *Israel and the Third World* (New Brunswick, N.J.: Transaction Books, 1976), pp. 182–199.

6. *Africa Research Bulletin* (hereafter *ARB*), 1970, p. 1820.

7. Samuel Decalo, "Africa and the UN Anti-Zionism Resolution: Roots and Causes," *Cultures et Development*, vol. 48, no. 1 (1976), p. 101.

8. Gitelson, "Israel's African Setback," p. 185.

9. Susan A. Gitelson, "Why Do Small States Break Diplomatic Relations with Outside Powers?" *International Studies Quarterly*, vol. 18, no. 4 (December 1974), p. 467.

10. OAU doc. Assembly of Heads of State and Government (AHG)/Res. 62 (VII).

11. Mohamed O. Beshir, *Israel and Africa* (Khartoum: Khartoum University Press, 1974).

12. From interview by Tullia Zevi, *Africa Report*, vol. 17, no. 7 (August 1972), p. 12.

13. *Africa Diary*, 26 November–2 December 1973, p. 6738.

14. Ghana Press Release, Information Section, Ghana High Commission, London, 29 October 1973.

15. For full details of the report, see *United Nations General Assembly Official Records* (hereafter *UNGAOR*), doc. A/8566.

16. For some details on the confusion that was attendant on the initiative within the OAU and African ranks at the UN in December 1971, see Ran Kochan, "An African Peace Mission in the Middle East: The One-Man Initiative of President Senghor," *African Affairs*, vol. 72, no. 287 (April 1973), pp. 186–196; Yassin El-Ayouty, "The OAU and the Arab-Israeli Conflict: A Case of Mediation that Failed," in Yassin El-Ayouty (ed.), *The Organization of African Unity After Ten Years: Comparative Perspective* (New York: Praeger, 1975), pp. 189–212.

17. *UNGAOR*, 26th Year, 2016th plenary meeting, 13 December 1971.

18. *Africa Report*, vol. 17, no. 7 (1972), p. 12.

19. *West Africa*, 15 October 1973, p. 1443.

20. *ARB*, June 1972, p. 2497.

21. *Foreign Report*, 16 May 1973.

22. *ARB*, September 1973, p. 2975.

23. Col. Baruch Bar-Lev, who headed the Israeli mission in Kampala in 1971, was reported in 1976 to have admitted that he "helped make Idi Amin President of Uganda." See *New York Times*, 17 July 1976.

24. *ARB* (Economic Series), July 14–August 15 (1972), p. 2433.

25. *Africa Confidential*, vol. 13, no. 5 (1972).

26. See *ARB*, December 1972, p. 2684.

27. *Africa Diary*, 1973, p. 6291.

28. Colin Legum, "Africa, the Arabs and the Middle East," in Colin Legum (ed.), *Africa Contemporary Record, 1973–74*, vol. 6 (London: Rex Collings, 1974, p. A5).

29. *Africa Diary*, 1968, p. 4173.

30. *ARB* April 1969, p. 1374; December 1970, p. 1967.

31. For details, see *Africa Diary*, 1972, p. 6258; *New York Times*, 12 January 1973.

32. Ibid., 19 March 1973.

33. From an interview in *Al Ahram*, cited in Phillippe Decraene, "Is the Romance with Israel Over?" *Africa Report*, May-June 1973, p. 20.

34. *ARB*, November 1972, p. 2676.

35. Ibid., February 1971, p. 2010.

36. Ibid., December 1972, p. 2705.

37. Ali Mazrui, "Black Africa and the Arabs," *Foreign Affairs*, vol. 53, no. 4 (1975), p. 732.

38. Ibid.

39. Victor LeVine and Timothy W. Luke, *The Arab-African Connection: Political and Economic Realities* (Boulder: Westview, 1979), p. 11.

40. *The African Stand Toward Israel*, Ministry of Information, no. 94, Cairo, December 1973, p. 24.

41. Susan Allen, "Suez: Who Wins When the Canal Opens?" *African Development* (April 1975), pp. 15–17.

42. *West Africa Pilot*, 20 May 1968.

43. *UNGAOR*, 25th session, 1890th plenary meeting, 29 October 1970, p. 3.

44. *The African Stand Toward Israel*, pp. 6–7.

45. Algerian Press Service, 23 October 1973, in *BBC Summary of World Broadcasts*, Part IV, 26 October 1973.

46. See World Jewish Congress, *African and Asian Media Survey: African and Asian Attitudes on the Middle East Conflict*, January 1974.

47. Nadelmann, "Israel and Black Africa," p. 197.

48. For text of the resolution, see OAU doc. AHG/Res 70 (X), 1973.

49. Legum, "Africa, the Arabs and the Middle East," p. A5.

50. *Jerusalem Post*, 24 and 29 September 1973.

51. *New York Times*, 26 November 1973.

52. *Lagos Radio*, 10 October 1973, cited in World Jewish Congress, *African and Asian Media Survey*, p. 23.

53. Ibid., p. 19.

54. For some of the official statements, see ibid.

55. Ibid., p. 24.

56. *Ghanaian Times*, 11 October 1973.

57. *Daily Nation*, 21 October 1973.

58. *New York Times*, 6 November 1973, p. 15.

59. Mazrui, "Black Africa and the Arabs," p. 736.

60. LeVine and Luke, *The Arab-African Connection*, p. 15.

61. Marie Syrkin, "Israeli-African Relations: The Fall from Grace" (unpublished), cited in LeVine and Luke, *The Arab-African Connection*, p. 16.

FOUR

The Era of
Non-Formal Relations,
1973–1978

Africa's relations with Israel reached their lowest ebb with the severance of diplomatic relations in October and November 1973. At the November 1973 emergency session of the ministerial council, called specifically to discuss the Middle East crisis and its impact on Africa, the OAU tied Africa's fortunes to the Arab-Israeli conflict for the first time. In a lengthy anti-Israeli declaration of policy,[1] the council said the African countries' break with Israel

> testifies to the one and indivisible nature of the struggle of the African and Arab peoples against the common enemy, imperialism, whose bridgeheads in Africa and the Middle East constitute a violation of their territorial integrity, a threat to their security and an impediment to their development.

The diplomatic rupture was defended as an attempt "to free [Africa] from colonialism [and] to eliminate apartheid and Zionism." The declaration stated that the conflict had "revealed the open collusion between the forces of aggression in Africa and Israel, armed and supported by imperialism and world Zionism." It went on to declare that the "struggle of the Palestinian people to recover their usurped land . . . is part and parcel of [their] overall struggle for self-determination against colonialism and racial discrimination." It recommended "that African states should take, either individually or collectively, within the framework of the OAU and other international bodies, and in particular in compliance with Chapter VII of the UN Charter, all requisite measures to put an end to Israel's defiance of the international community."

The council also adopted a twenty-two-paragraph anti-Israeli resolution on the Middle East. Apart from demanding "the immediate and unconditional withdrawal of Israel from all the occupied Arab territories," the resolution asked member states "to maintain the severance of relations with Israel" until it withdrew from all occupied territories and "until the recovery by the Palestinian people of their legitimate national rights."

The rupture of relations was greeted with anger in Israel. An editorial in *Ha'aretz* stated that Israel had "reason to react in anger to their [Africa's] lack of gratitude. . . . The haste to alienate us does not add to our respect for the African countries."[2] *Hatsofe*, the National Religious Party newspaper, declared:

> One of Israel's diplomatic errors was its great effort to establish close ties with the African states without first establishing whether these regimes were stable and mature enough to make the effort worthwhile. Careful consideration would have shown that the enormous sums spent in developing Africa would have been put to infinitely better use in absorbing immigrants and in reducing the social gap in Israel.[3]

The *Jerusalem Post* stressed that Israeli public opinion was "angry":

> If it were not occupied with more pressing concerns of the war, it would doubtless have been much more embittered and more volubly embittered. . . . If the ceasefire opens the path to political settlement in the Middle East, no doubt many of the African states will seek to renew their links with Israel—Israel will certainly be glad of it. But those links will never be the same again. The taste of betrayal at a time of crisis will remain.[4]

The paper's diplomatic correspondent, David Landau, concurred: "What is clear is that no matter how relations with Africa improve (they can scarcely get worse) at some time in the future, the original enthusiasm which spurred Israel's first overtures to Africa 15 years ago will not return."[5] *Ha'aretz* put it more bluntly: "If we come out of this war without being reduced in stature, the Africans will not be slow in seeking relations with us once again. But it is unlikely that the restoration of our position in Africa will be high on Israel's list of priorities for the near future."[6] Yaacov Shimoni, then assistant director of the Foreign Ministry, later described the situation as follows:

> Obviously Israel has been in a state of traumatic shock concerning her African relations since 1973. It would be foolish to deny that or to close one's eyes to it. We did our best to develop a structure of relationships with the emerging countries as they achieved independence from the mid-1950s. That framework, developed over a period of fifteen years or so, has somehow broken down. . . . Of course it cannot be totally repaired. Whenever we resume relations with African countries . . . they will never be the same again. Wounds of this kind leave scars.[7]

The general public was less restrained in its reaction. A Dr. Jacobsen remarked in a letter to the *Jerusalem Post:*

> I think that this eventual desire of these states [to renew diplomatic relations] should be met with complete indifference. More than that, we should refuse to renew the development assistance to any state which severed relations.
>
> The heavy burden of our taxation which most of us are willing to bear in order to repair the damages of this war would become intolerable if even a penny was spent to bolster the economy of those who let us down when the pinch came.[8]

A letter-writer from Tel Aviv deplored the "race between African countries to sever diplomatic relations with the State of Israel. It makes me wonder whether these countries have any independent foreign policy at all."[9]

In practical terms, however, many African leaders did not take their break with Israel as a very serious action. Yaacov Shimoni disclosed that after breaking relations, some African leaders informed Jerusalem that the step was only a political move and that they remained friendly toward Israel.[10] Many of them wanted ongoing projects of technical cooperation to continue. Even those who had missions in Israel saw no need to wind up their activities long after the break; at the end of November 1973 the Foreign Ministry had to remind the diplomats of the need to do so.[11]

However, after prolonged deliberations Israel decided to terminate bilateral programs with those countries that had broken relations. As Shimoni explained: "The Israeli Parliament and public opinion would not have accepted the idea that one should continue aiding from Israeli taxpayers' money, even in small amounts, countries that have just severed relations, i.e. taken the supreme step of hostility, short of war."[12] The disillusionment in Israel was so profound that President Senghor's offer to Israel to keep someone in Dakar as a consular agent was rejected.[13] And a Foreign Ministry spokesman stressed that Israel was not interested in being "represented by other countries in Africa."[14] Tamar Golan summed up the situation:

> Many African leaders who took this decision [to break relations] did not regard it as a final act. It was a dramatic gesture but every good play has several dramatic scenes. The Israelis were amazed when at the very time African leaders were severing ties, some also expressed the desire to continue with "business as usual." Others even asked that Israeli aid missions stay on. To the Israelis, this was hypocrisy at its worst. To the Africans, this was a way of saying "Don't take the act too seriously, the play goes on."[15]

Nevertheless, the Israeli government agreed to maintain "interest offices" in Côte d'Ivoire, Ghana, and Kenya, and bilateral programs with a few select countries were not broken.[16] The government was concerned about the possible negative impact of the severance of diplomatic relations on Israeli firms operating in Africa. Although the firms were not directed to wind up their activities, the government warned their management that it could no longer provide any protection or help for personnel employed in Africa.[17]

MULTILATERAL RELATIONS

On the multilateral level relations remained sour as African states continued to give unreserved support for Arab positions. Arab leaders decided at Rabat on 26–29 October 1974 that the PLO was the sole legitimate representative of the Palestinian people and that the organization should head "an independent national authority" to be set up on any Palestinian land that would be liberated.

The Twenty-ninth Session of the UN General Assembly in November 1974 became a forum for international endorsement and legitimation of this Arab decision. All black African states except Malawi and Swaziland supported the Assembly's breach of its own established procedure by agreeing to hear the PLO in the plenary session. The practice hitherto had been that all non-governmental organizations could be heard in any of the relevant seven standing committees of the General Assembly. Two other pro-Palestinian resolutions of importance were adopted by the Assembly with African backing. Except for Malawi and Swaziland, which abstained, black African states voted in favor of Resolution 3236 (XXIX), which reaffirms Palestinian "rights to national independence and sovereignty." The resolution also instructed the secretary-general to maintain contact with the PLO on all issues concerning the Palestinian question. In none of its resolutions did the Assembly concern itself with UN Security Council Resolutions 242 (1967) and 338 (1973) or with the security of Israel. However, most of the states, in explaining their votes, stressed that they upheld Israel's right to exist.

The Africans also overwhelmingly supported Resolution 3237 (XXIX), which gave the PLO observer status at the General Assembly and other UN agencies. In the past such observer status had been reserved for states. Subsequently, they endorsed the resolution which "strongly condemns all governments which do not recognize the right to self-determination and independence of peoples under colonial and foreign domination and alien subjugation, notably the peoples of Africa and the Palestinian people." The African states also supported Arab-inspired moves to exclude Israel from active participation in any of the UNESCO regional commissions and to condemn the archaeological excavations in Jerusalem.

At the OAU, the story was rarely different. Both the 1974 and 1975 summits passed strident condemnatory resolutions against Israel. In 1975 the PLO leader was invited to address the Assembly of Heads of State and the PLO was given observer status in the OAU. The assembly agreed "that the racist regime in occupied Palestine and the racist regimes in Zimbabwe and South Africa have a common imperialist origin, forming a whole and having the same racist structure and being organically linked in their policy aimed at repression of the dignity and integrity of the human being."[18]

Nonetheless, black African states refused to endorse an Arab proposal to expel Israel from the UN and to impose economic sanctions upon her. After a stormy eight-hour debate the ministerial council decided to send a proposal calling for the suspension (not expulsion) of Israel from the UN to the Assembly of Heads of State. The assembly dropped the suspension clause completely and merely agreed to a request of OAU member states to reinforce pressures against Israel, "including the possibility of eventually depriving it of UN membership." Even then, Zaire totally rejected both the suspension and the watered-down version. Ghana, Liberia, Senegal, and Sierra Leone expressed reservations.[19]

The disappointment felt by the African states in their dealings with the Arabs had started to affect Afro-Arab relations and the extent to which some of them were willing to go along with Arab demands vis-à-vis Israel. As indicated in Chapter 2, the Africans had expected the Arab states to generously reciprocate their break with Israel in 1973. They not only demanded oil at concessionary prices but equally expected substantial Arab financial support for their economies, which had been adversely affected both by drought and the crippling oil price hikes. The Arabs were, however, not prepared to meet any of the African demands. They refused concessionary oil prices and were not prepared to commit a substantial part of their petrodollars to African development.

The period from November 1973 to late 1975 was spent in a fruitless debate over how best to transfer the $200 million promised to ameliorate the impact of the quadrupled oil price on Africa. African states not only derided the loan as grossly inadequate, they also wanted it transferred for disbursement to the African Development Bank. But the Arabs were insistent on disbursing it through their own exclusive institutions—first through the Arab League, then centered in Cairo, and later through the Arab Bank for African Development. The Africans were also opposed to the setting up of exclusive Arab financial institutions for African development. They wanted all Arab development assistance channeled through the African Development Bank, whose membership includes nine Arab League members of the OAU. Alternatively, the Africans pressed for the setting up of joint institutions which would give both groups room to partake in the decision-making process on issues affecting African states. The total rejection of all African demands gave rise to criticism and suspicion as to Arab intentions in Africa.[20]

Besides, only a trickle of Arab money was finding its way to Africa. In the period of 1973–1975, when the need for compensatory aid to weak

African economies was greatest, the African members of the Arab League received nearly 90 percent of all OPEC aid going to the less developed African countries. Moreover, African countries with predominantly Muslim populations were favored in the disbursement of the little that was given to Africa. In addition, the terms of the Arab-OPEC aid generally hardened from 1974 to 1975. An Organization for Economic Cooperation and Development (OECD) study shows that in 1974 and 1975 the toughest terms were often extended to the poorest countries, those with a GNP per capita below $200, while the softest terms in 1975 benefited the richest recipients, those with GNP per capita over $1,000.[21] Even then, actual bilateral disbursement rarely exceeded between 35 and 45 percent of commitments and much of it took excessively long to materialize. Multilateral disbursement was about 59 percent during 1974 and 1975.[22]

An editorial in Kenya's *Sunday Nation* asked: "With such 'friends' who needs enemies?" It went on:

> The honeymoon between Africans and Arabs seems about over. The jubilant chants of solidarity which accompanied the dramatic break of diplomatic relations [with Israel] have now been replaced by cries of frustration and bitterness from African nations whose economies face collapse as a result of the astronomical increases in the prices of oil products. . . . The Arabs are doing what the bad old imperialists have been doing all along, giving aid so as to finance the purchase of products from the donor nations. The only difference is that there was a much closer relationship between the aid given by the Western nations and the volume of trade between them and developing countries.[23]

Reflecting on the concept of friendship between the Africans and the Arabs, the paper said: "Certainly it is a strange friend indeed who persists in a policy which spells the collapse of the economy of a friendly state, especially when the intended victim pleads for his survival as eloquently as the African nations have done." The paper then went on to argue for the resumption of ties by African states with Israel: "Why must African nations be the only friends of the Arabs who must have total diplomatic severance with Israel in order to qualify for friendship with Arab nations?"[24]

There were similar calls from several prominent Kenyan politicians, including Attorney General Charles Njonjo, Minister for Local Government James Osago, and Assistant Minister for Home Affairs Martin Shikuku.[25] Gabon, whose president had converted to Islam after a visit to Libya in 1973, in the ecstasy of the Afro-Arab honeymoon, expressed itself as disillusioned in 1974. President Omar Bongo stated: "The state of our relations with Arab countries is nothing but negative, with the exception of Algeria."[26] Even the commentary of Nigeria's Radio-Television Kaduna (which usually reflected pro-Muslim/Arab bias) on 25 June 1974 was critical:

> The impression has been created that the Arabs have taken and are still going to continue to take black Africa for a ride. In other words, while members of the OAU are taking all reasonable measures to support the cause of the Arabs, the oil sheiks, on the other hand, appear to pursue a policy capable of crippling the economy of Africa without showing serious concern.[27]

African dissatisfaction at the time was not only due to disappointment over aid and oil. The OAU was evidently annoyed by widespread reports of growing Arab economic and military cooperation with the racist and minority regimes in Southern Africa. Even Idi Amin, who was the African leader most uncritically supportive of the Arabs, was sufficiently alarmed to cable the Arab League secretary-general concerning "his dissatisfaction over the number of Arab states investing and doing business in South Africa." He went on to say that "Africa is today surprised at the behaviour of Arabs who have neglected Black Africa and had decided to do business with South Africa."[28]

A number of African leaders had also become apprehensive of what they regarded as the excessive Arab influence within the OAU. The acrimonious debates and the inconclusive ballots for an OAU secretary-general in Mogadishu in 1974 brought these feelings to the fore. At the summit the Arab members had used every means, including underhanded ones, to get the Somali foreign minister elected to succeed Nzo Ekangaki, who had just resigned over criticism of his handling of the oil crisis.

Commenting on the elections, the *Times of Zambia* alleged that there was "a spirited attempt by one group [the Arabs] to achieve a dominance of the organization which would have reduced it to a mouthpiece of that clique. . . . It must be recognized by all that no one group of nations can dominate the continent without endangering its survival as a political and economic entity."[29] Jean Pierre N'Diaya, a well-known African journalist, reacting to the elections, advocated the strengthening of cultural and other ties between black Francophones and Anglophones in the OAU. He went on:

> The strengthening of cultural ties implies the establishment of a "Black Peoples' League" which should embrace all peoples of African origin, in the same way the Arab League unites the Arab world. For only by such unity can Arab and African peoples find their true destiny.[30]

The invitation of Yasser Arafat to address the OAU summit in 1975 was another manifestation of increasing Arab influence which did not go over well with many Africans. One African observer asked:

> Can any of the Foreign Ministers who made this irresponsible decision to invite Arafat to address the Assembly of Heads of State of the OAU cite any occasion when any of the leaders of African liberation movements was invited to address the summit of the Arab League, to advise the best way the Arabs could contribute to the cause of the oppressed peoples of Africa still under colonial and racist rule?[31]

Despite all the criticism, African states continued to maintain their diplomatic boycott of Israel in support of the Arabs. This was in part due to current lack of interest on the part of the Israeli Foreign Ministry in exploiting the signs of disenchantment with the Arabs. The Israelis saw the rupture not only as totally uncalled for, but as something "done in a manner calculated to offend most, in the midst of the Middle East War." To them "it seemed futile to appear interested in rebuilding what most felt could never be replaced. Africa's 'betrayal' had underscored the worthlessness of reliance on the fickle Third World."[32]

At the UN the Africans continued to vote overwhelmingly for Arab-sponsored resolutions. An analysis of the 263 African votes on the seven most important resolutions on the Middle East during the Thirtieth Session of the General Assembly in 1975 shows a coincidence in African and Arab votes of 73.8 percent. Only 3 percent of African votes were at variance with those of the Arabs, while the absence and abstention of states account for the remaining 23.2 percent (see Table 4.1).

TABLE 4.1

VOTING RECORD OF SELECTED AFRICAN STATES ON SELECTED RESOLUTIONS ON THE MIDDLE EAST, 30TH SESSION OF UN GENERAL ASSEMBLY, 1975

	A/Res 3375 PLO	3376 Pales-tine	3414 Middle East	3419 Displaced Inhabitants	3525C Quneitra	3516 National Resources	3379 Zionism
Botswana	Y	Y	–	Y	Y	Y	A
Burundi	Y	Y	Y	Y	Y	Y	Y
Cameroun	Y	Y	Y	Y	Y	Y	Y
Cape Verde	Y	Y	–	–	–	–	Y
Central African Republic	–	–	A	–	A	A	N
Comoros	O	O	Y	Y	–	Y	O
Congo	Y	Y	Y	Y	Y	Y	Y
Côte d'Ivoire	Y	A	Y	Y	A	Y	N
Dahomey	Y	Y	Y	Y	Y	Y	Y
Equatorial Guinea	Y	Y	Y	–	Y	Y	Y
Ethiopia	Y	A	Y	Y	Y	Y	A
Gabon	Y	A	A	–	–	A	A
Gambia	Y	Y	Y	Y	–	–	Y
Ghana	Y	Y	Y	Y	Y	Y	A
Guinea	Y	Y	Y	Y	Y	Y	Y
Guinea-Bissau	Y	Y	Y	–	–	–	Y
Kenya	Y	Y	A	Y	Y	Y	A
Lesotho	Y	A	Y	Y	Y	Y	A
Liberia	Y	A	N	–	–	Y	N
Madagascar	Y	Y	Y	Y	Y	Y	Y
Malawi	A	A	A	A	N	A	N
Mali	Y	Y	Y	Y	Y	Y	Y
Mauritius	Y	Y	Y	Y	Y	Y	A
Mozambique	Y	Y	Y	Y	Y	Y	Y
Niger	Y	Y	Y	Y	Y	Y	Y
Nigeria	Y	Y	Y	Y	–	Y	Y
Rwanda	Y	Y	Y	Y	Y	Y	Y
São Tomé	Y	Y	–	–	–	–	Y
Senegal	Y	Y	Y	Y	Y	Y	Y
Sierra Leone	Y	A	Y	Y	Y	–	A
Swaziland	A	N	A	A	–	Y	N
Tanzania	Y	Y	Y	Y	Y	Y	Y
Zaire	Y	Y	–	Y	Y	Y	A
Zambia	Y	Y	Y	Y	Y	Y	A

Source: Compiled by the Research Department, Ministry of Foreign Affairs, Jerusalem, 1976.
Y=in favor, N=against, A=abstention, O=not yet member, –=absent.

The Africans maintained the broad support for the Arab position at the session until the Arabs suddenly decided to include a clause equating Zionism with racism in a resolution on the "Decade for Action to Combat Racism and Racial Discrimination" in the Third Committee of the General Assembly. A number of black African states tried unsuccessfully to stop the Arab inclusion of the clause in the draft resolution, which essentially dealt with the situation in Southern Africa. Ambassador Kamarake of Sierra Leone argued that

> the question of Zionism was basically a new element as far as discussion of the Decade . . . .was concerned. That element had not been introduced during the discussion in the Economic and Social Council or even in previous discussions of the Decade in the Committee. Moreover, he would like to draw the attention of the African Group, in particular, the African states south of the Sahara, to the fact that although the Assembly of . . . the OAU in . . . 1975 dealt with different forms of racism, that resolution had not been considered in the context of the Decade. . . . The same could be said of the Political Declaration adopted at the Conference of Ministers for Foreign Affairs of Non-aligned countries held in Lima in August 1975, to which reference was made in the fifth preambular paragraph of draft A/C.3/2159. In the light of these facts, his delegation appealed to the sponsors of the draft resolution and to the Committee as a whole to reflect on the situation and on the possibility that putting draft resolution A/C.3/2159 to a vote at the present time might divide the ranks of the OAU and of the non-aligned group.[33]

The Ethiopian delegate said the resolution would jeopardize the consensus which had emerged with respect to the Decade at a time when the goal appeared in sight. The introduction at the last minute of new objectives might sow confusion and disrupt the efforts which had been made to achieve unity, for to identify Zionism with apartheid was inconceivable.[34]

Some black African delegates emphasized the damage which the passage of the resolution could do to the main concern of the Africans at the UN—the issue of racism and racial discrimination in Southern Africa—as Western countries whose support was essential for the success of the "Programme for the Decade" had indicated, in no uncertain terms, that they would not support it. The Zambian delegate warned:

"Moves that may come in the way of universal support and participation cannot be welcomed."[35] The Kenyan delegate insisted that the matter should be dropped and then referred for further study. He lamented:

> Indeed, apart from expressions of anger and sometimes insults, or pleasure, depending upon the inclination of the speakers, what has been going on sheds little or no light at all on the subject. It is common practice for this Organization to request its organs to conduct studies and provide data on difficult issues on which the United Nations has been asked to take decisions. No adequate reasons have been given for rushing this definition through before some of us have had time to benefit from studies, both private and public.[36]

During the committee debate, Liberia suggested a postponement of the vote on the amendment until the following session. It was supported by Ghana, Nigeria, and Zambia.[37] Sierra Leone, supported by Zambia, formally introduced a motion calling for such a postponement. Although the proposal was rejected, thirteen African states were among the forty-five countries that supported it. These were: Botswana, Côte d'Ivoire, Ethiopia, Gabon, Kenya, Liberia, Malawi, Rwanda, Sierra Leone, Swaziland, Upper Volta, Zaire, and Zambia. Four others—Gambia, Ghana, Lesotho, and Togo—abstained. Cameroun, Cape Verde, Chad, the Congo, Dahomey, Guinea, Guinea-Bissau, Madagascar, Mali, Mozambique, Niger, Nigeria, Senegal, Uganda, and Tanzania opposed the motion. However, when a Libyan motion to close debate on the draft, intended to rush a vote on the motion, was put to a vote, only Côte d'Ivoire and Liberia opposed it. Botswana, Cameroun, Ethiopia, Ghana, Kenya, Lesotho, Mauritius, Rwanda, Sierra Leone, Swaziland, Tanzania, Togo, Upper Volta, Zaire, and Zambia all abstained.

The issue generated heated and often acrimonious debates both within and without the UN. The matter was made worse by Idi Amin who, ostensibly speaking on Africa's behalf in his capacity as the OAU chairman, not only attacked Zionism but went so far as to call for the expulsion of Israel from the UN and her extermination. *Afrique Nouvelle* (Senegal) described the speech as "the most racist act ever seen at the United Nations." *Daily Star* (Nigeria) condemned it as "palpably unimaginative and smack[ing] of sadism." But the remarks of United States UN Ambassador Daniel Moynihan infuriated African delegates at the UN. Speaking in San Francisco on 3 October 1975, Moynihan called Idi

Amin "this racist murderer" who was by "no accident" also president of the OAU. Tiamiou Adjibade, chairman of the African Group at the UN, reacted by accusing Mr. Moynihan of "an unfriendly act" toward the OAU.[38]

When the Zionism-racism amendment was finally put to the vote, only five black African states opposed it; twelve abstained and twenty supported it (see Table 4.1) The Mauritius delegate, Ramphul, attributed the small number of African states opposing it to Moynihan's speech:

> I am satisfied that I have done my best to bring about a compromise. I admit that I have failed. I have failed mainly because of two words that were used by two representatives of one country. They chose to describe the action of 70 independent, sovereign countries as obscene and, by implication, described those same countries as indecent and not to be counted among one's friends. Many are those delegations which would have changed their position were it not for those two words.[39]

The support of the majority of black African states for the Zionism-racism vote was not an indication of Africa's definitive policy on either Israel or Zionism. On many issues at the UN, delegates do have open instructions (as Ramphul's statement would suggest) and their votes consequently reflect their personal inclinations. Sometimes votes are cast in a particular context that would not warrant a conclusion outside that context. For instance, although Nigeria voted in favor of the Zionism resolution, her delegate to the UN Economic and Social Council conference in Abidjan, Côte d'Ivoire in July 1976 declared that Nigeria would actively work to expunge references to "Zionism as a form of racism from international resolutions."[40] Moreover, many states regarded their support for any anti-Israeli resolution not as a mark of hostility toward Israel but rather as a means of inducing her to reconsider some of her policies, particularly the occupation of Arab lands and the recognition of Palestinian rights. Hence most of the African delegates, while condemning Israel at the UN, often reiterated her right to secure and recognized boundaries.

The growing and demonstrative links between Israel and South Africa during this period damaged Israel's political standing in black Africa and was a major factor inhibiting those countries that were well disposed toward Israel from possibly reestablishing diplomatic links. This became particularly so after then-South African Prime Minister

Vorster's visit to Israel and the signing of wide-ranging and far-reaching agreements between them in 1976. Many Arricans regarded the visit as indicating something more intimate than normal diplomatic relations. The *Ghanaian Times* said that it should be seen as "an escalation of racist resistance to the African Liberation Movement." It further observed that Israel's "active cooperation with South Africa makes it impossible for an African country which is committed to the African Liberation Movement to extend sympathy to its cause in the Middle East." It suggested that in the light of such cooperation, the African states should take a closer look at Israeli business interests in Africa "and, if necessary, nationalize them."[41] The OAU was now convinced that Israel and South Africa were "allied to suffocate by all means the legitimate claims to the liberty, to the independence, to the dignity, of the black peoples of Southern Africa." It urged its members and members of the Arab League to do everything to "break the yoke of racism and Zionism."[42]

At the UN, the chairman of the Special Committee on Apartheid, Leslie O. Harriman of Nigeria, stated that the "Pretoria-Tel-Aviv axis has come to represent a serious menace to peace and freedom in Africa and the Indian Ocean."[43] The committee issued a report in September 1976 that was very critical of Israel. And from that year a separate resolution condemning the "Relations Between Israel and South Africa" began to be adopted by the UN General Assembly. The arguments of Israeli delegate Eilan did not persuade the Africans or the General Assembly. Eilan had pointed to the Anti-Apartheid Committee's own figures of $10.2 million as the value of Israel's trade with South Africa—a figure which he said "hardly exceeded the sums spent by Arab oil magnates on an average buying spree in the capitals of Europe. . . . Why should Israel be singled out in that fashion while countries whose trade with South Africa was far heavier went unmentioned?" He asked further: "Why had the report [of the committee] not mentioned, for example, that President Nyerere had charged the Arab oil-producing states with spending millions of dollars to buy gold from South Africa instead of using it to assist the liberation movements?"[44] On Vorster's visit, Eilan said:

> The report had emphasized the visit of Mr. Vorster and other
> South African leaders to Israel. However, Israel was not the only
> country to be visited by those leaders. . . . Israel had taken this
> occasion to reaffirm its opposition to apartheid, a policy which it

had opposed in the United Nations long before most of the African countries had achieved their independence and long before it had become politically fashionable and advantageous to do so.[45]

What Eilan seemed to have overlooked is that it was partly because of the previous demonstrative anti-apartheid commitment of Israel that the African states now singled her out for special criticism. Israeli-South African ties appeared to be on the upswing while even the republic's traditional Western allies were at pains to show that their relations with South Africa were less warm than before.

The 1976 resolution says, in part, that the UN secretary-general should "disseminate widely the report of the Special Committee Against Apartheid in various languages in order to mobilize public opinion against the collaboration by Israel with the South African racist regime." In another resolution, the General Assembly accused Israel, along with Britain, France, the United States, and West Germany, of supplying nuclear and military equipment and technology to South Africa and called on the five countries to refrain from extending facilities to South Africa "enabling it to produce uranium, plutonium and other nuclear materials."[46] The widespread resentment against Israeli-South African links contributed heavily to the almost unanimous support the Africans gave Arab-sponsored anti-Israeli resolutions during the Thirty-first and Thirty-second sessions of the General Assembly in 1976 and 1977 (see Tables 4.2 and 4.3)

BILATERAL RELATIONS

The picture was, however, different at the level of bilateral relations between Israel and black African states. A survey of bilateral relations does not indicate any implacable hostility toward Israel, as the strident anti-Israeli resolutions both at the OAU and the UN would have suggested. This is largely to be expected. First, as pointed out earlier, many African states did not sever their ties with Israel because of any bilateral conflict with her. While severing ties, many still regarded Israel as a friend. Second, bilateral relations can be (and usually are) conducted discreetly without all the publicity of multilateral diplomacy. And third, bilateral relations are conducted in an atmosphere devoid of such pressures as bloc "logrolling" that characterize diplomacy at the UN.

Although the break of relations caused a significant loss of interest

TABLE 4.2

VOTING RECORD OF SELECTED AFRICAN STATES ON SELECTED RESOLUTIONS ON THE MIDDLE EAST, 31ST SESSION OF UN GENERAL ASSEMBLY, 1976

	A/Res 31/20 Pales. Comm.	31/61 Middle East	31/61 Peace Conf.	31/106C Territories	31/106D Quneitra	31/110 Habitat	31/186 National Resources	31/6E Apartheid
Botswana	A	Y	Y	Y	Y	Y	Y	Y
Burundi	Y	Y	Y	Y	Y	Y	Y	Y
Cameroun	Y	Y	Y	Y	Y	Y	Y	Y
Cape Verde	Y	–	–	–	–	–	–	Y
Central African Republic	–	Y	Y	Y	Y	Y	Y	Y
Comoros	Y	Y	Y	Y	Y	–	–	Y
Côte d'Ivoire	A	Y	Y	Y	A	Y	Y	A
Equatorial Guinea	Y	Y	Y	Y	Y	Y	Y	Y
Ethiopia	Y	Y	Y	Y	Y	Y	Y	Y
Gabon	Y	–	–	Y	Y	Y	Y	Y
Gambia	A	Y	Y	Y	Y	Y	–	Y
Ghana	Y	Y	Y	Y	Y	Y	Y	Y
Guinea	Y	Y	Y	Y	Y	Y	Y	Y
Guinea-Bissau	Y	Y	Y	Y	Y	Y	Y	Y
Kenya	Y	A	Y	Y	Y	Y	Y	Y
Lesotho	A	Y	Y	Y	Y	Y	Y	Y
Liberia	Y	–	Y	A	A	Y	Y	–
Madagascar	Y	Y	Y	Y	Y	Y	Y	Y
Malawi	A	A	A	A	A	Y	A	A
Mali	Y	Y	Y	Y	Y	Y	Y	Y
Mauritius	Y	Y	Y	Y	Y	Y	Y	Y
Mozambique	Y	Y	Y	Y	Y	Y	–	Y
Niger	Y	Y	Y	Y	Y	Y	Y	Y
Nigeria	Y	Y	Y	Y	Y	Y	Y	Y
Rwanda	Y	Y	Y	Y	Y	Y	Y	Y
São Tomé	Y	Y	Y	Y	Y	Y	Y	Y
Senegal	Y	Y	Y	Y	Y	Y	Y	Y
Seychelles	–	–	–	–	–	–	–	–
Sierra Leone	Y	Y	Y	Y	Y	Y	Y	Y
Swaziland	–	A	A	A	A	Y	Y	A
Tanzania	Y	Y	Y	Y	Y	Y	Y	Y
Togo	Y	Y	Y	Y	Y	Y	Y	Y
Uganda	Y	Y	Y	Y	Y	Y	Y	Y
Upper Volta	Y	Y	Y	Y	Y	Y	Y	Y
Zaire	–	Y	Y	Y	Y	Y	Y	Y
Zambia	Y	Y	Y	Y	Y	Y	Y	Y

Source: Compiled by the Research Department, Ministry of Foreign Affairs, Jerusalem, 1977
Y=in favor, A=abstention, –=absent

TABLE 4.3

VOTING RECORD OF SELECTED AFRICAN STATES ON
SELECTED RESOLUTIONS ON THE MIDDLE EAST,
32ND SESSION OF UN GENERAL ASSEMBLY,
1977

	A/Res/5 Settlement	A/Res/20 Middle East	Res/40 Pales. Comm.	Res/91B Quneitra	Res/91C Territories	Res/105D Apartheid	Res/161 National Resources
Angola	Y	Y	Y	–	–	Y	–
Benin	Y	Y	Y	Y	Y	Y	Y
Botswana	Y	Y	Y	Y	Y	Y	Y
Burundi	Y	Y	Y	Y	Y	Y	Y
Cameroun	Y	Y	Y	Y	Y	Y	Y
Cape Verde	Y	Y	Y	Y	Y	Y	Y
Central African Republic	Y	Y	A	Y	Y	A	Y
Comoros	Y	Y	Y	Y	Y	Y	Y
Côte d'Ivoire	Y	Y	A	A	Y	A	A
Equatorial Guinea	Y	–	Y	Y	Y	–	Y
Ethiopia	Y	Y	–	Y	Y	–	Y
Gabon	Y	Y	Y	Y	Y	Y	Y
Gambia	–	Y	Y	Y	Y	Y	–
Ghana	–	Y	Y	Y	Y	Y	Y
Guinea	Y	Y	Y	Y	Y	Y	Y
Guinea-Bissau	Y	Y	Y	Y	Y	Y	Y
Kenya	Y	Y	Y	Y	Y	Y	Y
Lesotho	Y	Y	A	Y	Y	Y	Y
Liberia	Y	Y	A	A	A	A	Y
Madagascar	Y	Y	Y	Y	Y	Y	Y
Malawi	A	–	Y	A	A	A	Y
Mali	Y	Y	Y	Y	Y	Y	–
Mauritius	Y	Y	Y	Y	Y	Y	Y
Mozambique	Y	Y	Y	Y	Y	Y	Y
Niger	Y	Y	Y	Y	Y	Y	Y
Nigeria	Y	Y	Y	Y	Y	Y	Y
Rwanda	Y	Y	Y	Y	Y	Y	Y
São Tomé	Y	–	–	Y	Y	Y	Y
Senegal	Y	Y	Y	Y	Y	Y	Y
Seychelles	–	–	–	–	–	–	–
Sierra Leone	Y	Y	Y	Y	Y	Y	–
Swaziland	Y	–	–	A	A	A	Y
Tanzania	Y	Y	Y	–	–	Y	Y
Togo	Y	Y	Y	Y	Y	Y	Y
Uganda	Y	Y	Y	Y	Y	Y	Y
Upper Volta	Y	Y	Y	Y	Y	Y	Y
Zaire	Y	Y	Y	Y	Y	–	Y
Zambia	Y	Y	Y	Y	Y	Y	Y

Source: Compiled by the Research Department, Ministry of Foreign Affairs, Jerusalem, 1978.
Y=in favor, A=abstention, –=absent

by Israeli officials in Africa, particularly until 1977, it did not lead to a total break in contacts between Israeli officials and those of many of the states that severed ties. Shortly after the break, a number of African leaders became actively, but discreetly, involved in trying to promote a Middle East settlement. As early as April 1974 former President Senghor of Senegal spoke of his contacts with Israeli and Arab leaders and his "desire to promote an exchange of views."[47] In January 1977 the Israeli ambassador to London, Gideon Raphael, met Senghor. The following month the Senegalese leader arranged a meeting between Member of Knesset Arieh Eliav and the Palestinian representative in Paris. In May 1978 Shimon Peres, then chairman of the Labor Party, participated in a Socialist International conference in Dakar and held private talks with Senghor.[48]

President Houphouët-Boigny also met several times with both Israeli and Arab leaders in an attempt to encourage negotiations. In February 1977 he met Prime Minister Yitzhak Rabin in Geneva. In May he met Foreign Minister Yigal Allon in Paris, and in December he met Ehud Avriel, special advisor to Foreign Minister Dayan, and Hanan Aynor, then head of the African Department of the Foreign Ministry, during their tour of several African states following Sadat's visit to Jerusalem. Ehud Avriel also represented Israel at the coronation of Emperor Bokassa of the Central African Republic in December 1977.[49]

The upswing in diplomatic contacts between Israel and African states had by February 1977 aroused the Egyptians into believing that Sadat needed to launch a major diplomatic counter-offensive in Africa. Egypt was reported to have emphasized that African countries had severed their ties with Israel in 1973 "for as long as that country continues to occupy Arab territories and refuses to restore their legitimate rights to Palestinians."[50]

No single event demonstrated the close contact between Kenya and Israel better than the Israeli commando mission to rescue the hijacked hostages held at Entebbe Airport in Uganda. Some members of the Popular Front for the Liberation of Palestine (PFLP) had hijacked a Paris-bound Air France Airbus to Entebbe, Uganda, on 28 June 1976. The hijackers later released all passengers except Israelis and other Jews. In a lightning commando operation on 3 July, the Israelis rescued the hostages and killed the hijackers. Several Ugandan soldiers were killed and many of their jets destroyed in the process.[52]

Although the Kenyan government strenuously denied any complicity in the Israeli mission, it is widely believed that it did play a vital role in assisting the Israelis. Apparently Kenyan security forces had been approached about landing rights in Nairobi before the raid. To scout the Kampala airport security system, four Israeli Mossad agents and two Kenyans used a Kenyan police boat to cross Lake Victoria and land near Entebbe. Hours before the raid, an Israeli Boeing 707 hospital plane flew to Nairobi to wait for the hostages. Meanwhile, it also unloaded fifty Israeli paratroopers who were put on boats and sent to Lake Victoria, ready to move on Entebbe if necessary. After the successful rescue mission, the Israelis refueled and treated their wounded in Nairobi before flying home.[53]

Military and intelligence cooperation between Israel and some African states also continued despite the lack of diplomatic relations. However, it is difficult to formulate a complete picture of that aspect of interaction because of the secrecy in which it is normally conducted. The internal political situation in some African countries fostered continued collaboration. For instance, Kenya had, by early 1975, become so worried by developments in Idi Amin's Uganda, and by the increasingly assertive irredentist policies of the Barre regime in Somalia, that Kenyan authorities were reported to have asked for military advisors and tanks from Israel. Although the reports were dismissed as "speculation" by Kenya's Defense Ministry, [54] the Entebbe operations undoubtedly lent credibility to such reports.

Ethiopia is another country with whom close military and political cooperation continued despite the break in relations and the seizure of power in Ethiopia by a professed Marxist-Leninist military junta. With the overthrow of Selassie and the bloody conflicts within the Dergue, the ruling junta, there was almost a complete breakdown of internal stability in the country. This was compounded by the lethal ideological disputes among the revolutionaries both within and outside the Dergue. By early 1977 an official "terror campaign" had been launched to counter the terror of the opposition ("red" versus "white" terror). Many Ethiopian provinces and nationalities rose in secessionist rebellion against the Addis Ababa regime. On the external front, the ousting of Selassie and the establishment of a Marxist regime alienated Ethiopia from the U.S., her traditional arms supplier. The situation became aggravated with the human rights crusade of U.S. President Jimmy Carter, who, due to alleged gross violations of human rights by the Dergue, suspended vital military supplies to Ethiopia and withdrew American military personnel. Somalia saw an opportunity in the chaos that gripped Ethiopia to settle its irredentist claims through military appropriation of almost a third of Ethiopian territory. And the conservative Arab states, fearful of having a Marxist pro-Soviet country as a neighbor and anxious to convert the Red Sea into an "Arab Lake," intensified their support for the Eritrean secessionists and the other newly emerged counter-revolutionaries.[55]

Ethiopia turned to Israel, her second most important military ally before the severance of relations. The *International Herald Tribune*, quoting "well-placed Israeli and foreign officials," said Colonel Mengistu Haile Mariam asked for Israeli help in improving relations with the U.S. in 1977. Consequently Prime Minister Begin, as the first item in his first meeting with Carter, urged a reversal of U.S. policy toward Ethiopia, "much to the astonishment of the Americans."[56]

For Israel, the sale of weapons and other forms of military and political collaboration with Ethiopia was more than a commercial affair. Israel has an enduring strategic interest in Ethiopia, and the potential disintegration of the country heightened that concern.

By February 1977 French newspapers carried reports to the effect that Israel had air bases on two Ethiopian-owned islands in the Bab el Mandeb straits.[57] These bases helped the Israelis to protect their southern oil and cargo links via Eilat. In July the *Los Angeles Times* reported that Israel's advisors were fighting alongside Ethiopian troops in the battle for the Ogaden.[58] In August *Foreign Report* revealed extensive military cooperation between the two countries.[59] Israeli instructors were said to have formed and trained the new Seventh Division of the Ethiopian army, which had been fighting since the beginning of July in Eritrea. Israeli pilots were also said to be flying the Ethiopian strike force in the northern province. Israel also maintained a resident training establishment at Awash, 150 miles east of Addis Ababa. Courses were conducted by a team consisting of an Israeli colonel and a dozen other officers. About 350 Ethiopians attended each course, which lasted for three months and included training in the use of explosives and American-made rocket launchers, bayonet practice, and ambush techniques. All equipment, including tents, was supplied by the Israelis, and much of it was said to derive from booty captured from the Egyptians during the October 1973 war. In January 1978 Israel was also reported to "have given the tottering Ethiopian forces incalculable help in keeping American logistical equipment going."[60] And in early February U.S. government sources confirmed that Israel had given Ethiopia cluster bombs, aircraft-fired missiles, and napalm.[61]

Israeli military assistance was publicly acknowledged by Foreign

Minister Moshe Dayan in February 1978[62] in what Prime Minister Begin said was "a human error which anybody might have made."[63] Dayan's "slip" may, however, have been conscious as it was made when there was increasing Soviet activity in Ethiopia. The statement also turned out to be a most embarrassing revelation for the Ethiopian regime, which, as could be expected, reacted angrily. Its embassy in London described it as a "delicate and sinister act." It explained that as a result of American "deliberate policy" of delaying supplies to Ethiopia, the government had sent out arms-purchasing missions to Europe, Asia, Latin America, and the Middle East. "From among these, Israel was the one which offered the sale of limited amounts of ammunition and spare parts. Ethiopia, having no other alternative, had to buy the ammunition from Israel at an exorbitant price."[64] The government then terminated trade relations with Israel and expelled Israeli advisors.[65]

Israeli trade statistics also reveal that Israel continued to export to Africa sophisticated radio-telecommunication and electrical equipment which could be used (and most probably is used) for military purposes. Israel's Tadiran electronics firm was most prominent in this trade. About 80 percent of Tadiran's exports in 1978 were reported to be composed of military equipment. Among the countries that imported electronic equipment were Cameroun, Côte d'Ivoire, Ethiopia, Gabon, Ghana, Guinea, Kenya, Malawi, Nigeria, Rwanda, Senegal, Tanzania, and Zambia (see Table 4.4).

The departure of Israeli diplomats from black Africa did not lead to a corresponding departure of Israeli technical experts from the continent, although there was a drastic reduction in their number: in 1974 there were 49 Israeli experts as against 254 in 1972; and by 1977 there were only fourteen Israeli experts under cooperation agreements. All but two, who were "personally and publicly" requested by Bokassa in the Central African Republic, were serving in countries having diplomatic relations with Israel, i.e., Lesotho, Malawi, and Swaziland.[66] Requests by others for a continuation of the pre-1973 arrangements were rejected by Israel. However, Israeli experts continued to be sent to Africa under the auspices of multilateral agencies such as the UN, or of development funds provided by various Western countries.[67] In early 1977 there were over 100 Israeli experts working in Africa.

African trainees continued to be sent to Israeli institutions, although the vacancies available to them were reduced, as preference was given to Latin American countries which had been largely neglected in the 1960s but which, nonetheless, did not join the bandwagon of Afri-

TABLE 4.4

ISRAELI ELECTRONIC EXPORTS
TO SELECTED AFRICAN COUNTRIES, 1977–1978

Country	Product(s) from Israel	$US million 1977	1978
Nigeria	Total electronic imports	$ 3.096	$ 4.351
	(total imports)	(18.613)	(20.492)
	Radio/telecommunications apparatus	3.227	2.923
	Transmission and reception apparatus	.399	.764
	Special-purpose trucks	—	—
Ethiopia	Total electronic imports	4.450	2.010
	(total imports)	(9.860)	(7.569)
	Generators	.005	.012
	Electric motors	.116	—
	Primary cells and batteries	.378	—
	Accumulators	4.820	.718
	Tele. switchboards, exchange and parts	.043	—
	*Radio/tele. apparatus and parts	.365	.204
	*Transmission-reception apparatus and parts	.365	.204
	Electronic traffic control equipment	.015	—
	Switchboards and control panels	.003	—
	Electric circuits	.004	—
	Electric lamps	—	.007
	Mounted piezo-electric crystals	.005	—
	Thermionic valves	.003	—
	Electrical goods	—	.024
	Electrical wire and cable	—	.007
	Parts of jet engines	.034	.010
	Instruments to detect & measure radiation	.018	—
	Instruments to check electrical apparatus	—	.115
Kenya	Total electronic imports	—	.256
	(total imports)	(-)	(7.778)
	Radio/tele. apparatus and transmitter/receiver	—	.060
	Jeeps	—	.279
Côte d'Ivoire	Total electronic imports	.442	1.005
	(total imports)	(3.354)	(6.156)
	Radio/tele. apparatus	.285	.442
	Rectifiers	—	.465
	Transmitters	.070	.081

(Cont'd.)

Table 4.4—continued

Ghana	Total electronic imports	.445	.526
	(total imports)	(1.691)	(2.416)
	Radio/tele. apparatus	.309	.466
	Transmitter/receiver	.063	.048
	Jeeps	—	.012
	Special vans and trucks	.250	.058
Gabon	Total electronic imports	1.133	.276
	(total imports)	(2.025)	(.876)
	Radio/tele. apparatus	.040	.236
	Transmitter-receiver	.003	.143
	Rectifiers	—	.143
Tanzania	Total electronic imports	—	.332
	(total imports)	(–)	(5.830)
	Radio/tele. apparatus	—	.026
	Electric wire and cable	—	.170
Cameroun	Total electronic imports	.057	.161
	(total imports)	(.115)	(.228)
	Radio/tele. apparatus	—	.027
	Transmitter-receiver	—	.011
	Switchboard and control panel	.051	—
Senegal	Total electronic imports	.006	.874
	(total imports)	—	(.936)
	Radio/tele. apparatus	.006	.023
	Rectifiers	—	.851
Malawi	Radio/tele. apparatus	—	.400
Zambia	Total electronic imports	.037	—
	(total imports)	(2.829)	(1.576)
	Radio/tele. apparatus	.111	.009
	Transmitter and control panels	.024	.002
Rwanda	Total electronic imports	.037	—
	(total imports)	(0.069)	—
	Radio/tele. apparatus	.033	—
Guinea	Total electronic imports	—	.049
	(total imports)	(–)	(.058)
	Radio/tele. apparatus	—	.045
	Transmitter parts	—	.004

Source: Central Bureau of Statistics, *Statistical Abstracts of Israel*, derived from David Blumberg, "Bilateral Relations in the Absence of Diplomatic Ties: Africa and Israel in the Post-1973 Era," B.A. paper (Harvard University, Cambridge, 1981), pp. 39–41.

*Quantities supplied: one transmitter-receiver each year and 3,424 and 1,075 radio-telegraphic apparatuses, respectively. This strengthens the theory that the items were used by communications command bases and mobile units (perhaps walkie-talkies) for troops afield.

can and Asian countries in breaking relations with Israel.[68] Of the thirty-four African trainees at the Afro-Asian Institute during the months when their countries broke relations, only four (three Kenyans and one Mauritian) withdrew from their programs.[69] A former director of the institute, Akiva Egar, said:

> A number of African countries broke their ties with us and stopped sending trainees, but the majority, despite the break in diplomatic ties did not recall their trainees at the time and continued to send others when they finished their training. Among such countries are the largest and most important in Africa, such as Nigeria, Ghana, the Ivory Coast, Kenya, Sierre Leone, Togo, Upper Volta, the Central African Republic and others.[70]

The proportion of African students at the institute, however, dropped from 69 percent in the 1960s to 25 percent in 1975.[71] African participation in the institute's programs, however, began to take an upward turn from 1975 to mid-1977.

African tourists, mainly Christian pilgrims, continued to visit Israel. There were 9,451 of them in 1974, and the figures for 1975 and 1976 were a little short of 6,000 each year.[72] In 1977 twenty-seven clergymen from Angola, Cameroun, Ethiopia, Ghana, Kenya, Nigeria, Rhodesia, South Africa, Tanzania, and Zambia were in Israel for a special nine-week course on biblical tradition and community development sponsored by Israel's Inter-faith Committee and the Foreign Ministry.[73] In addition, the Tantur Institute of Advanced Ecumenical Studies near Bethlehem offered research facilities to prominent African clerics.

In most cases economic relations were also uninterrupted. Israel's exports to Africa more than doubled between 1973 and 1978 (see Table 4.5). Nigeria, Kenya, Côte d'Ivoire, Tanzania, Togo, and Ghana (in that order) became Israel's major black African trading partners. Israel continued to export a variety of manufactured goods such as fertilizers, chemicals, pharmaceuticals, industrial machinery, and electronics, and imported primary agricultural products such as timber, cocoa, and cotton. Consumer goods represented a relatively small percentage of trade; in 1978, for instance, agricultural products accounted for only 1.3 percent, clothing 1.0 percent, textiles 2.3 percent, and foodstuffs 3.8 percent. In contrast, chemicals and fertilizers accounted for 33 percent, electronic equipment for 17 percent, and machinery for 17 percent of trade. The pattern in trade flows begun in the late 1960s became more

TABLE 4.5

ISRAEL'S TRADE WITH AFRICA,
1973–1978 ($US m)

Year	Exports	Imports
1973	$30.2	$24.6
1974	40.9	42.5
1975	38.8	27.5
1976	43.1	29.8
1977	57.1	24.5
1978	72.5	31.8

Source: Central Bureau of Statistics, *Statistical Abstracts of Israel*, 1973–1978.

pronounced. Israel's exports to Africa far exceeded her imports. In 1978, for example, Israeli exports to Africa came to $72.5 million while imports amounted to only $31.8 million.

Koor, dealing primarily through its subsidiary Alda, was the most active Israeli trading company. During the period in question Alda provided service as middleman and import-export agent to other smaller Israeli firms. In addition, the Balton concern served as an umbrella, incorporating trading companies active in thirteen black African countries, namely Burundi, Cameroun, Côte d'Ivoire, Ethiopia, Ghana, Kenya, Liberia, Malawi, Mozambique, Nigeria, Rwanda, Tanzania, and Zambia. Israeli companies were also active in the service sector; notable among these were Solel Boneh, Tahal, Meir, Mekorot, Federmann, and Vered. However, the lack of diplomatic missions limited the activities of some of the companies in some states. In Cameroun, companies working on a hotel construction project left. In Ethiopia the new Marxist regime nationalized a major Israeli cotton firm, a leather works factory, and a pharmaceutical company, along with other major enterprises of other Western countries. Some companies left Ghana as well. But generally the companies were not seriously affected in those countries where they were well established; only where they acted strictly as managers and the like did they leave.[74] It is pertinent to add, however, that the worsening economic situation in some countries contributed to the decision of some of the smaller companies to leave Africa.

In a sense, therefore, while the post-1973 political and multilateral aspects of Afro-Israeli relations remained, on the whole, negative, Israel developed complex and profitable economic and other bilateral ties with Africa. However, unlike the earlier period, Afro-Israeli contacts became less diffused, with Israel concentrating its activities on a few select states. Also, while the thrust of contacts in earlier times was on aid and diplomacy, the post-1973 period witnessed emphasis on non-formal ties. Trade, economic, and cultural links became the dominant features of the period. Concomitantly, there was a significant difference in the character of the actors involved in Afro-Israeli relations. While the Afro-Israeli landscape in the pre-1973 era were dominated by diplomats and technical experts, the bulk of the post-1973 relations were initiated and executed by private businessmen, by semi-public and public corporations, by third-party companies, and by individual scholars and religious leaders.[75] Consequently, relations were intentionally low-key and reticent.

NOTES

1. See Colin Legum, "Africa, the Arabs and the Middle East," in Colin Legum (ed.), *Africa Contemporary Record*, Vol. 6, 1973–74 (London: Rex Collings, 1973), pp. A8–A12.

2. *Ha'aretz*, 26 October 1973.

3. Quoted in the *Jerusalem Post*, 5 November 1973.

4. *Jerusalem Post*, 26 October 1973.

5. Ibid., 20 November 1973.

6. *Ha'aretz*, 2 November 1973.

7. "Interview, Israel, the Arabs and Africa," *Africa Report* (July–August 1976), p. 51.

8. *Jerusalem Post*, 5 November 1973.

9. Ibid.

10. *Jerusalem Post*, 19 November 1973.

11. *Ma'ariv*, 29 November 1973.

12. "Interview, Israel, the Arabs and Africa," p. 54.

13. Interview with President Senghor in *Il Globo*, cited in *Africa Research Bulletin* (hereafter *ARB*), April 1974, p. 3215.

14. *Ma'ariv*, 29 November 1973.

15. Tamar Golan, "Israel and Africa: What Future After Mutual Disenchantment?" American Jewish Committee, Foreign Affairs Department, April 1975, p. 13.

16. Shimeon Amir, "Challenge and Response: Israel's Development Cooperation, 1974–75," in Michael Curtis and Susan A. Gitelson (eds.), *Israel in Africa and the Third World*, p. 236.

17. *Jerusalem Post*, 20 November 1973.

18. Assembly of Heads of State and Government (AHG), Res. 77 (XII).

19. *ARB*, August 1975, pp. 3720–3721.

20. See Olusola Ojo, *Afro-Arab Relations* (London: Rex Collings, forthcoming).

21. Maurice Williams, *Review of Development Cooperation Efforts and Policies of the Development Assistance Committee* (Paris: OECD, 1976), pp. 100–101, cited in Victor T. LeVine and Timothy W. Luke, *The Arab-African Connection: Political and Economic Relations* (Boulder: Westview, 1979), p. 23.

22. For more on the subject of Afro-Arab relations, see ibid.; Ojo, *Afro-Arab Relations*; Robert A. Mertz and Pamela M. Mertz, *Arab Aid to Sub-Saharan Africa* (Munich: Kaiser, 1983).

23. *Sunday Nation* (Nairobi), 16 June 1974.

24. Ibid.

25. See, for example, the *East African Standard* (Nairobi), 19 and 20 June 1974.

26. *West Africa*, 29 July 1974.

27. For the full text of the commentary, see Colin Legum, "Africa, Arabs and Oil," in Colin Legum (ed.), *Africa Contemporary Record*, vol. 7, 1974–75 (London: Rex Collings, 1975), p. A106.

28. *Daily Times* (Lagos), 5 February 1975. For some other reactions, see the *Standard*, 27 March 1975; Olusola Ojo, "South African-Arab Relations," *UFAHAMU*, vol. 2, no. 3 (1982), pp. 121–132.

29. *Times of Zambia*, 18 June 1974.

30. *Africa*, September 1974, p. 31.

31. *Zambia Daily Mail*, 25 March 1975.

32. Samuel Decalo, "Africa and the UN Anti-Zionist Resolution: Roots and Causes," *Cultures et Development*, vol. 48, no. 1 (1976), pp. 111–112. Confirmed by personal interviews and discussions in Israel, February-March 1985.

33. *United Nations General Assembly Official Records* (hereafter *UNGAOR*), Third Committee, 2133rd meeting, 17 October 1975, p. 107.

34. Ibid., 2134th meeting, 17 October 1975, p. 117.

35. *UNGAOR*, plenary meetings, A/DV 2400, pp. 88–90.

36. Ibid., pp. 78–80.

37. *UNGAOR*, Third Committee, 2133rd meeting, 17 October 1975, p. 54.

38. *ARB*, October 1975, p. 3811.

39. *UNGAOR*, plenary meetings, A/DV 2400, pp. 68–70.

40. *Jerusalem Post*, 14 July 1976.

41. *Ghanaian Times*, 13 April 1976.

42. *ARB*, April 1976, p. 4009. For more reactions, see *Jerusalem Post*, 7 June 1976.

43. *Afro-American* (Washington, D.C.), 18 September 1976.

44. *UNGAOR*, Thirty-first Session, Third Committee, 29th Meeting, 13 October 1976.

45. Ibid.

46. *Jerusalem Post*, 7 November 1976.

47. *ARB*, April 1974, p. 3215.

48. Edward Morgan, "A Survey of Israel's Political and Economic Relations with Africa Since 1977" (mimeo), 6 April 1979, p. 24.

49. *Le Monde*, 12 May 1977, and discussions with Hanan Aynor.

50. *ARB*, February 1977, p. 4340.

51. See *Africa Now*, October 1983, p. 40.

52. *ARB*, July 1976, pp. 4081, 4101–4105.

53. David Blumberg, "Bilateral Relations in the Absence of Diplomatic Ties: Africa and Israel in the Post-1973 Era," B.A. paper (Harvard University, Cambridge, 1981), p. 36.

54. *Daily Nation* (Nairobi), 29 April 1975.

55. See Olusola Ojo, "Ethiopia's Foreign Policy Since the 1974 Revolution," *Horn of Africa*, vol. 3, no. 4 (1980), pp. 3–12.

56. *International Herald Tribune*, 22 August 1983.

57. *Foreign Report*, no. 1525, 1 March 1978, pp. 4–6.

58. *Los Angeles Times*, 7 July 1977.

59. *Foreign Report*, no. 1499, 10 August 1977, pp. 4–5.

60. *ARB*, January 1978, p. 4703.

61. *Jerusalem Post*, 5 February 1978.

62. *ARB*, February 1978, pp. 4739–4740.

63. *Jerusalem Post*, 19 February 1978.

64. *ARB*, February 1978, p. 4740.

65. *Jerusalem Post*, 19 February 1978.

66. See Avil Gil, "Israel's 'Quiet' Relations with Black Africa," *Jewish Observer and Middle East Review*, 17 March 1977, p. 4.

67. Pesonal interview, International Cooperation Division, Ministry of Foreign Affairs, Israel, December 1984.

68. Interviews and discussions with Israeli Foreign Ministry officials and heads of some of the training institutions involved in cooperation assistance programs, November 1984 through February 1985.

69. *Jerusalem Post*, 3 December 1973.

70. Gil, "Israel's 'Quiet' Relations," p. 3.

71. Moshe Decter, *To Serve, To Teach, To Leave: The Story of Israel's Development Assistance Program in Black Africa* (New York: American Jewish Congress, 1977), p. 13.

72. *Statistical Abstract of Israel*, 1976, p. 117; 1977, p. 114.

73. *ARB*, August 1977, p. 4548.

74. Interview with Mr. Ilan Hartuv, Director, Economic Division, Ministry of Foreign Affairs, Israel, December 1984.

75. See Naomi Chazan, "Israel in Africa," *Jerusalem Quarterly*, no. 18 (1981), pp. 29–44.

FIVE

The Period of Gradual Rapprochement, 1979–1985

The peace process, which began with the late President Sadat's dramatic trip to Jerusalem in November 1977, produced the Camp David Accords in September 1978. The eventual signing of a peace treaty between Egypt and Israel in March 1979 ushered in an important stage in Afro-Israeli relations. This was not only because of the expectations of both Egypt and Israel regarding Africa, but also because of what the Camp David Accords and the peace treaty set out to achieve.

For the first time a principal power in the Arab coalition was prepared to engage in a direct dialogue with Israel, and was also willing to conclude a peace agreement with her. Furthermore, the image of an Israel that was intransigent, annexationist, and expansionist began to change when it became clear that she was willing to give up the whole Sinai without any attempt to exploit that aspect of UN Resolution 242 (1967) which speaks of "secure" boundaries, i.e., to retain any part of the territory captured from the Egyptians in 1967. Article 1 of the peace treaty commits Israel to "withdraw all its armed forces and civilians from the Sinai behind the international boundary between Egypt and mandated Palestine."[1] Under the treaty both Egypt and Israel also agreed to terminate the state of war between them and to "establish normal and friendly relations."

Equally important, the "Framework of Peace in the Middle East,"[2] signed at Camp David, recognizes the imperative to "involve all those who have been most deeply affected by the conflict" in the resolution of the Arab-Israeli conflict. Both parties therefore regarded the "Framework" and the treaty as only an important step in the search for a more comprehensive peace.

It thus looked as if the psychological and practical barriers to resolving the conflict in the Middle East, which had estranged African states from Israel, had been broken. But most of the Arab states reacted negatively to the Camp David Accords and the treaty. The Arab League summit meeting in Baghdad on 27 March 1979 decided on (1) a break of political and diplomatic relations with Egypt; (2) suspending her from the Arab League; and (3) moving the League's headquarters from Cairo to Tunis. The League Council, meeting at the level of Arab foreign and economic ministers, also decided to impose financial and technical sanctions on Egypt. Egypt was subsequently suspended from the Islamic Conference, which the Arab states dominate. They also wanted the African states to remain steadfast in their boycott of Israel and to take similar punitive measures against Egypt.

AFRICA'S REACTIONS TO CAMP DAVID
AND THE PEACE TREATY

The reaction of the black African states to both the Camp David Accords and the peace treaty was varied. Some reacted positively, some negatively, and others were equivocal. President Dauda Jawara of Gambia, addressing the fourth plenary meeting of the UN General Assembly in September 1978, said that

> the bold initiative taken last year by President Anwar El-Sadat of Egypt had generated hopes that a breakthrough was in sight. These peace efforts have been given a new impetus by the courageous, imaginative and timely initiative of President Carter of the U.S. which culminated in the agreements concluded at Camp David, which we hope will be a strong enough foundation for a final and definitive settlement in this long drawn-out conflict in the Middle East.[3]

The Côte d'Ivoire delegate believed that "the Camp David agreements have created the necessary conditions for the continuance of the dialogue and for negotiations between the parties and have made it possible to hope for a just and lasting settlement of the tragic Middle East problem. In our opinion they are an important step along the difficult road that should lead to peace."[4]

The Liberian delegate commended "the initiative taken by President Jimmy Carter in hosting this important meeting and the flexibility, goodwill and compromising spirit demonstrated by the parties concerned. The results of the meeting, no doubt, represent a significant step in the application of the principle of peaceful co-existence in the Middle East."[5] The Central African Republic described the accords as "highly constructive,"[6] and the Ghanaian UN delegate said they had "contributed to a better understanding of the fears and concerns of some of the contestants and laid a foundation for more productive future negotiations for a settlement."[7] The *Times of Zambia* was glowing in its praise:

> The outcome of the Camp David talks is a triumph of civilized negotiations between the leaders of Egypt and Israel. Jimmy Carter deserves all the praise that is being heaped on him for his role of peacemaker. But there is a long way to go yet. . . . Those Arab nations less mature than Egypt and with a built-in need to create trouble will have to be convinced of the benefits of peace. . . . The bravery of Sadat is the real reason for the peace that may yet come to the Middle East. He had the courage, the sagacity and the foresight to throw his whole political career into a peace settlement. He deserves the praise of the world. . . . We welcome [these] chances for peace and we pray that it will come soon."[8]

Predictably, the countries having diplomatic relations with Israel were full of praise for the achievement of Camp David. The remark of the Lesotho delegate to the UN was typical: "We believe that the Camp David agreements have provided for steps towards dismantling the edifice of hatred, bitterness and distrust in which the people of the Middle East have been locked for so many decades, and that they represent rays lighting the way toward relations based on friendship, to the benefit of all the peoples of the Middle East."[9]

The press as well as the spokesmen of the "radical-socialist" African countries reacted negatively to the agreements. These countries were more radically aligned with the "rejectionist" Arab states and the PLO. They included Angola, Benin, the Congo, Ethiopia, Madagascar, Mozambique, and Rwanda.[10] The Ethiopian UN delegate said the Camp

David agreements were "nothing but a sophisticated imperialist plot designed to exacerbate further the already difficult and complex situation in the Middle East."[11] Dos Santos Alves of Mozambique claimed:

> In the Middle East, imperialist intervention has gained fresh momentum and divisive maneuvers are increasing with the clear objective of destroying the liberation movement and the fight for emancipation of the Arab peoples.
>
> By fomenting conflicts between the Arab states and by seeking to isolate progressive forces, imperialism will enjoy the transient illusion of having been successful. But until the inalienable rights of the Palestinian people to a free, sovereign and independent fatherland under the leadership of the PLO, its sole legitimate representative, is implemented, and until the territory occupied by force in 1967 is returned, there will be no true peace in the Middle East.[12]

Angola argued that "the bilateral Camp David agreements arrived at under the tendentious auspices of the Carter Administration" could not contribute to a lasting solution of the problem.[13] Madagascar was even more uncompromising in its condemnation. Its UN delegate said that the Camp David Accords and the peace treaty had reduced Palestinian rights

> to the hypothetical enjoyment of an ill-defined autonomy. . . . Even the colonialists at the beginning of the century did not go that far in their retrogade policy. How can we therefore fail to condemn the separate and partial treaty which was the outcome of the Camp David agreements and which deals so cavalierly with the Palestinians? How can we accept that the future of a region. . . should be left to the whim of one, two, or three states which vie with each other in finding ingenious ways to control it politically, economically and militarily? How can we endorse the tripartite plot and betrayal of which the Palestinian people have been the victim? And, finally, how can we still let people believe that a peace process has been initiated at a time when the end result of that so-called peace has simply been the negation of the Palestinian nation and increased Israeli arrogance, aggression and extortion of Arab land?[14]

However, the vast majority of African states were equivocal or cautious about their reaction to Camp David. This was due partly to the strength of Arab opposition and partly to their uncertainty as to whether both Egypt and Israel would actually be able to deliver on the lofty intentions of Camp David. The Nigerian government's reaction was typical: "Turning to the Camp David accords, my delegation welcomes all initiatives in the direction of peace. All the same, we must remember that what we have is a framework and that the road to final peace is still both long and arduous."[15] Kentcha of Cameroun said his country believed that the agreements "reveal certain ambiguities, shortcomings and uncertainties."[16] The Senegalese delegate expressed the reason for many states' reservations:

> Senegal will always support every initiative capable of bringing peace and security to the Middle East, be the solutions found within the United Nations itself, or at some other level, in a multi-lateral or bilateral framework. . . . Nevertheless, we think that there can be no just and lasting peace without the effective participation of the Palestinian people, whose authentic representative is the Palestinian Liberation Organisation.[17]

At the OAU the Africans refused, despite Arab demands, to condemn the treaty and reprimand Egypt for making peace with Israel. Rather, President Tolbert of Liberia, which hosted the 1979 summit, hailed the treaty, and Senegal urged African support for Egypt "in this very difficult negotiation" but asked African states to refrain from having "contact with Israel as long as UN resolutions were not applied." When Sadat rose to speak, he was given a rousing ovation. Only Angola, Benin, the Congo, Madagascar, and Mozambique joined the Arab members in their walkout.[18] Even then, President Machel of Mozambique returned some minutes after Sadat began his speech.

The limits of the African position were not, however, tested until the Arabs introduced a resolution at the UN General Assembly in November 1979 (Res. 34/65) one of whose key operative paragraphs (para. 4) declared "that the Camp David accords and other agreements have no validity in so far as they purport to determine the future of the Palestinian people and of the Palestinian territories occupied by Israel since 1967." Egypt proposed that the operative paragraph be deleted from the draft resolution. Chad, Côte d'Ivoire, Equatorial Guinea, Gabon, Liberia, Mauritius, Niger, Swaziland, Togo, Uganda, Upper Volta, and Zaire voted in favor of the Egyptian proposal. Angola, Cameroun, the Central African Republic, Comoros, Kenya, Lesotho, Malawi, Nigeria, Rwanda, and Sierra Leone abstained. Only Benin, Burundi, Cape Verde, Ethiopia, Gambia, Ghana, Guinea, Guinea-Bissau, Madagascar, Mali, Senegal, and Seychelles joined the Arabs and the Soviet-bloc countries to defeat the motion. Even more African states voted in favor of a U.S. proposal that the adoption of the whole resolution require a two-thirds majority. Cameroun, the Central African Republic, and Malawi joined the states which had supported the Egyptian proposal to vote for the American motion; Lesotho, Nigeria, and Rwanda abstained. Many of the African states were absent.[19]

Nonetheless, the hope that the signing of the peace treaty would lead to the reestablishment of Afro-Israeli relations did not materialize. Although Israeli Foreign Ministry officials made a few contacts with African leaders after the Camp David agreements in 1978, there is no evidence of any serious and sustained Israeli diplomatic effort to induce African states into taking such action. On the contrary, the Israeli government was expecting the initiative for a resumption of ties to come from the African states since the initiative to sever such ties had been taken by them.[20] It also does not appear that the Israeli public at the time cared much about Israeli overtures to Africa; at least there was no pressure on the government to take that approach. Even as late as September 1983, when speculation was rife to the effect that a large number of countries would resume relations with Israel, the *Jerusalem Post* was telling the government that

> Israel should insist that those African states that voted to equate Zionism with racism explicitly disavow that act before exchanging ambassadors with Israel again. For if the severing of relations can be interpreted in purely political terms, the denunciation of Zionism cannot be treated with political equanimity. No state should be permitted to feel it can have normal relations with Israel without first disclaiming the historic obscenity of that resolution.[21]

Furthermore, although Egypt sought African support for Camp David and the peace treaty, she did not encourage African states to renew their ties with Israel. Foreign Minister Boutros Ghali even toured African states urging them not to take such a step.[22] In Monrovia in 1979, while President Sadat spoke glowingly of the Egyptian-Israeli peace process, he did not object to the OAU passing resolutions which heavily criticized Israel and which urged African states to maintain their diplomatic boycott of the country.[23]

Afro-Israeli relations, nonetheless, showed a marked improvement. The efforts of the Carter administration and of American Jewish organizations contributed to this. In 1978 the American Jewish Committee inaugurated a program of seminars, conferences, and informal meetings for Jewish and African intellectuals and diplomats intended to improve Jewish-African and Afro-Israeli relations.[24] And in September 1979 outgoing American UN Ambassador Andrew Young lobbied very strongly for renewed Afro-Israeli relations during his tour of several African countries.[25] Young got Liberian President Tolbert's assurances that he would discuss the issue with a number of his African colleagues to arrive at a coordinated African response. Young later revealed that Cameroun was the only country among those he visited that ruled out new contacts between Israel and Africa.

Thus, by the end of the decade, although formal diplomatic relations remained frozen, there were significant developments. In July 1979 the Histadrut and the Zaire Trade Union resumed formal cooperation, which had been suspended in the wake of Zaire's diplomatic rupture.[26] The peace process also revived public debate over Africa's diplomatic relations with Israel in many African countries, and in Ghana an Israel-Ghana Association, which included parliamentarians, was formed to promote relations.

THE BEGINNINGS OF CHANGE

The end of the 1970s and the beginning of the 1980s witnessed important changes in Africa's internal and external environments which worked positively for Israel in the continent. The economic malaise which had gripped several African countries since the early 1970s began to take alarming proportions. This was aggravated by the worsening food crisis caused by declining agricultural production and high population growth rate.[27] The political situation in many of the states hardly fared better. Economic difficulties posed direct threats to the stability of many regimes. The twin problems of economic decline and political instability had a profound impact on the foreign policies of the states. As Naomi Chazan observed: "The specter of severe food crises and concomitant security threats inevitably necessitated a re-evaluation of internal priorities and hence external alliances."[28] On the pan-African level, the solidarity of the early 1970s had evidently broken down as the OAU's experience with Chad and Western Sahara demonstrated.[29]

On the international level the disappointing returns from the North-South dialogue and from Afro-Arab contacts evoked increasingly vocal reservations regarding the continued utility of such contacts and of the external militancy that lay at their foundation. The readiness of the Arab states to frustrate Afro-Arab relations over an inter-Arab feud with Egypt, without the slightest consideration for black African sensitivities, further increased African frustration and resentment toward Arab policy in Africa.[30]

In addition, the late 1970s and early 1980s witnessed the intensification of great-power rivalry. The extension of that rivalry to Africa polarized African states as never before. They began to openly take positions with either East or West purely on the basis of friendship or alignment with the respective powers. The net result was that, unlike in the early 1970s, there was no longer a stigma attached to being pro-Western in general or pro-American in particular. In fact, the economic and political situation in several African states made leanings toward the West more attractive than ever, because of the anticipated benefits of such orientation. All this together with the changes of governments in Western Europe and the U.S. made the atmosphere in Africa more conducive to Israeli overtures and made the Africans more receptive.

These changes were complemented by a change in the Israeli government's hitherto reticent policy in Africa. Indeed, it decided to launch a diplomatic offensive in the continent. This became particularly evident at the beginning of 1981. The new Israeli policy was signaled by the appointment of David Kimche, who had spent much of his career in black Africa, as director-general of the Israeli Foreign Ministry.

The quest for diplomatic relations with Africa gathered momentum with the appointment of Yitzhak Shamir and Ariel Sharon as foreign and defense ministers, respectively. Both Shamir and Kimche launched a vigorous campaign to woo black African leaders, and relations with Africa once again became a major foreign policy concern in Israel. Israel was now willing to mobilize resources, both economic and military, to promote diplomatic rapprochement. The importance attached to military matters in this diplomatic initiative led to the establishment of a joint committee of the foreign and defense ministries in order to coordinate their activities in Africa. Although primary attention was focused on the more important subregional powers with whom Israel had maintained fruitful economic relations, and on pro-Western states some of whom felt threatened by Libya, the authorities decided "to exploit every opportunity and pursue every possibility."[31]

For Sharon, relations with Africa were more than a mere diplomatic matter; they had strategic implications as well. In a paper, "Israel's Strategic Problems in the 1980s," Sharon identified Israel's sphere of strategic and defense interests as stretching from Pakistan, Turkey, and Iran across the Arab world deep into Central Africa and southward to South Africa. He believed Israel should be actively involved in the conflict between the West and the Soviet Union. His ideas were in agreement with President Reagan's plans to build a strategic consensus among pro-Western states to contain the Soviet Union.[32] To buttress efforts to establish military links, Sharon employed a personal advisor on arms sales and attempted to curb activities of private arms entrepreneurs.[33]

Israel also sought the assistance of both the United States as well as France in her bid to "reenter" Africa. The Reagan administration favored an Afro-Israeli rapprochement, which it believed would help solidify African leanings toward the West. The military sales component of the Memorandum of Understanding signed in November 1981 by Israel and the United States is largely aimed at Africa and Latin America. It provides for Third World countries to purchase Israeli arms and services, which will be paid for out of American foreign military sales credits.[34] In a November 1982 meeting with the then Israeli ambassador to the United States, Moshe Arens, Vice-President George Bush agreed to support Israel's case in his subsequent visit to five African states. Former Secretary of State Haig was also known to have been helpful in this regard.[35] In December 1983 U.S. Assistant Secretary of State for African Affairs Chester A. Crocker told a gathering of about 100 Jewish community leaders that the U.S. was conducting regular and close consultations with Israel on African issues.[36] France also gave a commitment in December 1981 to help Israel in restoring ties with Africa. And the issue figured prominently in discussions between President Mitterrand and Israeli leaders during the former's visit to Israel in 1982.[37]

EXPANSION OF AFRO-ISRAELI RELATIONS

The year 1981 saw the beginning of a flurry of diplomatic contacts between Israeli and African officials, particularly in Europe and at the

UN. One of the first acts of David Kimche on assumption of office was to visit Africa. Some of the former Israeli ambassadors to Africa were dispatched to their former posts to reopen a dialogue. Several countries, including the Central African Republic, Côte d'Ivoire, Gabon, Ghana, and Liberia, indicated a willingness to enter into negotiations with Israel. In June 1981 an agreement was reached with the Central African Republic. However, the overthrow of President Dacko in a military coup in September 1981, as well as the "second coming" of Flight Lieutenant Jerry Rawlings in Ghana in December 1981 and his subsequent turning to Libya for support,[38] dashed hopes of renewed ties between Israel and these states.

In November 1981 Ariel Sharon embarked on a secret mission that took him to the Central African Republic, Côte d'Ivoire, Gabon, Liberia, Malawi, Senegal, and Zaire. During the visit secret military protocols were signed with the Central African Republic, Gabon, and Zaire.[39] Yitzhak Shamir also met with six African foreign ministers in the UN General Assembly that autumn. It appears that at this stage Sharon was involved in a struggle with the Foreign Ministry for primacy in the "new" African policy. Foreign Ministry officials were critical of the publicity that followed Sharon's "secret" visit. There was evidently lack of coordination between Shamir and Sharon.[40] Nevertheless, shortly after Sharon's visit Israel opened interest offices in the Central African Republic, Gabon, Togo, and Zaire.

Consultations continued, with more active French support and intensified American Jewish organizational diplomacy. In Washington at the beginning of December 1981, Mobutu of Zaire announced his intention to resume relations with Israel once the Israeli withdrawal from Sinai was completed in April 1982. This was followed on 4 December by a meeting between Mobutu and representatives of four major American Jewish organizations, namely the American Jewish Committee, the American Jewish Congress, the American-Israel Public Affairs Committee, and the Anti-Defamation League.[41]

Mobutu held consultations with several black African leaders in an effort to work out a coordinated response to the new Israeli diplomatic offensive. However, these did not bear any fruit, principally because of the embarrassment caused to the African leaders by the extensive leaks about their contacts "emerging from Sharon,"[42] and also because they were angered by Israel's decision in December 1981 to extend Israeli civil jurisdiction to the Golan Heights. The OAU condemned this move as "a step aimed at retarding the peace process in the Middle East."[43] David

Kimche had to rush to Washington to try to enlist the support of the United States in smoothing things out with the Africans.[44]

Further consultations were held in early 1982. The Inter-Parliamentary Union conference in Lagos in April 1982, from which the Arabs had unsuccessfully attempted to exclude Israel, provided another opportunity for Israeli officials to meet with African leaders. By May 1982 a Saudi newspaper, *Al Madina*, alleged that Côte d'Ivoire, Kenya, and Nigeria were "attempting to convince a number of African countries to restore their relations with Israel" and that African countries were "coming under increased Zionist, Euro-American pressure."[45]

On 15 May 1982 Zaire unexpectedly announced that it was restoring full diplomatic ties with Israel. The announcement stressed that the final withdrawal of Israel from Sinai in April had removed the reason for the severance of ties. Mobutu's decision was, however, influenced by other considerations. Militarily, he was becoming increasingly concerned both with the incompetence of his bodyguards and the hesitance of the French to render assistance. But the real catalyst behind his action was his country's economic problems. The Zairois economy was troubled by the collapse of world prices for such key Zairois mineral exports as cobalt and copper. This was aggravated by years of wasteful, corrupt, and inefficient administration. The American administration, which had done much to prop up both the Zairois economy and Mobutu's personal rule, was becoming increasingly critical of his human rights record, of his ostentatious life-style, and of the corruption of his government. This came to a head during the May 1982 hearings of the congressional Foreign Affairs Committee, when the House slashed the aid earmarked for Zaire from $20 million to $4 million. The announced cut in aid infuriated Mobutu, who then repudiated all US assistance.

Resumption of ties with Israel now looked very attractive. Mobutu could benefit from Israel's technical and military assistance. In addition, he saw in the pro-Israeli American Jewish lobby a powerful lever to put pressure on Washington, where his most outspoken critics on Capitol Hill had been Jewish congressmen. Mobutu's action was well received by American Jewish leaders, who subsequently helped him to establish ties with members of the administration, Congress, and with businessmen.[46]

However, the Arabs reacted swiftly and angrily. Arab League Secretary-General Chedli Klibi described Zaire's action as "a grave violation of the principle of Afro-Arab solidarity." The League states, except Sudan, broke diplomatic relations. The Arab Bank for African Development (BADEA) and other Arab national financial institutions immediately canceled loans. Morocco immediately withdrew its 1,500 troops, which had helped to keep Mobutu in power since the violent assault on Shaba by Katangese rebels in May 1978.

Mobutu retorted by denouncing the "massive Arab interference and criticism," and made it clear that Zaire had no intention of following any slave caravan with "its whips and turbans." He stated bluntly that just as American dollars had not made Zaire "bend its knees, the ignoble maneuvering with petrodollars" would not succeed.[47] He stressed that the Africans had not fought European colonization and neocolonization "only to bend their necks beneath the yoke of Arab neocolonization and the pressures of the turbaned emissaries who run backwards and forwards across black Africa." Mobutu dismissed Chedli's claim that Zaire's action went against Afro-Arab solidarity as mere slogan touting, a "decoy and a trap, a policy of a wagon and a locomotive with the Arabs being the engine and Africans the wagon. The Arabs move or stop the train at will and the Africans blindly follow." He went further to accuse the Arabs of racism in their attempt to arrest the development of Afro-Israeli relations. He wondered why other countries "except the black African states" had the right to freely associate with Israel.[48]

Black African reaction, on the other hand, was generally mute. Although a few of the states, like Cameroun, Côte d'Ivoire, and Togo, which were expected to follow in Zaire's footsteps announced that they would not do so, most African states (with the exception of the Congo and Mauritius) refrained from directly attacking Zaire. On the other hand, some African newspapers were very critical of "economic arm-twisting of the kind practiced by BADEA."[49]

The failure of black African states to follow Zaire's lead can be explained by three major factors. First, Mobutu had apparently not coordinated his action with the African leaders with whom he had held consultations earlier on. Hard pressed by economic and military considerations, which were made urgent by the decision of the U.S. House of Representatives to slash American aid, Mobutu was probably more anxious than the other leaders and was also possibly impatient at what he regarded as their "foot-dragging." Many of the states were angered by his unilateral decision and did not wish to be seen as merely following his lead.

Second, the Arab states intensified their diplomatic counter-offensive, backed with threats of economic sanctions and promises of financial rewards. In early June 1982 Arab League emissaries, including the secretary-general, embarked on a tour of several black African countries, among them those they thought might follow Zaire—Cameroun, Gabon, the Central African Republic, and Kenya.[50] The secretary-general of the Conference of Islamic Organizations, based in Jeddah, met with African ambassadors resident in Jeddah and gave them notes for their home governments "stressing the political and legal consequences of the Zairois decision."[51] Promises of aid were made to several countries. In Uganda, there was quick normalization of relations with Obote and promises to release some funds promised to Idi Amin. In Zambia, whose president was in the midst of a tour of the Gulf states when Mobutu announced his decision, BADEA promised to provide a large-scale loan for the development of agriculture and small industries. Its chairman, Chedli Ayari, told Kenneth Kaunda in August that the OPEC Fund for International Development was prepared to lend him $15 million for agricultural development. He added that "more aid will be available from Arab countries in reward for Zambia's support for Arab causes." The Saudi Fund later promised to provide a credit of $74.4 million to finance agricultural ventures.[52] Similar promises of aid were offered to Niger, Sierra Leone, and others. The Arabs also increased their pressure on Kenyan industrial concerns suspected of having Israeli connections. Nigeria, which was facing serious financial problems as a result of the world oil glut, and which was unwilling to accept the harsh conditions of the International Monetary Fund (IMF) for loans, was promised emergency relief to the tune of one billion dollars.[53] The importance attached to Arab financial weapons was emphasized by the state secretary of the Ghana Foreign Ministry, Obed Asamoah: "Although the Israelis have technical know-how which Ghana could use should relations be re-established between the two countries, it could not make up for the loss of economic aid to Ghana from Arab countries."[54] Similar views were heard from Kenya. The *Daily Nation* noted that the Arab states were "more important to us than Israel, not just because of their oil and petrol dollars but also as potentially huge markets for our produce."[35]

And third, twenty-three days after Zaire's initiative, Israeli tanks rolled into Lebanon in what she labeled Operation Peace for Galilee. The invasion and the massacres of Palestinian refugees at Sabra and Shatila by pro-Israeli Lebanese militia forces provoked worldwide condemnation and gave serious pause to those countries which had been considering upgrading their relations with Israel. The OAU condemned the invasion as a "deplorable act." Upper Volta said that as a result of the invasion, "the resumption of normal diplomatic relations between Upper

Volta and Israel was out of the question."[56] The war effectively suspended contacts between Israeli and African officials for a time.

Nevertheless, improved relations between African states and Israel
became manifest in many international conferences, even in the period
of the Lebanese War. In June 1982 the Africans objected to an Arab
draft resolution at the OAU summit calling for Israel's expulsion from
the UN. In his summation the Kenyan president and chairman of the
meeting expressed the hope that in the future, issues not directly concerned with Africa would not be imposed on the OAU and would not
divert attention from the major problems of the continent.[57] In August
1982 both Togo and Zaire abstained on a Soviet-sponsored UN Security
Council resolution calling for military sanctions against Israel in reaction to the events in Lebanon.[58] Later in the year many African states
joined the West in defeating an Algerian-Saudi Arabian draft resolution
at the International Telecommunications Union conference in Nairobi
which would have barred Israel from future meetings of the union.[59]
Another attempt to expel Israel from a special session of UNESCO on 23
November was also foiled.[60] And the Executive Committee of the International Union of Local Authorities agreed, "with the support of Nairobi's mayor," to host their 1983 meeting in Haifa, Israel.[61]

Israel was, however, determined to show through Zaire that it paid
to resume diplomatic ties with her, although Foreign Ministry officials
indicated they would have wished their reentry into Africa had been via
a country that enjoyed greater respect in the continent. Sharon told his
cabinet colleagues that Israel's posture in Africa would be upgraded
when Zaire's neighbors saw the effective assistance being given to
Mobutu. He said that once Africans compared what the Arab states and
Israel were capable of providing, the prospects of Israel's political come-
back would be vastly enhanced.[62]

Israel and the American Jewish lobby quickly interceded on Zaire's
behalf in Washington to help secure higher levels of American aid and
to improve its image in American opinion.[63] More importantly, the bilateral Israel-Zaire relations widened and deepened. The exchange of ambassadors in June and July 1982 was followed by a series of top-level official visits, including a four-man delegation in October in which General Tamir, chief advisor to Sharon, and General Barak,
deputy army chief of staff, participated. These contacts culminated in a
visit by Shamir late in November 1982.

Shamir was accompanied by an entourage of eighty-five officials
that included industrial, agricultural, and military experts. During the

visit cooperation agreements, as well as an agreement to negotiate landing rights for El Al in Kinshasa, were signed. Under one of the agreements Israel consented to grant scholarships to sixty Zairois students to study agriculture in Israel, to conduct mobile courses for farmers in the provinces, and to open a sophisticated agricultural demonstration center in Enselle. Israel also agreed to encourage the expansion of private investment in Zaire.[64]

Shamir's visit was followed by another one by Sharon in January 1983, in which Sharon signed a series of military accords with Mobutu.[65] One of the agreements dealt with a five-year plan for upgrading Zaire's internal and external defense system, including its security services. Israel agreed to suppy the Zairois force with artillery, mortars, and communications equipment. Mobutu also announced that Israel would replace Belgium in training his army's crack Camaniola Division, based in the strategic Shaba province close to the Angolan and Zambian borders where most of Zaire's mineral reserves are located. The agreement also provided for the expansion of the Special Presidential Brigade from 3,000 to 7,500 and for Israeli support in establishing a new artillery batallion and for naval training. Mobutu disclosed that the expenses would be paid "fifty-fifty" by both Israel and Zaire and denied that he was being given captured PLO weapons from Lebanon. It was also disclosed in 1984 that Israel was providing training for the president's bodyguards and intelligence agents.[66]

Relations between the two countries have since continued to grow. High-level official contacts remain a feature of the relationship, including a five-day visit in January 1984 by Israeli President Chaim Herzog and a well-publicized six-day visit to Israel by Mobutu in May 1985.

Contacts between Israeli and black African officials were resumed in the spring of 1983. In March senior black African diplomats at the UN met with officials of the World Jewish Congress in New York in what were described as "warm discussions aimed at laying the groundwork for a renewed era of normalization between Africans and Jews."[67]

The diplomatic scene began to brighten for Israel with her agreement in May 1983 to withdraw her troops from Lebanon under the Israel-Lebanon troop withdrawal accord. In July Shamir flew to Geneva to hold talks with Houphouët-Boigny.[68] These contacts received a boost with the visit of Hillel Shlomo, a former Israeli ambassador, to Conakry as the personal guest of Sekou Toure, then chairman of the Conference of Islamic Organizations and a leader who had been noted both for his radicalism and his staunch pro-Arab stand.[69] Extensive negotiations were also initiated with the Central African Republic and Liberia. On 20 June Liberia's military ruler Samuel Doe announced that he would seek the approval of his ruling National Redemption Council to start a dialogue with Israel. A delegation from the Central African Republic headed by Finance Minister Slyvan Bangui was in Israel in early August, as was a Liberian delegation led by its defense minister. It was also reported that "one of the most militantly pro-Palestinian [African] leaders had requested Israel's technical aid."[70] On 14 August Liberia announced it was resuming ties with Israel. A week later Doe and an entourage that included six ministers made a well-publicized four-day visit to Israel, thus becoming the first African head of state to arrive in Israel since the visit of the OAU's "wise men" in November 1971.

Doe's motives in restoring ties with Israel were not unconnected with problems in his bilateral relations with the United States and the internal Liberian security situation. It has been suggested that he took the decision partly to win Jewish support and placate the United States, which was pressing for a return to civilian rule as a condition for continuing miltary support.[71] Major John G. Rancy, then U.S. secretary of state for presidential affairs, had suggested in a letter to Doe in March 1983 that "given America's past record in supporting the State of Israel, and knowing the role Jews play in the economic and political affairs of the U.S., it is my belief that re-establishing ties with Israel will win you enormous support in American circles."[72] Furthermore, by July 1983 Doe had begun to take the perceived Libyan threat to Liberia's internal stability very seriously. He dismissed a number of pro-Libyan figures, including Foreign Minister Boima Fahrbulleh. The Begin government used the "Libyan card" by providing access to the Mossad's extensive intelligence materials on Libyan activities in Africa. It was disclosed that the main demand made by Liberia as a quid pro quo for reestablishing ties was a breakdown of all Israeli classified assessments of Libyan actions and intentions in Africa. Such materials were given to a three-man delegation which paid a secret visit to Israel late in July. The delegation was also given intelligence material about "the recent dispatch of Libyan agents to Niger and the Central African Republic and about activities of Libyans and Cubans based in Ghana."[73]

Cooperation agreements covering health, agriculture, and infrastructure were signed during Doe's visit. Israel agreed to help reactivate Liberia's agricultural company, Agrimeco, and to encourage its firms to participate in local road construction schemes. Agreements were also reached on cooperation between the two countries' central banks. El Al also agreed to provide two Boeing 707 aircraft gratis and to help manage Air Liberia and maintain its facilities. Liberia has continued to receive Israeli assistance. In September 1984 Israel agreed to provide advice and send experts to help repair Liberia's naval ports and installations, and in October the Liberian justice minister, Jerkins Scott, signed a $30 million agreement with the Israeli Heftziba Company under which the company would have rights to the cutting and exporting of timber from Liberia.[74]

Liberia's renewed ties once again heightened speculation that other African states would take similar action. President Eyadema of Togo congratulated Liberia for her action, saying she had set the pace for other West African states.[75] And in November 1983, during a visit to the United States, he said that the reason for his country's break with Israel no longer held.[76] The Ivorian leader also indicated that he would resume ties once Israel established a timetable for withdrawal from Lebanon.[77] France was also reported to be cooperating with Israel in consolidating a plan for economic assistance to Africa.[78]

The resolution of the power struggle in Upper Volta in favor of the late pro-Libyan Thomas Sankara froze the issue of renewed ties with Israel, which had looked very promising at one stage. Although the two countries agreed to have an Israeli interest office in Quagadougou, no such office has been established to date, and in April 1984 the government accused Israel of being implicated in an abortive coup staged by opposition leader Joseph ki-Zerbo.[79] The overthrow of the civilian government in Nigeria in December 1983 also removed public pressure on the government for normalization of relations with Israel; the Babangida administration's decision to take Nigeria into the Islamic Organization Conference became public in January 1986.

Nonetheless, events in some other African countries have fostered close Israeli-African ties. The gradual tilt of Mozambique toward the West, and its accommodation of South Africa with the signing by the two countries of a non-aggression pact on 18 March 1984, has led to Mozambique's softening its opposition to Israel. Shortly after the signing of the pact with South Africa, Mozambique National Airlines concluded an agreement with Israeli and South African businessmen according to which a weekly charter flight would operate between Mozambique and Israel.[80]

Furthermore, the new military regime in Guinea has moved close to Israel. In June 1984 during his visit to France, Prime Minister Drara Traore said that his government was considering the question of relations with Israel.[81] Israel has since opened interest offices in Conakry. By August 1984 Foreign Minister Shamir could claim (after another round of talks with Houphouët-Boigny in Geneva) that Israel was "close to the moment." He implied that it was only the desire of African states "to act as a bloc within the OAU" that had delayed some countries from renewing ties. He disclosed that "Hardly a week goes by when there isn't someone here from Africa."[82] Since then Cameroun, Côte d'Ivoire, and Togo have renewed their diplomatic ties with Israel.

Improved Afro-Israeli relations continued to be manifest at international forums. In March 1984 Israel was accepted to the ILO Asian region with "wide support from trade unionists from Asia, Africa and Latin America."[83] At the end of September African delegates joined their Western counterparts to quash anti-Israeli resolutions at the Inter-Parliamentary Union (IPU) meeting in Geneva. First, Syria failed in its attempt to put on the agenda a draft resolution assigning all the blame for the Arab-Israeli dispute to Israel. Then a Kuwaiti draft on colonialism and racism which equated Zionism with racism was struck off when six of the ten-member drafting committee, including Cameroun, Zambia, and Zimbabwe, decided to delete all references to Israel. And finally, a Soviet draft declaring that equal rights for women were impeded by "colonialism, racism and Zionism" was also amended in the committee by deleting references to Zionism.[82] In the UN the Decolonization Committee agreed to delete the names of Israel and the United States from a resolution that identified the two countries as the principal military suppliers of South Africa. Similar African support was obtained during the IPU meeting in Lome, Togo, in April 1975.[85]

The pattern of Israel's military, economic, and technical cooperation, noticeable in the post-1973 period, became more pronounced, and with more African states getting involved. Israel's arms sales to Africa have served the dual purpose of furthering the economic interests of her armaments industry and winning friendship for her. The stress has, however, been on using arms sales as a tool to promote diplomatic rapprochement. Most of the recipients of Israeli arms were pro-Western countries, particularly those who felt internally and externally threatened by pro-Soviet regimes and Libya. Besides Liberia and Zaire, Gabon, the Central African Republic, Kenya, Lesotho, Swaziland, and Habre's Chad have received some form of military assistance from Israel.[86] In 1982 Nigeria was listed among countries that bought sophisticated weaponry, and in 1983 she purchased paramilitary equipment worth about $7 million. It is also rumored that Nigeria's internal security service, the National Security Organization, is trained by the Mossad.[87] Military cooperation with Kenya has also been cemented. The Stockholm International Peace Research Institute revealed arms transfers from Israel to Kenya in 1979, 1980, and 1983.[88]

It is also interesting to note that, despite the harsh condemnation of Israel and the publicity that was attendant on the Ethiopian government's decision to "terminate" military cooperation in February 1978, military contacts between the two did not end. It is reported that only the "less essential technicians" were sacked in 1978; the key advisors remained.[89] At the beginning of 1985 reports of Israeli arms supply and military training assistance to Ethiopia became widespread again. It was revealed that there was extensive military and intelligence cooperation between the two countries and that arms supply by Israel was resumed in 1983. By January 1985 arms worth some $20 million had been supplied. The arms transfers were linked to alleged Ethiopian agreement to allow the "exodus" of Ethiopian Jews to Israel.[90] The disclosure of the airlift of some 7,000 Ethiopian Jews from Sudanese refugee camps once again created tension and prompted strong Ethiopian verbal attacks against Israel.

Economic exchanges have expanded despite Arab pressure.[91] Israel now trades with over thirty black African states, although her key partners remain Nigeria (which accounts for about half of Israel's total African trade), Kenya, Gabon, Côte d'Ivoire, Tanzania, Zaire, Zambia, and Ethiopia. The bulk of Israel's trade with Africa is conducted by semi-public firms, notably Koor and Motorola. Koor generally trades through its American and European subsidiaries. Tadiran, Amcor, Teva Pharmaceuticals, and other private Israeli companies continue to be active in the continent. Israel continues to export to Africa more than she imports from it (see Table 5.1). The items of trade remain generally the same. The trade figures, however, do not include arms trade and trade in diamonds, uranium, or oil, which some sources claim to have become an article of trade between Gabon and Israel since the late 1970s.[92]

The trade figures also do not reflect the important role which Israeli construction companies continue to play in various African states. Contracts have been implemented in Cameroun, the Central African Republic, Côte d'Ivoire, Gabon, Ghana, Kenya, Nigeria, Togo, and Zaire. Israeli companies engaged in contractual work in Africa employ between 3,000 and 4,000 Israelis, and Africa has become the major source of demand for Israeli engineers, construction workers, and agricultural experts.[93] Solel Boneh remains the largest Israeli construction

TABLE 5.1

AFRICA'S TRADE WITH ISRAEL,
1979–1982 ($US m)

Year	Exports	Imports
1979	$19.7	$75.4
1980	19.5	111.7
1981	15.3	124.1
1982	25.0	111.8

Sources: Central Bureau of Statistics, *Statistical Abstract of Israel*, 1983; *Foreign Trade Statistics Quarterly*, 1981.

company in Africa. In 1983 it employed over 15,000 African workers in various countries. The company, whose worldwide net profit in 1983 amounted to $773 million, has over 74 percent of its activities concentrated in Africa. Nigeria remains its largest client. At the end of December 1983 the *Jerusalem Post* reported that the company operated five Hebrew schools, for Israeli children, in three countries.[94] The increasing financial difficulties of many African states, particularly from the late 1970s, forced the company to become increasingly involved in "turnkey" projects in which the contractor takes on enhanced responsibilities. These include planning, design, long-term financial arrangements, supply of equipment and, in many cases, management of the completed project during the running-in period. In the case of hotels, this sometimes involves training of domestic personnel. Thus, by mid-1984 Nigeria alone owed Solel Boneh $120 million.[95]

Other Israeli firms, such as Ashtrom, Azurim, Tahal, Federman, Hiram-Zeevi, and Zehariah Druker, have continued to be involved in African projects. However, the general economic decline in most African states has seriously affected the operations of these and other foreign (as well as indigenous) trading and construction firms. As a result, from 1984 Solel Boneh began to reduce the scope of its work in Africa and to move to North and Latin America.[96]

Cultural exchanges and tourism continued to grow during this period. Visits by African pilgrims to the Holy Land increased as did visits by Christian leaders for courses and religious conferences. Academic exchanges continued and African athletes, even from countries without formal diplomatic relations, began to participate in the Israeli Hapoel Games. The Central African Republic, Côte d'Ivoire, and Kenya participated in the 12th International Hapoel Games in Jaffa in April 1983. In 1984 three distance runners from Zaire took part in a mini-marathon in Jerusalem. And in the cultural area, the Israeli Bat-Dor Dance Company made a successful tour of Zaire and Kenya in 1983 despite the stiff political pressure on Kenyan authorities from the Arabs.[97]

The growing improvement in relations with African states has inevitably led to an increase in Israel's technical assistance operations. However, these operations remain limited due to budgetary constraints. The budget of Israel's Division of International Cooperation was only $1 million in 1982; an extra half million dollars had to be found to finance the aid package for Zaire in 1982. In fact, in August 1982 officials of the Central African Republic left Israel disappointed at the amount of aid they would be likely to get for restoring relations.[98]

Because of Israel's own economic difficulties, the Israeli government had to look for external sources, mainly in the United States and the Scandinavian countries, to fund its technical assistance programs. American Jews and the U.S. government have been pressured to assist. David Kimche made several visits to Washington in order to gain support for a plan whereby the U.S. would substantially finance Israel's assistance programs along the lines of the Egyptian-Israeli-U.S. arrangement, under which Egypt enjoys Israeli agricultural assistance through two trilateral projects funded to the tune of $8 million by the U.S. Agency for International Development.[99] In April 1984 specific legislation was introduced in Congress for the transfer of $20 million for Israeli economic development projects in the Third World.[100] Later in the year Congress also approved a $2 million package for setting up the U.S.-Israel Cooperative Development Research Program, which provides U.S. funding for Israeli research aimed at solving "serious development problems in Third World countries."[101] Holland, the Swedish International Development Agency, and the German-based Christoffel Blindenmission have also channeled additional funds to Israel to sustain some of the assistance programs.[102] German Economic Cooperation Minister Jurgen Warnke also indicated, after a week-long visit to Israel, that Israel and West Germany had agreed to expand joint Third World projects.[103] Israel has thus managed to increase the budget for short-term courses run in Israel, thereby enabling more African students to participate. In 1984 there were over thirty such courses.

NOTES

1. For the full text of the treaty, see "Documents on Palestine," in *The Middle East and North Africa 1983–84* (London: Europa Publications, 1983).

2. For the text of the framework, see ibid., pp. 66–68.

3. *United Nations General Assembly Official Records* (hereafter UNGAOR), 33rd Session, plenary meetings, 1978, p. 27.

4. Ibid., p. 484.

5. Ibid., p. 228.

6. Ibid., p. 606.

7. Ibid., p. 500.

8. *Times of Zambia*, 20 September 1978. For more African press comments, see Susan Aurelia Gitelson, "African Press Reactions to the Camp David Summit and to the Israel-Egypt Treaty," *Geneve-Afrique*, vol. 17, no. 1 (1979), pp. 183–195.

9 *UNGAOR*, 33rd Session, plenary meetings, 1978, p. 541.

10. See Naomi Chazan, "Israel in Africa," *Jerusalem Quarterly*, no. 18 (1981), p. 132.

11. Ibid., p. 602

12. Ibid., p. 272.

13. Ibid., p. 478.

14. *UNGAOR*, 34th Session, plenary meeting, 1979, pp. 278–279.

15. *UNGAOR*, 33rd Session, plenary meeting, 1978, p. 431.

16. Ibid., p. 339.

17. Ibid., p. 360.

18. See *Jerusalem Post*, 18 July 1979; *Africa Research Bulletin* (hereafter ARB), July 1979, pp. 5,326–5,330.

19. UN doc. A/Res 34/65, 83rd plenary, 29 November 1979.

20. *Africa Confidential*, vol. 22, no. 2, 14 January 1981, p. 8.

21. "An African Policy," *Jerusalem Post*, 18 July 1979.

22. *Jerusalem Post*, 22 March 1984.

23. See *ARB*, July 1979, p. 5335; see also *Jerusalem Post*, 18 July 1979.

24. See Richard L. Sklar, "Africa and the Middle East: What Blacks and Jews Owe to Each Other," in Joseph R. Washington, Jr. (ed.), *Jews in Black Perspectives: A Dialogue* (Cranburg, N.J.: Associated University Presses, 1984), p. 142.

25. *ARB,* September 1979, pp. 5424–5425.

26. *Jerusalem Post,* 15 July 1979.

27. See Olusola Ojo, "Africa's Food Crisis and Afro-Arab Relations," *Ife Social Sciences Journal,* vol. 5, nos. 1–2 (1982), pp. 137–153.

28. Naomi Chazan, "Israel and Africa in the 1980s: The Dilemmas of Complexity and Ambiguity," paper presented at the International Conference on Africa and the Great Powers, University of Ife, June 1983, p. 2.

29. Amadu Sesay, Olusola Ojo, and Orobola Faschun, *The OAU After Twenty Years* (Boulder: Westview, 1984).

30. See Olusola Ojo, "Afro-Arab Relations in the 1980s and Beyond," *Jerusalem Journal of International Relations,* vol. 8, no. 4 (1985).

31. Chazan, "Israel and Africa in the 1980s."

32. Ignacio Klitch, "Israel Returns to Africa," *Middle East International,* 4 June 1982, p. 12.

33. See Chazan, "Israel and Africa in the 1980s," p. 10.

34. Israel's annexation of the Golan Heights in December 1981 led to the temporary suspension of the Memorandum of Understanding, but it was reinstated on 17 May 1983 as part of the agreement for the partial withdrawal of Israeli troops from Lebanon.

35. See David Levenfeld, "Israel and Black Africa," *Midstream,* February 1984, p. 9.

36. *Anti-Defamation League News* (New York), 23 December 1983.

37. *Jerusalem Post,* 10 December 1982; see also Klitch, "Israel Returns to Africa," p. 12.

38. Rawlings has since accused Israel of involvement in the subsequent coup plots against him. See *New African,* September 1983, p. 42.

39. *African Business,* April 1983, p. 17. See also *Jerusalem Post,* 29 November 1981.

40. *Jerusalem Post,* 10 December 1981. Shamir and Sharon have long been rivals for the leadership of the Likud Party.

41. See Sklar, "Africa and the Middle East," p. 142.

42. *Jerusalem Post,* 27 January 1982.

43. *ARB,* December 1981, p. 6295.

44. *Jerusalem Post,* 30 December 1981; see also *Jeune Afrique,* 23 December 1981, p. 13.

45. Cited in the *Jerusalem Post,* 16 May 1982.

46. *Jerusalem Post,* 11 August 1983.

47. *Africa,* July 1982, p. 44.

48. See *Weekly Review* (Nairobi), 4 June 1982; *West Africa,* 31 May 1982, p. 1447; *Africa,* July 1982, pp. 44–45.

49. For a sample of the African press reaction, see *Africa Economic*

Digest, 16–22 September 1983; *New African*, July 1982, pp. 38–39; *Africa Now*, December 1983.

50. See *Africa Economic Digest*, 9 June 1982, pp. 8–9.

51. *Weekly Review*, 28 May 1982.

52. *Africa Economic Digest*, 20–26 August 1982, p. 25, 1–7 January 1983, p. 19. In May 1983 Saudi Arabia, Kuwait, and other Gulf states were reported to be considering imports of Zambia's poultry products. And Zambia agreed to allow the PLO to open a diplomatic mission there. See ibid., 13–19 May 1983; *Jerusalem Post*, 25 August 1983.

53. For more details, see *New African*, June 1982; *Africa Economic Digest*, September 1982, March and April 1983; *Africa*, December 1982. (See also Chapter 6.)

54. *ARB*, May 1982, p. 6472.

55. Ibid., p. 6473.

56. For more details of the African reaction, see *ARB*, June 1982, p. 6508.

57. *Daily Nation*, 26 June 1981, cited in Arye Oded, "Africa, Israel and the Arabs: On the Restoration of Israeli-African Diplomatic Relations," *Jerusalem Journal of International Relations*, vol. 6, no. 3 (1982–83), p. 54.

58. *Jerusalem Post*, 8 August 1982.

59. *Weekly Review*, 12 November 1982, p. 30.

60. *International Herald Tribune*, 24 November 1982.

61. *Jerusalem Post*, 26 November 1982.

62. Ibid., 21 January 1983.

63. Ibid., 1, 2 December 1982.

64. See ibid.; *African Business*, April 1983, pp. 16–17.

65. For more details, see *Jerusalem Post*, 21 January, 9 February 1983; *Ha'aretz*, 20 January 1983.

66. *Jerusalem Post*, 22 January 1984.

67. Ibid., 20 March 1983.

68. *New African*, September 1983, p. 42.

69. Sekou Toure's Guinea had been the first African state to break diplomatic relations with Israel in June 1967.

70. *Jerusalem Post*, 18 August 1983.

71. *The Middle East*, January 1985, p. 38.

72. Ibid.

73. *The Times*, 23 August 1983.

74. For more details, see *Africa Economic Digest*, 2 September 1983, p. 10; ibid., September 1983; *Jerusalem Post*, 25 October 1984.

75. *International Herald Tribune*, 7 September 1983.

76. *West Africa,* 7 November 1983, p. 2596.

77. John Tomlinson, "Israel's Cooperation with Black Africa," *Focus* (Britain-Israel Public Affairs Committee), March 1984. See also *International Herald Tribune,* 1 February 1985.

78. *Ma'ariv,* 5 October 1983.

79. See *West Africa,* 2 April 1984; *New African,* August 1984, p. 32.

80. *Jerusalem Post,* 29 March 1984.

81. Ibid., 14 June 1984.

82. Ibid., 7 August 1984.

83. Ibid., 2 March 1984.

84. Ibid., 1 October 1984.

85. Ibid., 28 October 1984.

86. For details, see *New African,* September 1983, p. 42; *Africa,* February 1982, p. 48.

87. *Jerusalem Post,* 11 June 1982; *The Middle East,* January 1985, p. 387; see also Chapter 6.

88. *SIPRI, World Armament and Disarmament Yearbook, 1980* (London: Taylor and Francis, 1980), p. 148; *SIPRI, World Armament and Disarmament Yearbook 1983* (London: Taylor and Francis, 1983), p. 320.

89. *Foreign Report,* no. 1525, 1 March 1978, p. 5.

90. See *Jerusalem Post,* 3, 8 January 1985.

91. For example, in 1979 the Kenyan government reacted heatedly to activities of the Arab League's Central Boycott Office in Damascus directed against Kenyan firms alleged to be trading with Israel. A government statement said they constituted a "serious breach of diplomatic privileges and immunities enjoyed by the Arab League Office in Nairobi" and warned the office not to interfere in its internal affairs. It went on to stress that "the Kenyan Government can never accept that the Arab states, or any other state for that matter, has a right to dictate to Kenya who to trade or not to trade with." *ARB* (Economic and Technical Series), 15 October-14 November 1979, p. 5294.

92. Discussions in Israel, January 1985.

93. *Ma'ariv,* 21 April 1982, cited in Chazan, "Israel and Africa in the 1980s," p. 6.

94. *Jerusalem Post,* 28 December 1983.

95. Ibid., 5 June 1984.

96. Interview with Yaakov Shur and Jacob Levar of Solel Boneh, Haifa, 28 January 1985.

97. For details, see Leon Hadar, "Imbroglio in Nairobi," *Jerusalem Post,* 19 May 1983.

98. Discussions in Israel, November 1984–March 1985.

99. For details, see *Jerusalem Post*, 28 December 1984. For Shamir's appeal to American Jews, see *Ma'ariv*, 1 December 1982.

100. *Jerusalem Post*, 20 April 1984. The legislation was not passed by Congress. Legislation for $10 million in aid has since been introduced.

101. *Jerusalem Post*, 28 December 1984.

102. Discussions in Israel, January-February 1985.

103. *Jerusalem Post*, 5 June 1985.

SIX

Israel and South Africa

HISTORICAL LINKS

The links between Israel and South Africa predate the establishment of the State of Israel in 1948. South African leader General Jan Christian Smuts played an important role in the British government's acceptance of the concept of a Jewish homeland in Palestine, put forth in the Balfour Declaration of 1917. Although an Afrikaner, his friendship with Chaim Weizmann, president of the British Zionist Federation and later Israel's first president, strengthened the bonds between the two states. In fact, South Africa was one of the first countries to accord formal recognition to the State of Israel. And in the Arab-Israeli war that ensued immediately after the proclamation of Israel's independence, South Africa supplied Israel with "food, medical supplies, money, arms, uniforms, and fighter aircraft." In addition, several hundred Jews from South Africa went to fight,[1] and the Jewish community in South Africa contributed proportionately more volunteers than any other Jewish community in the world.[2] In 1950 Israeli Foreign Minister Moshe Sharett visited South Africa, and in 1953 South African Prime Minister Daniel Francois Malan was the first head of government to pay an official visit to Israel.

The pro-Zionist sentiments of General Smuts, however, were not shared by a significant segment of his fellow Afrikaners. In fact, prominent members of the Nationalist Party did not hide their anti-Jewish sentiments. The Afrikaners' secret society, the Broederbond, was instrumental in closing South African borders to Jewish refugees from Nazi Germany in the late 1930s, and prominent Nationalist leaders, including the late President John Vorster, were Nazi sympathizers during World War II and were interned for the duration of the war.[3]

Jews within South Africa suffered social and political discrimination: they were not allowed membership in the Nationalist Party until 1954; neither could they apply for membership in social clubs. As one scholar observed:

> There were periods when "the Jew" was used as a bogy in Nationalist Party political propaganda. During the decade of the 1940s and 1950s, the so-called "Jewish" capital was a convenient scapegoat on which was fastened the responsibility for the economic ills of the country. The Nationalist Party press frightened the electorate with "Hoggenhaimer," the symbol of Jewish capitalism, who was depicted in political cartoons as an obese Semite financial magnate and presumed to be the financial cornerstone of the Botha-Smuts Party.[4]

The existence of this large Jewish community of about 120,000 in South Africa has been a factor that links Israel with South Africa and which thus affects Israel's African policy. The effect of the diaspora on Israel's policies was suggested dramatically by Shabtai Rosenne, a senior Foreign Ministry official:

> Israel is a Jewish state. The only Jewish state in the world; it was reestablished deliberately by the Jewish people as a Jewish solution to the Jewish problem, which scarred the history of mankind for over 2000 years. This is the cardinal feature dominating all Israel's policy, domestic and foreign. This makes Israel unique. Without full appreciation of this elementary factor, it is impossible to understand Israel or any aspect of Israel's policy—domestic and foreign.

The South African Jews are very prominent in South Africa's economic and political life. The community is one of the wealthiest Jewish communitites in the world on a per capita basis. Its zeal for the Zionist cause has also been greater than that of any other community. It is the highest per capita contributor to the State of Israel in the world, with an average total of over $120 million a year—in absolute figures, a contribution second only to that of the American diaspora. Moreover, the rate of emigration to Israel of South African Jews has been very high—far higher than that of Jews from the U.S. Many South African-born Israelis have been prominent in Israel's political life. Among them are Abba Eban, former foreign minister and more recently chairman of the Knesset Foreign Affairs and Defense Committee, and Arye Pincus, who in 1966 was elected chairman of the Jewish Agency in Jerusalem, the controlling body of the World Zionist Organization. Prominent among the Israeli UN delegation in 1961, for example, were South African-born Israelis: Michael Comay, head of Israel's permanent mission at the UN, who was a former secretary of the South African Zionist Organization and an officer in the South African army during World War II; Arthur Lurie, Israeli ambassador to Canada; and Arye Pincus.[5]

Thus, over the years very close personal, communal, normative, and financial links have developed between South African Jews and Israel. South African Jewry has also exhibited an intense interest in internal Israeli politics, as the South African Zionist Movement replicated party divisions within Israel itself. These linkages have often exposed South African Jewry to charges of dual loyalty by the Afrikaners.

It is also estimated that there are "as many as 25,000 Israelis who live in South Africa, proportionally the largest Israeli community in the world."[7] The inflow of Israelis to South Africa has increased significantly in the last decade as economic contacts between the two countries have increased.

Yet the position of the Jewish community has not, until recently, been politically secure. The victory of the Nationalist Party in the 1948 elections heightened fears of the community's exclusion from the mainstream because of the anti-Semitic prejudice of the party. However, although many South African Jews have been prominent in the opposition that grew in the 1960s,[8] the Board of Deputies, the establishment that speaks for the organized Jewish community in South Africa, decided early in the 1950s not to become involved in the controversies surrounding the apartheid policies of the South African government. Pragmatic self-interest seemed to have dictated their reluctance to provoke the wrath of the ruling oligarchy. This position was clearly enunciated by Rabbi M.C. Weiler at the Eighth International Conference of the World Union of Progressive Judaism in London in 1953:

> The Jews as a community had decided to take no stand on the native questions, because they were involved with the problems of assisting Jewry in other lands. South African Jewry was doing more to help Israel than any other group. The community could not ask for the government's permission to export funds and goods and, at the same time, object to the government.[9]

Leslie Rubin, a liberal Jew who was a senator representing African interests in the South African parliament from 1954 to 1969, went even further:

> In fact, it is an open secret in South Africa that the board [Board of Deputies] does all it can to discourage individual Jews from opposing government policies. I am told more than once in a while in Parliament that my prominence as a critic of apartheid and spokesman for the African people was an embarrassment to the Board of Deputies. Other Jews in public life experienced similar attempts to persuade them to tone down their opposition to the government.[10]

The board has thus, in a way—partly because of the welfare of the Jewish community in South Africa itself, and partly because of its Zionist support for Israel—taken pains to ensure that the Jewish community was not regarded automatically by the Afrikaners as being basically opposed to their continued rule. It has thus played a not insignificant role in promoting relations between Israel and South Africa.

THE EARLY YEARS

Neither the South African government's assistance to Israel in the 1948 Arab-Israeli war nor the presence of South African Jewry within the Republic deterred the Israeli government from publically condemning South African racist policies. This was hardly surprising; it seemed only natural that the new state would identify with the aspirations of the South African non-white population for racial justice. Indeed, the first generation of Israeli leaders, such as David Ben-Gurion, Moshe Sharett, Levi Eshkol, and Golda Meir, not only were prominent in the liberation movements that campaigned against British colonial rule in Palestine but also viewed themselves and their party as an integral part of the international socialist movement.[11]

At the UN Israel identified with every anti-apartheid measure from 1952, when India first introduced a draft resolution condemning racial discrimination and apartheid and demanding equal rights for all South African races. Admittedly, as the few African members of the UN were then not able to bring sufficient pressure to bear on the organization, the resolutions condemning apartheid were mild.

The anti-apartheid stance of Israel at the UN did not, therefore, seriously affect Israeli-South African relations, nor did it affect the position of South African Jewry. Although it did cause some irritation, the South African government did not take it as anything different from similar moral opprobrium against its policies expressed by other friendly states. South African Prime Minister Malan maintained a highly emotional enthusiasm for the State of Israel. In 1956 Shimon Cooper, president of the South African Zionist Federation, was appointed to the judiciary; in 1958 Premier Verwoerd appointed another Jew, Perce Youtar, as deputy minister of justice of the Transvaal Province.

All that changed in the early 1960s. With the emergence of a sizable number of African independent states, the demand grew strong for more militant anti-apartheid and anti-colonial measures in the UN. The period also coincided with Israel's reassessment of its foreign policy with a view to establishing a considerable presence in the emergent African states. Israel, anxious to court the friendship of the new black African states in the face of mounting Arab diplomatic efforts to isolate it, began to show more positive support for the cause of African liberation.

In July 1961, when the president of Upper Volta, Maurice Yameogo, visited Israel, a joint communiqué issued by him and Prime Minister Ben-Gurion condemned racial discrimination and South Africa's apartheid policy as an infringement upon the rights and dignity of the people and "detrimental to the interests of its African majority." In November of that year Israel voted in favor of a UN General Assembly resolution which called on the world body to apply sanctions against South Africa owing to its apartheid policy, although Israel withheld its support for a clause which demanded the expulsion of the South African racist regime from the UN. It supported a similar resolution in 1962, and in 1966 Israel voted with the UN majority to terminate South Africa's mandate over Namibia. In addition, there is evidence that in the early 1960s Israel gave assistance to some African liberation movements. It was reported in September 1962 that Angolan nationalists were undergoing military training in Israel. And in June 1967 the Portuguese Command in Mozambique alleged that some of the captured nationalist fighters of the Front for the Liberation of Mozambique (FRELIMO) had been trained in Israel.[12]

The tough new Israeli position caused some debate within Israel and created opposition to her foreign policy. The pro-South African lobby within Israel drew attention to the danger for Israel and South

African Jewry which it felt was inherent in the UN call for sanctions. It was argued that if the Security Council could approve international intervention against North Korea and sanctions against South Africa, it could similarly bring action against Israel. It further reminded the government that Israel could not be certain that the U.S. would use her veto power in the Security Council to prevent the UN from imposing sanctions against Israel, as it was the combined Soviet and American threat to use Security Council sanctions in 1956 that had forced Israel to retreat from Suez and Sinai.[13] Dr. Haim Yakhil, director-general of the Israeli Foreign Ministry from 1960 to 1964, recalled in 1966: "On no issue do I remember more discussions than on apartheid among issues not directly concerning Israel's vital interests. Since 1961, this has been so."[14]

However, the government was convinced that it was doing the proper thing. Prime Minister Ben-Gurion, justifying the November 1961 UN vote to the Knesset, asserted that: "Israel would have been untrue not only to the moral imperative of Judaism, but also to its own vital interests, if it had failed to support the vigorous condemnation of South Africa's apartheid policy at the UN Assembly."[15] And in 1962, Golda Meir declared that Africans "have the right—and justly so—to expect Israel's support in their fight for liberty and freedom."[16] Besides, Israeli leaders believed that their action would not hurt the South African Jews seriously. In reply to a question on the subject at the Knesset in November 1961, Ben-Gurion said:

> That was the reason for our votes at the UN—to avoid difficulties for African Jews. After 1960 we changed because we didn't want to alienate the new African countries. We knew the Jews there wouldn't suffer very much. The South African government was angry but not against the Jews there—against Israel.[17]

Relations between South Africa and Israel deteriorated rapidly after this UN vote for sanctions. Verwoerd reacted heatedly, drawing unfavorable parallels between Israel and South Africa. He said the Jews had taken Israel from the Arabs after the Arabs had lived there for a thousand years: "In that I agree with them, Israel like South Africa is an apartheid state."[18] Most of South Africa's ire, however, was indeed directed against its own Jewish community which it accused of dual loyalties. The South African government immediately stopped the transfer of Zionist funds to Israel and restricted commercial cooperation.[19] Israel's imports from South Africa declined from $20.8

million in 1960 to $14.5 million in 1962. The decline in exports was even more pronounced: from $15.5 million in 1960 to $8.72 million in 1962.[20]

Undeterred by the South African reaction, Israel took additional measures to demonstrate her opposition to the South African government. In August 1963 she informed the UN Special Committee on Apartheid that she had taken measures to ensure that no arms, ammunition, or strategic materials would be exported to South Africa from Israel. In the same year she withdrew all her senior diplomats from Pretoria and announced that they would not be replaced, reducing the Israeli delegation to the level of chargé d'affaires.[21] Official visits were not promoted, and even at international conferences personal relations between diplomats of the two countries became the exception rather than the rule.

THE ERA OF QUIET NORMALIZATION OF RELATIONS

The Arab-Israeli war of June 1967 marked a turning point in Israeli-South African relations. It created the atmosphere for a thaw in relations between the two states, eliciting a strong response of solidarity with Israel not only among South African Jews but also among the entire white South African population.[22] As in previous military confrontations between Israel and the Arabs, many South African Jews volunteered for service in Israel.[23] The *Rhodesian Herald* reported that the South African Jewish community raised $30 million for Israel's war effort in 1967,[24] and the government lifted the embargo it had placed on the transfer of funds to Israel because of the latter's anti-apartheid policies at the UN. Other non-Jewish bodies also contributed funds to assist Israel.

Many white South Africans began to discern a community of interests between themselves and the Israelis, and even a certain parallel between their situations. The South African press drew parallels between the Arab-Israeli conflict and South Africa's position in Africa. The *Sunday Telegraph* saw both countries as states that were engaged in a life-and-death struggle against communism and atheism.[25] *Die Burger*, an organ of the National Party in the Cape Province, evinced similar sentiments:

> Israel and South Africa have a common lot. Both are engaged in
> a struggle for existence and both are in constant clash with the

decisive majorities in the United Nations. Both are a reliable pair of strength within the region, which would without them fall into anti-Western anarchy. It is in South Africa's interest that Israel is successful in containing her enemies who are among our own most vicious enemies; and Israel would have all the world against it if the navigation route around the Cape of Good Hope should be out of operation because South Africa's control is undermined. The anti-Western powers have driven Israel and South Africa into a community of interests which had better be utilized than denied.[26]

The South African Jewish Board of Deputies concurred. *Jewish Affairs*, its official organ, commented:

The argument that Israel and South Africa have a basic community of interests in the Middle East and further south has more than a grain of truth in it. The strong ties between the two countries are closer than ever since the 1967 War, are inseparable from their geographical and strategic position, from their anti-communist outlook and from all the realities of their national existence. In short, the destinies of the two countries are so different in many ways, but so alike in a much more meaningful sense than any enemy propagandist could conceive or, for that matter, would be happy to see.[27]

South Africa's moral and financial support for Israel during the war led to a thaw and subsequent improvement in the relations between the two countries. Various organizations committed to strengthening of relations sprang up. In Israel, the Friends of South Africa Society under the patronage of Menachem Begin, then a cabinet minister, was formed in 1968. In South Africa, the South African Foundation launched the Israeli-South African Man-to-Man Committee. These associations included prominent businessmen and politicians among their members, and were instrumental to the growth of both political and commercial contacts between the two countries. During the period between 1967 and 1971 Israeli visitors to South Africa, under the aegis of one of these organizations or Jewish bodies, included prominent politicians and officials like Shimon Peres; Adin Talbas, deputy director of Israel's Ministry of Commerce; Meir de Shalit, then director-general of Israel's Ministry of Tourism; former prime minister Ben-Gurion; former army intelligence chief Chaim Herzog; and Menachem Begin.

Commercial interaction between the two countries began to show marked improvement. In 1968 Israel sent a trade representative to South Africa, and in 1969 an Israeli-South Africa Trade Association was established. In August of the same year Zim, the Israeli shipping line, reported a 50 percent increase in the Israel-South Africa route since the June 1967 war, and further announced expansion plans to cope with this increase. Trade exhibitions were held to promote more trade. In 1970 South Africa advanced a credit line of $15 million to Israel.[28]

Israeli imports from South Africa jumped from $3.3 million in 1967 to $27.7 million in 1973. South Africa's share of total Israeli trade with Africa increased from 14 percent in 1967 to 40 percent in 1973 (see Table 6.1).

Israeli exports included textiles, clothing, chemicals and pharmaceuticals, while imports consisted of wool, asbestos, industrial diamonds, and metals. Diamonds remained the most important Israeli import from South Africa, as South Africa is the largest producer of uncut diamonds. For Israel the diamond-cutting industry is not only a large complex employing over 50,000 workers, it is also the country's most important source of foreign currency. In 1967 exports of cut diamonds totaled $102 million, and in 1968 they accounted for over 34 percent of the value of Israel's exports. By 1970 Israel had become one of the heaviest buyers of South African diamonds and one of the world's leading diamond-cutting centers. By 1972 exports of cut diamonds alone amounted to $385 million.[29]

TABLE 6.1
ISRAEL'S TRADE WITH SOUTH AFRICA,
1967–1973 (in $U.S. m)

Year	Imports	Exports	% of all Africa
1967	3.30	4.00	14%
1968	5.24	5.66	18
1969	5.80	8.19	21
1970	10.22	10.69	29
1971	7.97	9.40	24
1972	11.59	8.81	26
1973	27.49	11.96	40

Source: Central Bureau of Statistics, *Statistical Abstracts of Israel*, 1967–1973.

The period also witnessed the beginning of military cooperation between the two states. There was eagerness in South Africa not only to learn from Israel's experience in containing terrorism but also to benefit from the country's advances in military technology. Contacts between the general staffs of both countries became frequent, and the exchange of military delegations became commonplace. In October 1967 General Mordechai Hod, the chief-of-staff of the Israeli Air Force, was reported to have explained the lessons of the June war in detail to the South African Staff College.[30]

In June 1969 prominent former Israeli defense chiefs were in South Africa. They included former intelligence chief Herzog and General Aharon Doron, commander of Tel Aviv civil defense during the June 1967 war. And when former prime minister Ben-Gurion was in South Africa in May in connection with Zionist fundraising activities, and visited Vorster, he was accompanied by Colonel Joseph Golan, a former military attaché in Paris. A Tanzanian newspaper reported in March 1968 that a large group of Israeli military experts were in South Africa training South African forces.[31]

There were also reports of arms trade, although these were often difficult to verify. The Jewish Telegraphic Agency, in a report from London, revealed that:

> The South African Government has begun to organise the export of tanks to Israel, marking a new stage in their cooperation. The South African tank is a 65-ton giant, armed with a heavy gun, and designed according to the model of the new British tank. This is an apparent reference to Britain's Chieftain tank, which Israel has been trying to buy from Great Britain.[32]

In April 1971 the *New York Times* reported that South Africa was manufacturing the Israeli-designed Uzi submachine gun under license from Belgium. It further reported "wholly unconfirmable" rumors that Israel had made blueprints of the French Mirage fighter available to South Africa.[33] As the South Africans had set up a state-owned arms manufacturing company, Armscor, in 1968 to assist in reducing their dependence on external sources for their defense needs, it is plausible that they sought Israeli assistance to develop their own weapons systems.

However, Israel continued to express her abhorrence of the South African apartheid system, sometimes causing strains in their relationship, although the vigor with which she had pursued her anti-apartheid measures waned.[34] In November 1967 the Israeli UN delegate, Joel Barromi, walked out on the South African representative when the latter rose to defend apartheid in the General Assembly. The following year the new Israeli delegate, Yosef Tekoah, argued that South Africa had forfeited its right to continue to administer the territory of Namibia. And in June 1971 the Israeli government's offer of £10,000 to the OAU Liberation Committee—which the OAU rejected—led to an almost total break in Israeli-South African relations.

The weakening of Israel's political position in Africa, particularly from 1972, witnessed a corresponding improvement of relations with South Africa. In addition, there was less reluctance to make many of these contacts public. In 1972 Israel allowed South Africa to open a consulate-general in Tel Aviv. In the same year two Israeli companies, Tadiran and Elta, signed contracts for the delivery of electronic equipment to South Africa.[35] Political, financial, commercial, and cultural ties continued to increase. Among important South African figures who visited Israel before the Yom Kippur War were Connie Mulder, minister of the interior; Eschel Rhodie, secretary of information; and General Hendrik Van de Bergh, chief of South Africa's Bureau of State Security.[36]

THE OCTOBER 1973 WAR

The outbreak of another round of hostilities between Israel and her Arab neighbors in October 1973 had important consequences for Israel's domestic politics and foreign policy in general, and particularly for her relations with both black Africa and South Africa.[37] The Arab oil embargo altered the relations between Israel and her traditional allies in the West. Israel was shocked to see that most of her Western friends were prepared to "forsake" her if and when their own interests seemed to be served by such a policy.[38] Even her socialist allies in Europe refused refueling rights for American planes that ferried supplies to Israel in the critical periods of the war. Moreover, as we have seen, all but four African states broke their diplomatic ties with her in the wake of the war and Israel suddenly found herself short of firm friends. In the heat of emotion, the "defection" of the Africans was interpreted as a "betrayal."

In contrast, the support South Africans and the South African government gave to Israel was spontaneous and far-reaching. Although the South African government formally declared her neutrality in the war, Minister of Defense Botha promised that "within our means, and without declaring war," his government would find ways to assist Israel. He added: "There is a deep feeling on the part of thousands of South Africans for Israel, in her battle against the forces supported by communistic militarism, which also poses a threat to us." He disclosed that his country was deeply concerned about the role of the Soviet Union in the war, which he said was "most significant" and could have far-reaching consequences for South Africa.[39] Yitzhak Unna, Israeli ambassador in Pretoria, later commented:

> Western countries with whom we had traditional ties suddenly started swooning in the direction of the Arabs the moment there was a whiff of oil in the air. They left us in the lurch . . . [but] your Prime Minister publicly sent a message of encouragement to Israel in what were, for us, dark days.[40]

Many Jews from South Africa volunteered to help in some way, as did Jews from the United States and Western Europe. Many of these volunteers served in non-military functions in kibbutzim and moshavim. Julius Weinstein, chairman of the South African Zionist Federation, said that many doctors, including orthopedic, plastic, and general surgeons as well as anesthetists, worked in hospitals throughout Israel. The London *Daily Telegraph* even reported that South Africa had sent a number of Mirage jets and volunteer pilots to Israel during the war to acquire combat experience,[41] although this was vigorously denied by both countries. The planes were alleged to have rounded the West African coast by using the airfields in Portuguese-controlled Angola and Guinea-Bissau before joining the U.S. planes dispatched to Israel via the Azores.

The South African Jewish community raised funds to support Israel. Although the total amount was not disclosed, one scholar put the figure at more than $30 million.[42] Weinstein indicated that the amount collected was twice as much as that raised in 1967. He further disclosed that support had come not only from Jews but from Africans, Afrikaners, and the English-speaking section of the population.[43]

On the Israeli domestic political front, the war resulted in a major shift with consequent repercussions for Israeli-South African relations. Following the resignation of Prime Minister Meir in the aftermath of the war, a new generation of Labor Party leaders came to power:

In contrast with the older generation of Labor Pary leaders, such as Ben-Gurion, Sharett, Eshkol and Golda Meir, who viewed themselves and the party they led as an integral part of the international socialist movement and shared its emotional outlook on questions of decolonisation and relations with the Third World, the new Premier, Yitzhak Rabin, and many of the younger generation of leaders who came to power with him were pragmatists who were generally left cold by ideological considerations when they clashed with the dictates of realpolitik in a world which was growing progressively more hostile to Israel.[44]

The new leaders felt little inhibition in warming up toward South Africa, which was itself only too glad to exploit the isolation of Israel to foster closer relations. Nor was there any serious dissent on this score in Israel. References were often made to the "unprofitable returns resulting from the Israeli efforts in Black Africa" to justify Israel's South Africa policy.[45] Moreover, practical military, political, and economic concerns outweighed other considerations at this point.

The period following the 1973 war witnessed a gradual deterioration of the Israeli economy. The rate of inflation in Israel, estimated to be 30 percent in 1976, reached four figures in the 1980s. Israel needed a strong currency, raw materials for her industries, as well as more outlets to reduce her high annual trade deficits. Because of the unstable situation in the Middle East, Israeli leaders sought to reduce their dependence on Middle Eastern oil. Most of Israel's needs were then met by Iran and occupied Sinai. From the early 1970s Israel had planned to convert her three oil-burning electric plants into coal-burning ones. An agreement for the supply of coal by South Africa had already been signed in 1971. The quadrupling of oil prices after 1973 made Israel accord top priority to the issue; the price of oil was then about three times the price of South African coal.

Moreover, the continued condemnation in the UN of South Africa's "racism," Israeli "imperialism," and the Israeli-South African "unholy alliance" merely reinforced the "siege mentality" in Israel that had resulted from the growing feeling of isolation. "Both countries increasingly see themselves as surrounded by enemies, a target for ill-informed opinion, outposts of civilization at either end of the African continent—strongly anti-communist and pro-Western."[46]

The philosophical underpinnings of this "new" relationship were thus clearly established. Prime Minister Yitzhak Rabin defined it in

1976: "Both our countries have in common the problem of initiating dialogue, co-existence and stability in our respective parts of the world in the face of foreign-inspired instability and recklessness."[47] It was hardly surprising that as the world moved to isolate them the two countries should draw closer together, no matter what reservations individual consciences may have had about the relationship. The feeling in Israel was that as a beleaguered country she should be the last in the world to reject the proferred friendship of any state.[48]

On the political front relations between the two states were upgraded to ambassadorial level in March 1974. Israel ceased to vote consistently against South Africa at the UN. There were exchanges of high-ranking visitors. After the 10 November 1975 Zionism-racism vote at the UN, when the defection of black Africa to the anti-Israel Arab bloc seemed final, Israel agreed to the appointment of Charles Fincham as South Africa's first ambassador to Israel, and Prime Minister Rabin had no reservations about responding favorably to South African overtures to invite Prime Minister Vorster for an official visit to Israel in 1976. This was done despite the opposition of the Israeli ambassador in Pretoria. This period also coincided with President Ford's reevaluation of American Middle East policy in 1975, which led to America's cutting off aid to Israel for a period of seven months. Cultivation of close ties with South Africa served an added function in terms of trying to reduce Israeli dependence on the U.S.[49]

During the much-publicized Vorster visit in April 1976 a series of agreements on commercial, trade, scientific, fiscal and, in all probability, military cooperation were signed. A joint ministerial committee which would meet at least once a year was set up. The South Africans in particular were elated over the pact with Israel. A Johannesburg radio commentary claimed that Vorster's visit had "catapulted South Africa's foreign policy into an entirely new dimension."[50]

The pragmatic, non-ideological approval of the Rabin government was taken a step further by the right-wing Begin government which came to power in June 1977. The South African government expressed delight at the election of Begin, who had visited South Africa and was chairman of the Israel-South African Friendship Society.[51] Soon afterwards, South African Foreign Minister Botha visited Israel and reaffirmed South Africa's support for it.

Throughout its seven years in office Begin's Likud government did not exhibit the same unease with its South African association as did key figures in the Labor Party leadership. "Under the Likud government of Mr. Begin . . . a proper disregard has been displayed towards the public image of the alliance, and the emphasis has been on substance."[52] Visits to South Africa by Israeli officials were commonplace, and visits to Israel by South African officials were made public.

However, after the inauguration of the coalition government of Shimon Peres in September 1984, there was a noticeable change in the conduct of relations with South Africa. Peres seemed more concerned about the public-image aspects of Israeli ties with South Africa than had any government since Golda Meir's. He did not meet with Foreign Minister Botha during the latter's "private" visit to Israel in November 1984.[53]

ECONOMIC RELATIONS

Economic relations between the two countries have blossomed through a series of trade agreements, the establishment of joint projects, the formation of joint bodies aimed at promoting trade links, and the appointment of missions. By August 1975 it was reported that the number of joint ventures and "know-how" agreements had increased significantly, facilitated by the South African decision to permit its citizens to participate in projects in Israel approved by the Israeli Investment Authority (such approval entitles the enterprise to tax benefits and grants or loans). General Meir Amit, former Israeli chief of intelligence and head of Koor Industries, disclosed in South Africa that such projects included the participation of the state-owned South African Railways in a rail project in Israel and the construction of an Israeli plant in South Africa to desalinate sea water for drinking and irrigation. He further disclosed that a joint venture in the manufacture of agricultural chemicals, including insecticides, would start operation the following year, and that an oil tank farm for the storage of oil under tight security conditions was being built in Israel.[54]

However, the landmark in the development of economic ties was reached with Vorster's visit. During the visit he concluded agreements aimed at the encouragement of investment, development of trade, scientific and technical cooperation, and joint utilization of South African raw materials and Israeli know-how and manpower.[55] The agreements were described in South Africa as the "most far-reaching of [their] kind South Africa has ever concluded with another country."[56]

Steps were taken to implement the agreements. In September 1976 a high-level South African trade mission visited Israel.[57] Arnon Gafny, governor of the Bank of Israel, was in South Africa in 1977, and in February 1978 Israeli Finance Minister Simcha Ehrlich made a well-publicized week-long visit to South Africa—the first ever by an Israeli cabinet minister. He said to representatives of South African business that because of its duty-free policy toward industrial goods, Israel could offer South African investors an "attractive packet" for the export of industrial goods to both the European Common Market and the U.S.[58] In a joint communiqué in Cape Town, at the end of his talks with South African Finance Minister Owen Horwood, Ehrlich announced agreements on arrangements "that would enable South Africa to participate more directly in financing and developing the infrastructure of Israel's economy and in the development of specific industrial plants." Specifically, South Africa would permit South African individuals or companies to invest a further R44 million in Israel and would grant the latter a credit of R37.5 million.[59] Soon after Ehrlich's visit the South African government, in an unprecedented move, decided to allow its citizens to buy dollar-denominated Israeli bearer bonds. The bonds were to be used by the Israeli government to finance infrastructural projects.[60]

Ehrlich's visit was followed by that of a delegation of Israeli businessmen. In June there was also a strong contingent of South African businessmen at the ISRATEC '78 export trade show in Jerusalem. Visits by ministers became commonplace—for instance, Owen Horwood's visit to Israel in 1980 and visits by Energy Minister Yitzhak Moda'i and Finance Minister Yoram Aridor to South Africa in February and March 1983, respectively. Aridor's visit was believed to have signaled a "major deal" in the offing.[61]

Coal became an important element in the commercial transactions between the countries. After four years of what Johannesburg's *Sunday Times* labeled "top secret negotiations" between the Israeli government and the Transvaal Coal Owners' Association, a long-term agreement to bring in $23 million worth of South African coal annually to Israel's Hadera power plant was signed in January 1979.[62]

All these agreements have had a pronounced effect on trade between the two countries. Although according to International Monetary Fund figures trade between the two forms a small proportion of the overall trade of either country, representing only 0.5 percent of South Africa's imports and 0.6 percent of its exports, the increase in absolute figures is remarkable. From a level of $27.5 million in 1973 , the figure had by 1982 jumped to $245 million (see Table 6.2). These figures

TABLE 6.2

ISRAEL'S TRADE WITH SOUTH AFRICA,
1973–1984 (in $U.S. m)

Year	Imports	Exports	Balance of Trade for Israel
1973	27.5	11.9	−15.6
1974	43.4	28.7	−14.7
1975	38.4	39.3	0.9
1976	45.2	34.9	−10.3
1977	51.9	23.9	−28.0
1978	80.4	37.5	−42.9
1979	151.1	48.2	−102.9
1980	116.9	79.1	−37.8
1981	103.2	98.6	−4.6
1982	166.0	78.6	−88.2
1983	169.6	82.8	−86.8
1984*	128.5	68.3	−60.0

Source: Statistical Abstracts of Israel, 1973–1984; Foreign Trade Statistics Quarterly, 1973–1984.
*Figures for January to September.

do not take into account trade in diamonds, which are purchased through the Central Selling Organization in London, or in military equipment. Ephraim Raviv, Israel's economic and commercial counselor at the Pretoria Embassy and director of Israeli trade and tourism in South Africa, emphasized that "There are [also] the undisclosed trade items—the value of which nobody is prepared to venture even an anonymous guess. . . . One thing is certain—South Africa is a highly-valued client of Israel's electronic industry."[63]

For South Africa, trade with Israel has become an invaluable bridgehead into both the European Economic Community and the U.S. market, to which Israel has preferential access. Goods manufactured in Israel, or having a minimum 40 percent Israeli value-added coefficient, are eligible for duty-free entrance into the EEC, and Israeli-manufactured products are allowed duty-free entry into the U.S. under the Generalized Preference System.[64] Consequently, the South African Iron and Steel Corporation (ISCOR) and Israel's Koor Metal Industries formed ISKOOR in 1975, which imports semi-processed iron and steel from South Africa to Israel for further processing and then for export to Europe and the U.S.

Tourism has also increased. The South African Tourist Corporation has offices in Tel Aviv and Jerusalem, and the Association of South African Travel Agents held their eighteenth annual congress in Israel in 1977. The number of tourists from South Africa to Israel grew slightly from 15,000 in 1972 to 16,669 in 1975; then in 1976 it jumped by 23 percent to 20,831. In 1980 26,056 South African tourists visited Israel, while the figure for 1982 was 18,443. Israeli tourism to South Africa also staged a spectacular jump from 2,680 in 1972 to 7,285 in 1975.[65] However, the number of Israeli tourists visiting South Africa often fluctuates with the political situation in Southern Africa. For instance, there was a decline of about 13 percent in 1976 due principally to the unstable conditions in Southern Africa—the Soweto riots, the escalating war in what was then Rhodesia, and the Angolan civil war. However, since 1979 there has been an annual average of about 10,000 Israeli tourists visiting South Africa.

Cultural and sports exchanges have also become more frequent. In 1973 and 1974 the Israel Philharmonic Orchestra as well as Israeli fashion models toured South Africa. Some Israeli singers have performed in South Africa, as have the Jerusalem Song and Dance Ensemble and the Bat-Dor and Batsheva dance troupes. There have also been some South African productions in Israel, including the Johannesburg Youth Ballet, the Free State Choir, and several plays. In sports there have been some exchanges in rugby, golf, and tennis. However, most of those involved are teenagers who usually have not participated in team competitions, as many of the international federations to which Israel belongs do not sanction team competition between member states and South Africa. It should not be overlooked that criticism of these contacts in Israel has been unrelenting.[66]

MILITARY COOPERATION

It is the military cooperation between Israel and South Africa that has attracted the most publicity in recent years. The full extent of this cooperation is not known, as such matters are often shrouded in secrecy by both sides. Much of what is written is speculative. Any disclosure of such ties is often immediately denied. Another difficulty relates to the subjective nature of some of the sources on Israel-South African military ties. As many of these are part of the propaganda designed to further isolate Israel in the Third World, particularly in Africa, the information is often exaggerated. Israeli-South African military ties are portrayed, for instance, as the backbone of the South African military machine. Other countries with more extensive and more central roles in the development and maintenance of the South African military often go unmentioned.

Nevertheless, it is possible to discern the nature of the Israeli-South African military cooperation, and there is no doubt that such cooperation has increased since 1973. Israeli-South African military ties are of four broad types: arms transfer, intelligence cooperation, technology transfer, and nuclear training and cooperation.

The list of Israeli-made weapons in the South African arsenal seems substantial. The Stockholm International Peace Research Institute's 1980 *Yearbook* noted the rapid growth in the development of the Israeli arms industry and trade in the 1970s. Israel's arms exports in the 1960s were less than $10 million per year, but by 1976 the figure had reached an estimated $300 million and in 1980 about $1 billion. South Africa was listed as the largest buyer of Israeli arms in 1980, accounting for 35 percent of total arms exports.[67]

Shortly after the 1973 war there were reports of South Africa's interest in Israel's supersonic fighter plane.[68] There were also reports that Israel was selling to South Africa Gabriel sea missiles as part of a program to increase the strength of the South African fleet from 27 to 43 vessels. These reports coincided with the visit to South Africa of three former Israeli generals—Moshe Dayan, Chaim Herzog, and Meir Amit.[69] Amit was alleged to have disclosed during the tour that senior Israeli officers were giving lectures to South African officers in modern warfare and counter-intelligence techniques and that Israel was cooperating with South Africa in the field of military electronics and manufacture.[70] South Africa's Air Force General R.H.D. Rogers admitted that his country's casualties during the Angola debacle in 1975-76 were light because his country had adopted the Israeli strategy of evacuating the wounded from the front. Israeli military experts were reported to have assisted the South Africans on that occasion.[71]

The South African experience during the Angolan war also led to an increase in military cooperation with Israel. Having found that some of its equipment was inferior to that of Cuba, it sought the sophisticated weapons systems of Israel. During Vorster's visit to Israel in April 1976 military cooperation featured prominently on the agenda of his discussions with Israeli leaders, although both sides attempted to play down this aspect of the visit.[72]

Military and defense officials were prominent in Vorster's delegation, and his visit included tours of naval bases near Sharm-el Sheikh and of Israeli aircraft plants near Tel Aviv. Before the end of the year, the South African navy had purchased three Reshef patrol boats and had arranged to build three more under license at dockyards in Durban. The engineers who were to supervise the project were trained in Israeli dockyards.[73] The navy was also reported to have added two Dvora patrol boats and an unknown number of Aliya missile-carrying vessels. All three classes of vessels were equipped with Gabriels. Six more Reshefs were ordered at the end of 1977.[74]

It was also revealed in 1977 that Israel's cooperation with South Africa involved the armor-plating of both countries' tanks. Israel had trouble getting the special hardened steel it required for its Merkava tanks. In exchange for this hardened steel, the Israelis agreed to modernize 150 South African Centurion tanks. They made available to South Africa the process by which they were producing a new kind of armor-plate which is "more impenetrable than that which is available to the world's other armies, which [they believe] can resist most, if not all, of the anti-tank weapons in current use."[75] *The Economist* also reported in 1977 that South Africa had put up money for the next generation of Israeli warships, a new version of the Reshef, and that delivery of the first four or five was scheduled for 1979–80.[76]

Israeli technicians were reportedly helping South Africa to modernize its air force. Aircraft computers were being replaced with more advanced and sensitive models, some of them specially adjusted for operations against ground targets. South African planes were fitted with new armaments—air-to-air and air-to-ground rockets and gadgets for misleading missiles (particularly anti-aircraft shoulder missiles). South Africa's helicopters were fitted out for strikes against ground targets and were adapted to carry light cannon, heavy machineguns, and night warfare equipment.[77] South Africa showed keen interest in buying Israel's Kfir jets, and an agreement to supply up to twenty-four Kfirs was alleged to have been concluded.[78] However, the American approval needed before such a sale could go through, as the planes have American engines, was not forthcoming.

By the time the UN Security Council imposed an arms embargo against South Africa in November 1977, the range of Israeli-made equipment was quite varied.[79] A few days later Foreign Minister Moshe

Dayan said South Africa was a "good friend" of Israel and that Israel would "not leave her to the mercy of fate,"[80] a statement which was generally interpreted to mean that Israel would not comply with the embargo. However, because of criticism generated by Dayan's statement, on 7 November the government of Israel denied that it intended to violate the UN sanctions.[81] Dayan stated that if measures were going to be taken against Pretoria, Israel would not violate them. He insisted, however, that Israel was entitled to maintain relations with Pretoria just as other countries did.[82]

There have, however, been many reports indicating that Israel was not implementing the UN sanctions. Israel's main electronics companies, Tadiran and Elbit, combined to assist South Africa in building its own electronics industry. Tadiran is also said to have established a subsidiary in South Africa for the manufacture of electronic devices for counter-intelligence. In addition, there was a joint production project between Rotoflight Helicopters of South Africa and Chemavir-Nasok of Israel to build the Scorpion helicopter. The *African Intelligence Digest* reported that Israel provided South Africa with Arava early-warning aircraft as a replacement for its aged British-built propeller-driven Shackletons.[83] And in June 1983 the *Rand Daily Mail* reported that a remote-controlled drone shot down by Mozambique that week was a South African spy plane designed by Israel. The pilotless Israeli-designed IAI Scout was on a mission for the South African Defense Forces' military intelligence branch. The paper also revealed that a similar drone was believed to have been used to gather intelligence before the South African air strike on 23 May 1983 on alleged bases of the African National Congress (ANC) near Maputo.[84] Furthermore, when Defense Minister Sharon visited South Africa in 1981, he was reported to have made a secret trip to South African troops in Namibia along the border with Angola.[85] Again, when Finance Minister Aridor left for a ten-day visit to South Africa and the Far East, there were speculations in Israel that "military and security affairs, including arms deals, could be the fulcrum of the talks."[86] And in 1984 *Ha'aretz* reported that South Africa had shown interest in military computers used in the Israel Defense Forces and that she had "already begun purchasing a variety of projects."[87]

There are also indications of continued cooperation in military training and intelligence. In January 1983 the Angolan government alleged that Israelis were training UNITA rebels.[88] In June General Coustard Viljoen, chief of the South African Defense Forces, claimed that documents the Israelis unearthed in Tyre during the summer 1982 Israeli invasion of Southern Lebanon proved conclusively that the ANC had links with "other international terrorist organisations."[89]

The most closely guarded area of the military collaboration has been that of nuclear development. Contrary to widespread reports, Israel has never been the main, or even one of the main, South African mentors in this field. As Zdenek Cervenka and Barbara Rogers in their book *The Nuclear Axis* conclusively prove, France, Great Britain, the U.S., and West Germany have been the "main abetters in this enterprise."[90] Nevertheless, Israel has been involved to some extent in South Africa's nuclear development.

Speculation about Israel's nuclear collaboration with South Africa became widespread and particularly after Vorster's visit in 1976.[91] Israel was alleged to have supplied South Africa with nuclear technology, especially information on its laser enrichment process, in return for uranium.[92] It has been claimed that Israeli personnel have been seen at the South African Valindaba uranium enrichment plant near the Palindaba atomic research facility.[93] In February 1977 an exiled white South African journalist was reported to have uncovered strong indications of an influx of Israeli nuclear physicists into Pretoria over the past eighteen months.[94] South Africa was also reported to have used Israeli consultants to advise on safety aspects of commercial reactors.[95]

What is said to have conclusively proved Israel's involvement was a nuclear-bomb explosion deep in the southern Indian Ocean close to Prince Edward Island revealed by the U.S. Vela satellite in September 1979. Some sources have even speculated that the test was designed to try out a neutron bomb. But Israel's role in the venture was minute compared to that of Britain, Canada, France, the U.S., and West Germany.[96] The *Washington Post* of 8 December carried another report by Jack Anderson detailing a joint project by Israel, South Africa, and Taiwan to develop a strategic cruise missile. In May 1982 *Ha'aretz* reported on the achievement of the joint Israeli-South African nuclear development program. According to the report, the two countries have developed a neutron bomb and were developing a cruise missile with a range of 2,400 km and a nuclear gun.[97]

An outgrowth of Israeli-South African relations has been Israel's involvement with the so-called independent "bantustans," particularly Ciskei, Transkei, and Bophuthatswana. Although Israel, like other nations of the world except South Africa, does not recognize the "independence" of these "homelands," there has been a substantial growth of commercial, industrial, technical, and even military contacts with them. Lennox Sebe, "president" of Ciskei, is a regular visitor to Israel; in November 1983 he visited Israel for the third time that year. The "president" of Bophuthatswana is also a regular visitor to Israel. In one such "private" visit in September 1983, which he made in the company of a large entourage that included his "minister of construction," he described Israel as "a great and important friend."[98] Ciskei and Bophuthatswana maintain a "trade mission" in Tel Aviv. They fly the flags of their respective "countries" there, and their "official representatives" claim to be employees of each "country's" "foreign ministry."[99]

Some prominent political figures in the former Likud regime, including former finance minister Yoram Aridor, have important commercial interests in Ciskei. Aridor was reported to have signed contracts for the establishment of two factories there during one of his visits in 1983.[100] Among the construction and investment projects organized by the Ciskei Trade Mission are the building of a hospital and two schools by the Israeli Gur Construction Company, the construction of a textile factory with investment by the Israel Discount Bank, and educational and agricultural development projects run by Degem Systems and Agridev—Israel's state-owned agricultural development company operating through a local subsidiary, Agricamel. In addition, at least thirteen Israeli doctors and their families were in Ciskei on contract in June 1984.

In Bophuthatswana Israelis have helped to establish and run the Bophuthatswana Television Service,[101] and were "becoming involved in a big way in the development of soccer." The 60,000-seat Independence Stadium in Mbabatho, the capital, was designed by a Tel Aviv architect, and a Tel Aviv coach traveled several times a year to the homeland in his capacity as non-resident "soccer coach."[102]

In addition, there have been persistent reports from European sources that cooperation extends to the military sphere. Lennox Sebe was reported to have signed weapons and military assistance agreements with the Israeli government during one of his visits in 1982. The reports were later confirmed by Sebe's former military advisor, who admitted that he had accompanied Sebe to Israel "on an arms-buying mission."[103] Although the Israeli government denied these reports, in an interview on Israeli television on 11 November 1983 Sebe himself confirmed that Israel would provide his "republic" with military aid.[104] *Ma'ariv* also reported about the same time that Ciskei air force pilots were training in Israel. The *Jerusalem Post* later revealed that eighteen "Ciskeians" who would form the nucleus of a planned Ciskei air force had been trained in the country for about a year. The head of the private Herzliya flying school where they were training confirmed the presence of the pilots but insisted that they were training to fly commercial planes and that "his contract with the Ciskei government has no military connotations."[105]

Despite attempts of the Likud government under Shamir toward the end of 1983 to play down these relationships, claiming the hosting of bantustan dignitaries by official and quasi-official agencies had been done "out of ignorance," the presence in Israel of the "official representative" of these bantustans does not make the government's decision to cut off relations[106] look genuine and resolute. However, the firm stand of the Foreign Ministry against all forms of contact with the bantustans seems to be yielding some fruit. In April 1985 the Foreign Ministry was able to pressure some members of the Knesset who had earlier agreed to attend the opening of the Ciskei parliament to cancel the trip.[107]

A new pattern of Israeli-South African relations, which first became noticeable during Shamir's administration in 1983, thus became pronounced with the increased efforts of the National Unity government to cultivate the friendship of black African states. Increased international criticism of South Africa, as the political situation in that country deteriorates, is an additional reason for the Israeli government to want to maintain some political distance from South Africa. Political relations have therefore become low-key, even reticent, although economic contacts continue unaffected.

NOTES

1. See Kunirun Osia, *Israel, South Africa and Black Africa: A Study of the Primacy of the Politics of Expediency* (Washington: UPA, 1981), p. 2; James Adams, "Strangers and Brothers: The Unlikely Alliance Between Israel and South Africa," *Sunday Times* (London), 15 April 1984, p. 33.

2. Ibid.

3. Yosef Goell, "A View from Jerusalem," *Africa Report*, vol. 25, no. 6 (November-December 1980), p. 22.

4. Osia, *Israel, South Africa and Black Africa*, p. 14.

5. Shabtai Rosenne, "Basic Elements of Israel's Foreign Policy," *India*

Quarterly, vol. 17, no. 4 (October-December 1961), cited in Michael Brecher, *The Foreign Policy System of Israel: Setting, Images, Process* (London: Oxford University Press, 1972).

6. Discussions with H.S. Aynor.

7. Adams, "Strangers and Brothers," p. 33.

8. Ibid.

9. Quoted in Alfred T. Moleah, "The Special Relationship," *Africa Report*, vol. 25, no. 6 (November-December 1980), p. 14.

10. Leslie Rubin, "Dialog: South African Jewry and Apartheid," *Africa Report*, vol. 15, no. 2 (February 1970), p. 24.

11. Brecher, *The Foreign Policy System of Israel*, Chapters 12 and 13.

12. See Olusola Ojo, "Israeli-South African Connections and Afro-Israeli Relations," *International Studies*, vol. 21, no. 1 (1982), p. 38.

13. Discussions with H.S. Aynor.

14. Quoted in Brecher, *The Foreign Policy System of Israel*, p. 145.

15. Quoted in Goell, "A View from Jerusalem," p. 18.

16. Ibid.

17. Quoted in Brecher, *The Foreign Policy System of Israel*, p. 234.

18. Quoted in Moleah, "A Special Relationship."

19. Ojo, "Israeli-South African Connections," p. 38.

20. Central Bureau of Statistics, *Statistical Abstracts of Israel*, 1960–1962.

21. *Keesings Contempory Archives*, 23–30 November 1963, p. 19757; Africa Diary, 12–18 October 1963, p. 1390.

22. See Peter Hellyer, *Israel and South Africa: Development of Relations 1967–1974* (London: Palestinian Action, 1975) p. 9.

23. See ibid., p. 8; Osia, *Israel, South Africa and Black Africa*, p. 28.

24. *Rhodesian Herald*, 26 February 1968.

25. *Sunday Telegraph* (Johannesburg), 18 June 1967.

26. Quoted in Hellyer, *Israel and South Africa*, p. 22.

27. Quoted in ibid., p. 22.

28. See ibid., pp. 11–24; Osia, *Israel, South Africa, and Black Africa*, p. 22.

29. See Central Bureau of Statistics, *Statistical Abstracts of Israel*, 1967–1973; Y. Kashim, "Zionist-Racist Alliance," *International Affairs* (Moscow), April 1975, p. 67; Osia, *Israel, South Africa and Black Africa*, p. 23.

30. Hellyer, *Israel and South Africa*, p. 10.

31. Cited in Ojo, "Israeli-South African Connections," p. 41.

32. *Jewish Telegraphic Agency*, 20 January 1970.

33. *New York Times*, 30 April 1971.

34. Naomi Chazan, "The Fallacies of Pragmatism: Israeli Foreign Policy

Toward South Africa," *African Affairs*, vol. 82, no. 327 (April 1983), p. 172.

35. Patrick Fitzgerald and Jonathan Bloch, "Alliance Among Outlaws," *The Middle East*, May 1983, p. 32.

36. See Hellyer, *Israel and South Africa*, pp. 22–24.

37. See Colin Legum (ed.), *African Contemporary Record, 1973–74*, vol. 6 (London: Rex Collings, 1974), p. B463.

38. Fitzgerald and Bloch, "Alliance Among Outlaws," p. 32.

39. Hellyer, *Israel and South Africa*, p. 25.

40. *Jerusalem Post*, 24 February 1974, p. 3.

41. *Daily Telegraph* (London), 31 October 1973.

42. Adams, "Strangers and Brothers," p. 33.

43. *Jerusalem Post*, 24 February 1974, p. 3.

44. Goell, "A View from Jerusalem," p. 21.

45. See *Jerusalem Post*, 13 April 1974, p. 8.

46. Adams, "Strangers and Brothers," p. 33.

47. *South African Digest*, 30 April 1976, quoted in Benjamin Beit-Hallahmi, "Israel and South Africa 1977–1982: Business as Usual and More," *New Outlook*, vol. 26, no. 2 (March-April 1983), p. 31.

48. See, for instance, *Jerusalem Post* editorial, 11 April 1976, p. 10.

49. See *The Economist*, 5 November 1977.

50. See *Africa Research Bulletin* (hereafter *ARB*), April 1976, p. 4009; *ARB* (Economic Series), 15 March–14 April 1976, p. 3836; *The Times* (London), 14 April 1976.

51. Chazan,"The Fallacies of Pragmatism," p. 74.

52. Beit-Hallahmi, "Israel and South Africa," p. 31.

53. *Jerusalem Post*, 4 November 1984.

54. *ARB* (Economic Series), 15 July–14 August 1975, p. 3579. Koor Chemicals and South African Sentrachem's joint subsidiary—Agbro—started manufacturing herbicides in 1976 under an Israeli licensing arrangement.

55. *Jerusalem Post*, 13 April 1976, pp. 1, 2.

56. *ARB*, April 1976, p. 4009.

57. *Jerusalem Post*, 2 September 1976, p. 1.

58. Cited in Osia, *Israel, South Africa and Black Africa*, p. 26.

59. *Jerusalem Post*, 12 February 1978; *Financial Times*, 14 February 1978.

60. *ARB*, February 1978, p. 4600.

61. *Jerusalem Post*, 8 February and 3 March 1983.

62. See ibid., 15 January 1979, p. 2.

63. Cited in Moleah, "The Special Relationship," p. 16.

64. *African Intelligence Digest*, 20 September 1984, p. 7.

65. *Statistical Abstracts of Israel*, 1972–1982.

66. See *Jerusalem Post*, 11, 14 September 1975; 8, 27 August 1982; 24 July, 13 December 1983. See also Chazan, "Fallacies of Pragmatism," p. 182.

67. Stockholm International Peace Research Institute, *World Armaments and Disarmament, SIPRI Yearbook 1980* (London: Taylor and Francis, 1980), pp. 85, 86.

68. *Africa Confidential*, vol. 17, no. 8, 16 April 1976.

69. *Jerusalem Post*, 8 September 1974.

70. UN document no. 17464, 1975.

71. *Daily Telegraph* (London), 3 April 1976.

72. *Jerusalem Post*, 13 April 1976.

73. *The Guardian* (London), 8 November 1977.

74. Fitzgerald and Bloch, "Alliance Among Outlaws," p. 32.

75. *Foreign Report*, 2 November 1977, p. 1.

76. *The Economist*, 5 November 1977.

77. See *Foreign Report*, 2 November 1977, p. 1; *Africa Confidential*, vol. 19, no. 16, 4 August 1978.

78. *Foreign Report*, 2 November 1977, p. 1.

79. *New York Times*, 8 August 1976.

80. *ARB*, November 1977, p. 4656.

81. Ibid.

82. BBC *Summary of World Records*, Part IV, *The Middle East*, 9 November 1977.

83. *African Intelligence Digest*, 20 September 1984, p. 7; see also *SIPRI 1980 Yearbook*, p. 87.

84. Cited in the *Jerusalem Post*, 3 June 1983.

85. *New York Times*, 14 December 1983.

86. *Jerusalem Post*, 1 March 1983.

87. *Ha'aretz*, 31 January 1984.

88. *Jerusalem Post*, 16 January 1984.

89. *International Herald Tribune*, 7 June 1983, p. 1.

90. See Zdenek Cervenka, "The Conspiracy of Silence," *Africa*, no. 125 (January 1982), pp. 12–16; idem, "The West and the Apartheid Bomb," ibid., pp. 18–19; see also Robert Manning, "The Pretoria-Washington Axis," ibid., pp. 16–18.

91. Legum (ed.), *Africa Contemporary Record*, 1976–77, vol. 9, p. B853.

92. *Africa Confidential*, 4 August 1978.

93. Chazan, "The Fallacies of Pragmatism," p. 188.

94. *Jerusalem Post*, 17 February 1977.

95. *Christian Science Monitor*, 3 December 1981. See also Chazan, "The Fallacies of Pragmatism," p. 189.

96. For details, see Cervenka, "The West," p. 18.

97. For details, see Beit-Hallahmi, "Israel and South Africa," p. 34.

98. *Jerusalem Post*, 27 September 1983; Ha'aretz, 4 June 1985.

99. *Jerusalem Post*, 29 November 1983; *Ha'aretz*, 4 June 1985.

100. *Jerusalem Post*, 20 June 1984.

101. Ibid., 20, 27 May 1983.

102. Ibid., 27 May 1984.

103. Ibid., 20 June 1984.

104. Ibid., 12 November 1983.

105. See ibid., 13, 17, 19 November 1983, June 1984. For other revelations, see Adams, "Strangers and Brothers," pp. 33–34.

106. See *Jerusalem Post*, 29 November 1983.

107. See ibid., 8 April 1985.

SEVEN

Nigeria and Israel

Nigeria's ties with Israel predated her independence in 1960. In the late 1950s, many important contacts were established between Nigerian and Israeli officials through their joint participation in meetings of the labor and socialist movements. As a result of these contacts a number of Nigerians were encouraged by the Israelis to visit their country. This was at a time when Israel was reevaluating her policy toward the Third World in general.

The provisions of the 1954 Nigerian Federal Constitution made it possible for the constituent regions of the Federation to develop their own "foreign policies." Although the central government was granted specific powers relating to foreign policy, defense, and foreign trade, issues like higher education, tourism, and industrial development were left to the regions. Each of the three regions was allowed to establish autonomous commission offices in London and to develop contacts with foreign governments in pursuit of its own social and industrial development.

Regional delegations were often dispatched overseas to negotiate loans and other forms of assistance. On one such trip, a ministerial delegation headed by Chief Akindeko, minister of agriculture and natural resources from the western region, came to Israel in 1958 to observe cooperative movements. Besides negotiating cooperation agreements in the field of agriculture and cooperatives, the delegation negotiated the setting up of a number of joint ventures with Israeli concerns. As a result, two companies were jointly established in 1959 by the western regional government and Israeli firms.[1]   These were the Nigersol Construction Company and the Nigerian Water Resources Development Company. Similar visits were made by delegations from the eastern region with similar results.

By 1960 the southern regions (i.e., east and west) had established very friendly ties with Israel. Their leaders were fascinated with a number of Israeli institutions, such as the moshav and the kibbutz. They soon initiated ambitious agricultural settlements and training programs. Dozens of full-fledged moshavlike settlements were established, though on a private enterprise basis as opposed to the Israeli collective system. The Israelis also introduced poultry farming in 1960.[2]

The northern Nigerian political leadership, however, was not as friendly toward Israel. Their party, the Northern Peoples Congress (NPC), wanted close contacts with Muslim countries. In fact, Alhaji Ahmadu Bello, leader of the NPC and governor of the predominantly Muslim north, exhibited implacable hostility toward Israel. This is not surprising, as a number of the northern political elite often saw themselves and their region as part of the Muslim world and, to an extent, as having an affinity with the Arab world. Bello, in his autobiography, traced his own lineage to the Prophet Mohammed. Another key northern leader, Zanna Bukar Dipcharima, claimed Egyptian origins. The northern leadership was generally very exposed, and receptive, to Arab pressure. And there were allegations of covert Egyptian support for the NPC even before independence.[3]

Although the NPC became the senior partner in the immediate post-independence coalition government headed by Bello's deputy, Alhaji Tafawa Balewa, the federal government was left with little choice but to establish formal relations with Israel. First, Nigeria had a delicate federal structure composed of three regions, which were demarcated along tribal lines with the Hausa/Fulani predominating in the north, the Ibo in the east, and the Yoruba in the west. Moreover, political parties were by and large regional/tribal entities—the NPC in the north, the Action Group (AG) in the west, and the National Council for Nigeria and the Camerouns (NCNC) in the east.

Second, this structure was further complicated by the variegated religious map of the country, which to a large extent reflected the tribal/political divisions of the country (the north being predominantly Muslim and the southern regions predominantly Christian). Although the Yoruba west contained a significant Muslim population, these Muslims were different from their northern brothers socially and culturally. Most of them were not very puritanical in their religious observance; hence, their religious affinities with the Muslims did not become a political asset for the Arabs in their campaign against Israel in Nigeria. On the other hand, Nigerian Christians are often very sentimental about Israel, many tending to see the creation of the State of Israel as a fulfillment of biblical prophecy. The religious diversity, therefore, made it imperative for the government to keep religious issues out of politics in order to maintain the fragile unity of the country.

Third, the NCNC (the junior partner in the federal coalition), whose leaders had established links with Israel, favored a non-aligned policy for the country. And non-alignment was generally understood by the leaders as meaning one had no natural enemies. In the context of the Middle East, it was interpreted to mean absolute neutrality between the Arabs and Israelis in their conflict. The doctrine which came to be accepted as one of the guiding principles of Nigeria's foreign policy was underlined by the prime minister: Nigeria would "remain on friendly terms with every nation which recognizes and respects our sovereignty, and we shall not blindly follow the lead of anyone."[4]

Fourth, the government accorded top priority to the social and economic development of the country. It welcomed assistance from any country that was ready to contribute toward that objective. This was further underlined by the almost total dependence on external sources for financing the 1962–1968 National Development Plan. Although Nigeria's policy was said to be guided by the non-alignment approach of its leaders, the bulk of the country's political, economic, and cultural ties in the first years of independence were with the West, particularly Britain. Unnecessary antagonism toward the State of Israel would probably have lost Nigeria a good deal of Western goodwill.

And lastly, since the NPC did not have a majority in the House and had to enter a coalition with the NCNC, it had no choice but to accommodate some of the views of its junior partner. And the NCNC was categorical on the need to continue relations with Israel. Thus at independence, despite the pro-Arab orientation of the NPC, the overriding need for national unity and economic development dictated Nigeria's "open-door" diplomatic policy.

Following Nigeria's independence Israel established formal relations and opened a mission in Lagos. The fruitful cooperation that existed between her and the two southern regions was intensified. Their joint companies—the Nigersol Construction Company, the Nigerian Water Resources Development Company, the Eastern Nigeria Construction and Furniture Company, and the Eastern Nigeria Water Planning and Construction Company—continued to be heavily involved in construction and water development projects in both regions. Many government educational buildings and hotels were built, including faculty

buildings of the University of Ife, presidential hotels at Enugu and Port
Harcourt, and the Premier Hotel at Ibadan. A number of important
road construction projects were undertaken in both the east and the
west in the 1960s and early 1970s.[5] Some of these roads became show-
pieces for the country. Some road construction projects were also undertaken for the federal government, including the reconstruction and
resurfacing of 600 kilometers of main roads in the west, completed in
1962; the construction of 160 kilometers of main roads in the east, completed in 1964; and the Ijebu-Ode and Ife-Ondo roads, completed in 1971.
Virtually all the major water works projects in the west throughout the
1960s were carried out by the Nigerian Water Resources Development
Company.[6]

The success of these companies evoked some antagonism from certain anti-Israeli quarters. In January 1963 the *Nigerian Tribune* reported a
campaign, allegedly promoted by the competitors of the two companies
in the west, charging that they were receiving "preferential treatment"
and were being dominated by Israelis.[7] This was in spite of the fact that
the government of the western region had a 60 percent interest in each
of the companies. The two companies soon became deeply entangled in
the political crisis that gripped Western Nigeria from 1962. For almost a
year their operations were paralyzed. They were seen as political in-
struments of Chief Awolow's faction, which the central government was
keen on keeping in political limbo. The federal government appointed a
Lagos high court judge, Justice G.B.A. Coker, to head an investigation
into the financial affairs of the companies. The commission, however,
absolved the Israelis of any malpractices. It concluded:

> We are satisfied that . . . the Israeli partners have done their best
> to promote the business of the two companies . . . and indeed we
> have no strictures to make with respect to the activities of the
> two companies, except with respect to the ways in which the
> companies have been used by persons to whom we have referred
> [the Nigerian chairman of the board and some Nigerian officials]
> for the achievement of their selfish and maybe criminal
> purpose.[8]

Nigersol never recovered from the 1962 political crisis, and in 1971 it went
into voluntary liquidation.

Other Israeli companies also flourished in Nigeria. These included
Utigas, which supplied domestic gas; Coastal Shipping and Agencies;

Zim; and Dizengoff (Nigeria), a wholesale and retail company that imports Israeli goods such as pharmaceuticals, building materials, and electrical appliances.

Close cooperation was not, however, limited to the southern regional governments. As noted earlier, Israeli companies enjoyed the patronage of the federal government as well. Between 1960 and 1963 Israel loaned £5.2 million to the federal government, although the loans were used only by the latter and three southern regions (a third region—the mid-west—was carved out of the west in 1963).[9] In fact, when the first loan agreement for £3 million was signed shortly after independence in 1960, the northern Nigerian government denounced it and vowed not to accept any part of it. Israel also took part in the First Nigerian Trade Fair in Lagos in 1962 (which the Egyptians boycotted).[10]

Throughout the 1960s Nigeria enjoyed technical assistance from Israel in the form of training Nigerian personnel in Israel and the dispatch of Israeli experts to work in Nigeria. Israel was seen to be contributing to the economic development of the country. Conversely, the negative response of Arab states, as evidenced by their application of the Arab boycott to Nigerian enterprises [11] and their non-participation in the Trade Fair, merely portrayed them as only interested in injecting their Middle East regional feud into Nigeria and having no sympathy for Nigerian aspirations. In fact, the sum total of their demands on the country amounted to a negation of the main objectives set out in the National Development Plan. Thus, ties with Israel came to be accepted as a fruitful example of the diversification of Nigeria's external relations. However, the hostility of the northern political elite exerted a major constraint on the federal government's policy toward Israel. To maintain a balance, the government refused to have an embassy in Tel Aviv.

Relations were further enhanced by visits by officials of both governments. The most memorable of these was one made by Golda Meir to Nigeria in 1964. The Arabs, directly through their ambassadors and their wives and indirectly through the northern political elite, had opposed the visit. Their opposition was so heated that Mrs. Meir recalled that she almost canceled the visit while in Nairobi on her way to Lagos. But the visit went ahead nonetheless, and it turned out to be a very successful one for Mrs. Meir.[12] The Arab action evoked a very strong protest from the federal government; the southern papers—the *Daily Times*, the *Express*, the *Daily Sketch*, and the *Tribune*—condemned the Arab action as an abuse of Nigerian hospitality.[13]

At the United Nations Nigeria maintained strict neutrality and rarely contributed to the debates on the Middle East question at the General Assembly. On the few occasions in which she intervened, it was to urge moderation and accommodation.[14]

THE NIGERIAN CIVIL WAR

The military coup d'etat of January 1966, and the subsequent civil war that engulfed the country for about thirty months between 1967 and 1970, had a profound impact on Nigerian-Israeli relations. At first everything suggested closer ties. The most implacable anti-Israeli leader, the Sardauna, had been killed in the coup. The federal government, headed and dominated by the NPC, had been overthrown. In its place was a military junta headed by General Ironsi, who was said to have established friendly ties with many Israelis during his days as commander of the the Nigerian troops in the Congo (Zaire)[15] and was also an Ibo Christian. The coalition of the two southern parties, the AG and the NCNC, during the turbulent last two years of the civil administration—the United Progressive Grand Alliance (UPGA)—was quick to welcome the coup, and many of Ironsi's advisors were evidently favorably disposed toward UPGA. The AG and NCNC were, of course, traditionally friendly toward Israel.

However, before Ironsi could settle down even to tackle domestic affairs, not to mention foreign policy issues that were not pressing—like the question of having a mission in Israel—his regime was overthrown. He and many Ibo military officers and civilians were killed in the counter-coup that brought General Yakubu Gowon to power. Nonetheless, the Ironsi government had managed to take an important step which had a far-reaching impact on the conduct of foreign policy: it had abolished the "independence" of the regions in terms of foreign policy and had closed down their "mini-embassies," so that the different regions could no longer take such opposing stands. From then on only the federal government could authorize agents to foreign countries, take any foreign policy initiatives, or even speak on foreign policy.

The country rapidly moved to the brink of civil war after the July 1966 coup. All attempts to forestall the outbreak of war failed with the secession of the eastern region as Biafra in May 1967. However, on the eve of the declaration of Biafra's secession the country was split into twelve states (ostensibly to make for a more efficient administration, but in fact to render the declaration of secession difficult as the east was split into three states, with the non-Ibo minority tribes having their own states). The north was split into six states, thus ending the monolithic structure that had given no room for dissent.

Although Gowon is a northerner, he is a Christian, and he and his government did not show any hostility toward Israel simply because it was at loggerheads with its Arab neighbors. It was rather the Israeli attitude toward his government during the civil war that caused strains in relations. As early as December 1966 the *New Nigerian* alleged that the Israelis were giving military training and weapons to the Ibos.[16] Denial of the allegation by the Israeli mission in Lagos did not dispel the suspicion of Lagos authorities that Israel was sympathetic toward the Ibos and was possibly helping them. Such suspicions were only logical. After all, the conflict was portrayed at that stage as one between the Ibos (east) and the Hausa/Fulani (north). The Ibos had been good friends of the Israelis, with whom they had developed close technical and personal ties; in contrast, the northern leadership had been implacably hostile. A defeat of the Ibos could have meant the political neutralization of a reliable ally on the Nigerian political scene and the consequent ascendancy of Arab influence in Nigeria. That could have had a reverberating effect on Israeli influence in other African states, as many African states were (and still are) influenced by the Nigerian position on certain foreign policy issues. Also, it was not difficult for the Ibos to draw a parallel between their own situation and the persecution of the Jews in order to invoke Israeli sympathy.

Throughout the war the suspicion remained that Israel was not committed to the cause of the federal government. In 1969 General Gowon told the new Israeli ambassador in Lagos, Ben Yaacov, that he hoped he would make an "accurate interpretation" of the situation in Nigeria in order to improve understanding between the two countries.[17] The suspicion of Israeli support for secessionist Biafra was confirmed shortly after the war by Israeli Foreign Minister Abba Eban, who said that "Israel had exerted itself to such an extent in providing aid to the former secessionist regime that if another dozen or 20 countries had done so, the result of the war would have been different."[18]

The reaction of the press, including those who were traditionally sympathetic to Israel, was swift and angry. Many called for a break in diplomatic relations and the expulsion of Israelis from the country. However, the federal government merely summoned Ben Yaacov to the Foreign Ministry and handed him a protest to his government. The Nigerian government was committed to complete reconciliation with both its internal and external opponents. It had achieved its objective of keeping the country together. Feuding over external support for "deceased" Biafra, Gowon may have believed, would amount to a dissipation of energy and could possibly lead to loss of goodwill. Besides, the level of Israeli aid to Biafra was definitely not as significant as that of France or even some African states that formally recognized Biafra. To have singled out Israel for retaliation would have appeared selective, and this could have enhanced internal cleavages.

In contrast to the Israeli role, Arab states, particularly Algeria and Egypt, were solidly in support of the federal government. Their backing was not limited to diplomatic support within the OAU, where the federal government fought the most important diplomatic battle of the war, but also extended to material assistance. The Algerians were said to have acted as an indispensable channel to the Russians when Nigeria's traditional friends in the West refused to sell arms needed for the war. Egyptians flew some of the Soviet MiG jets, and Egypt also supplied arms and ammunition to the federal government.[19]

The diplomatic battle was particularly crucial, as some African states argued that the war could not be regarded as an internal affair—an argument the federal government used to prevent external recognition of Biafra. It was the endorsement of this position by the OAU that prevented the issue from being raised at the UN and in other international forums. It should be pointed out that the Arabs were not just defending a sacred principle of the inviolable sanctity of state sovereignty and territorial integrity enshrined in the OAU Charter. After all, many of them had abused, and continue to abuse, that principle with reckless abandon in Eritrea, in the Ethiopian-Somali conflict over the Ogaden, in Chad, and in Western Sahara. It was the political calculations in the context of the Arab-Israeli conflict that were the decisive motif of Arab action. Some others, like the Saudis, possibly saw a proselytization of the Ibo land with the eventual defeat of Biafra. Many of them no doubt fell victim to a tendency to oversimplify the civil war as a Muslim-Christian conflict.

The Arab support, nevertheless, resulted in greatly improved relations between Nigeria and the North African Arab states. Shortly after the war, in a "thank you" tour of those countries that had assisted Nigeria, Gowon visited Algeria, Egypt, and the Sudan. In Algeria Gowon and Colonel Boumedienne pledged in a communiqué to support all liberation struggles in Africa, the Middle East, and Southeast Asia.[20] The warmth in the Nigerian-Arab relations could also be felt in the vastly increased commercial ties between Egypt and Nigeria. In 1966 Nigeria exported goods worth only £29,545 to Egypt. This rose to £187,000 in 1968 and to £1,487,923 in 1970. Imports grew even faster, from £109,008 in 1966 to £971,348 in 1968 and to £15,971,500 in 1970.[21] And in 1971 Nigeria joined the Arab-dominated oil cartel—the Organization of Petroleum Exporting Countries (OPEC).

Nigeria continued to maintain relations with Israel, although the Israeli role in the civil war had strained these relations. Moreover, the war itself had led to the termination of joint ventures in the east. Nonetheless, the removal of the old political elite and the breakup of the north into many states provided Israel with an opportunity to extend its relations northward. By 1971 the Israeli ambassador had not only visited most of the northern states from which he had been banned in the 1960s, but certain of these states, such as Kwara, the North Central, Benue Plateau, and North Eastern States, were enjoying one form of Israeli technical assistance or another.[22]

At the UN Nigeria continued to stress her neutrality in the Arab-Israeli conflict. She indeed believed that her friendly ties with both sides could enhance her mediatory role in the conflict, and from 1967 she became more active in the efforts to find a solution to the Middle East problem. Nigeria even submitted a peace proposal in 1967,[23] although nothing came of it. And the leader of the Nigerian delegation, Chief Anthony Enahoro, hinted that he would visit Cairo and Tel Aviv to encourage the peace process.[24] Significantly, Nigeria did not support any of the one-sided draft resolutions at the emergency session of the UN General Assembly in 1967, and her delegate explained that Nigeria's support for the non-aligned draft was due to the country's backing of some of the principles enuciated in it.[25] With respect to its voting behavior at the UN on the Middle East conflict between 1967 and 1972, Nigeria recorded twenty-five votes against, two in favor of, and twelve abstentions on one-sided draft resolutions at the General Assembly. The two votes cast for the so-called "one-sided" draft refer to votes on clauses in the non-aligned draft. However, because of the very staunch support Israel had on the continent during the period, Nigeria was ranked as one of the ten African states most sympathetic towards Egypt.[26]

The greater commitment of Nigeria to African affairs after the civil war resulted in a shift in the country's Middle East policy in favor of Egypt. The continued Israeli occupation of Egyptian land was totally unacceptable to the Nigerian government. After all, the country itself had just ended a grueling thirty-month war over sovereign territorial issues. In addition, there were genuine fears that South Africa might occupy part of the territories of the Front-Line States—an area that had moved to the forefront of Nigeria's diplomacy since the end of the war. From 1970 Nigeria became more critical of Israel over this issue. However, within the OAU Nigeria spearheaded a collective African mediatory role in the conflict, and Gowon was a member of the OAU mission that visited Israel in November 1971.

Israeli-Nigerian relations also suffered as a result of the leadership role in Africa which Nigerian leaders assumed, particularly after 1972 when the need for a unified African position on a range of Third World economic issues had never been more pressing. Nigeria's statements on the Arab-Israeli conflict became increasingly pro-Arab. This was the case at the 1972 and 1973 OAU summits and at the September 1973 non-aligned conference in Algiers. In May 1973 Gowon described the continued Israeli occupation of Egyptian land as an "intolerable provocation" and urged other African states to support Egypt within the OAU and in other international forums.[27] He ruled out, however, the severance of ties with Israel and was very critical of Arab pressures, particularly Gaddafi's attempts to force African states to take such action. Nonetheless, on arrival from Algiers in September 1973, he warned that Nigeria would review relations with Israel if the latter continued to be "arrogant" in the face of world opinion: "When I go to the General Assembly of the UN in October, I will make our sincere pleas to Israel hoping there will be a change of heart. . . . Otherwise it will be clear that they don't want our friendship."[28]

THE OCTOBER 1973 WAR

The outbreak of another round of hostilities in the Middle East in October 1973 further complicated Nigerian-Israeli relations. Gowon laid the blame for the outbreak of the war squarely on Israel, claiming the war could have been averted if Israel had withdrawn from Arab territories in accordance with the 1967 UN resolution.[29] He called in the Israeli ambassador on 12 October to express Nigeria's anxiety over the fact that Israel had in fact crossed the 1967 cease-fire line on the Syrian front and that Israeli air action was resulting in civilian casualties.[30] He warned that further deterioration in the situation would jeopardize the friendly relations between the two countries.

However, he still opposed the severance of ties. At the UN he urged African states, during a closed-door meeting with the African Group, to give diplomatic support to Egypt for any moves in the world body that would restore to Egypt her territories.[31] But pressure continued both from within the country and from the Arabs. The *New Nigerian* insisted that a break with Israel was the only action consistent with Nigeria's national experience and leadership in the OAU. Gowon was persistently reminded of the contrasting roles of Egypt and Israel during the civil war.[32] At the annual reading from the Koran in Kaduna, the grand qadi of the northern states, Alhaji Abubakar Gumi, assured the Arabs that the Nigerians were behind them in their struggles with Israel. There was also alleged strong pressure from senior army officers from the north.[33]

Gowon was hoping that a cease-fire would help to ease these pressures. He met with the Israeli ambassador, as well as with the U.S. and Soviet ambassadors to press their governments into taking firm action to stop the war. The 22 October cease-fire agreement reached at the UN seemed to have encouraged Gowon not to bow to pressure. But when there were confirmed reports that the Israeli army had violated the cease-fire and consolidated its presence on the west bank of the Suez Canal, Gowon angrily accused Israel of breaking faith with Nigeria. In cutting off diplomatic relations with Israel on 25 October 1973, the Nigerian government explained that "Israel by its violation of the UN ceasefire and occupation of more Egyptian territory had shown itself unworthy of diplomatic relations."[34]

There were, of course, other considerations. Gowon was chairman of the OAU at the time. The OAU was an important regional instrument which Nigeria hoped to use in the realization of many of her foreign policy objectives in Africa. And since the end of the civil war she had consciously begun to strengthen the prestige of the organization. There was a clear possiblity that all of this would collapse if she became isolated over the Arab-Israeli conflict. Before Nigeria broke ties with Israel, all but ten other African states that eventually severed ties with her had already done so. And with Ethiopia—which had both strategic and close historical/cultural ties with Israel—breaking off relations on 23 October, Gowon's position became untenable.

The decision to break relations, although welcomed by "radical" groups and some newspapers, provoked criticism in some quarters. The *Nigerian Tribune* argued that it would have been better to have retained relations. It regretted that Nigeria was not playing an active role in the search for peace in the Middle East, a situation it attributed to the "folly" of breaking ties with Israel: "Nigeria, like all other countries who broke relations with Israel, is only watching from the distance. We have not even been consulted by the friends we back." It added that nobody had had the courtesy to ask Gowon, as chairman of the OAU, for an opinion.

"And no wonder," it continued, "the Middle East is an Arab problem. It is not an African affair. It is not the business of the OAU." It went further to regret that Nigeria and other African countries had "played their last card" by breaking off ties and thereby deprived themselves of the opportunity to influence the course of events in the Middle East.[35]

The break in relations in 1973 certainly marked the lowest ebb in Nigerian-Israeli relations. Unlike in some other African countries, Israel did not even retain an "interest officer" in Lagos. Thereafter, Nigeria often joined with most other African countries in passing condemnatory resolutions against Israel at international forums, including the 10 November 1975 Zionism-racism resolution. At the UN Nigeria did not, however, exhibit any implacable hostility toward the State of Israel, although it did criticize some of her policies. For example, at the height of the Afro-Arab "romance," Nigeria told the General Assembly that the reality of Israel's existence as a state should be acknowledged and that a realistic settlement in the area should guarantee Israel's security within agreed-upon borders.[36] Nigeria, together with most other African states, also frustrated Arab attempts at the 1975 Kampala OAU meetings to get the organization to recommend the expulsion of Israel from the UN.

Even the change of guard as a result of the 1975 coup and the attempted coup of February 1976 that brought Generals Mohammed and Obasanjo, respectively, to power, did not result in a negative change of policy toward Israel. The greater commitment of the new leadership to a political change in Southern Africa even resulted, in a way, in a lessening of the diplomatic attack on Israel. The seemingly intractable Rhodesian and Namibian situations, the Angolan civil war, the South African intervention in that war on the side of the UNITA/FLNA alliance against the MPLA government in Luanda, and the worsening of the apartheid situation in South Africa (marked by the Soweto riots and the killing of Steve Biko) made both the Mohammed and Obasanjo regimes more committed to ending colonization and racism in Africa. But they both realized that excessive and often one-sided attacks against Israel at international forums discouraged the support of Western powers in their anti-apartheid campaign. Nigeria also refused repeated Arab requests to allow the PLO to open an office in Lagos.

At least two of the three topmost men of the Obasanjo administration—Generals Obasanjo and Danjuma—were not known to be anti-Israeli per se. As military officers, it must have been difficult for them not to have had some private admiration for the Israeli military record in the Middle East. And as Christians, they probably lacked the antipathy toward Israel of some Muslim leaders.

However, the spectacular growth of Israeli-South African relations, as evidenced by reported military, economic, and political ties which culminated in the much-publicized visit of the South African premier to Israel in April 1976,[37] discouraged a review of Nigerian-Israeli relations. As noted earlier, Nigerian leaders were committed pan-Africanists, and General Obasanjo is known to have have followed the South African situation with more than keen interest even before he became second-in-command to General Mohammed. Israeli-South African ties could therefore not have been taken lightly in Lagos. The Nigerian press was also very critical of the ties. The *Daily Express*, in an editorial in June 1978, drew a sharp parallel between Israel and South Africa: if Nigeria reopened ties with Israel, it asked, "will it deny it to their bedfellow, the Dutch in South Africa?"[38] The Arab states and the PLO wasted no time in taking advantage of the Israeli-South African ties.

However, the general disenchantment with the direction of Afro-Arab relations in Africa as a whole, which had become apparent by 1975, led to some pressures on the government for a review of relations with Israel. This disenchantment even sparked off a public debate on Nigerian-Israeli relations. Chief Akindeko, a veteran politician, argued that it was time Nigeria reconsidered her relations with Israel. He added that Nigeria "should be able to play a preponderant role in reconciling contradictions in the Middle East rather than succumb to pressure group politics and petro-dollar diplomacy."[39] In May, a former commissioner of health under Gowon made a similar plea.[40] On the other hand, the *New Nigerian* opposed any change in policy because of Israel's role in the civil war and the need to support Egypt. It added: "The Israelis themselves have by the recent general elections demonstrated their preference for continued occupation by voting into power the extremist Likud party." The controversy was endless.[41]

Nonetheless, non-formal relations between the two countries continued unimpeded, and in some cases underwent significant improvement. Israeli construction and engineering companies, like Tahal and Solel Boneh, continued to enjoy active federal and state government patronage. The list of housing, hospital, hotel, educational, and industrial facilities, public buildings, and public works projects completed by Solel Boneh between 1975 and 1982 is very impressive.[42] Other Israeli companies also remained active.

Nigerians continued to be sent to Israeli institutions such as the

Afro-Asian Institute of the Histadrut in Tel Aviv, the Mount Carmel Center in Haifa, and the Settlement Studies Center in Rehovot. The Jerusalem-based Inter-Faith Committee and the Tantur Institute of Advanced Ecumenical Studies near Bethlehem continued to host Nigerian clerics.[43] Informal pilgrimages to the Holy Land continued, and from 1980 they became subsidized by the federal government.[44] Academic exchanges also continued.

Trade between the two countries has increased phenomenally over the years (see Table 7.1). In fact, Nigeria by itself accounts for about 50 percent of Israel's trade with black Africa.

THE EGYPTIAN-ISRAELI CAMP DAVID ACCORDS

The late President Sadat's peace moves with Israel sparked off another round of debate over Nigeria's continued diplomatic boycott of Israel. As early as January 1978 some commentators started arguing that the policy of diplomatic isolation was no longer justified in view of Sadat's peace moves.[45] This was also the basic position of people like Mr. Tanko Yusuf, former Nigerian ambassador to China, Korea, and Vietnam, and Justice Adewale Thompson.

However, apart from the Israeli-South African links which continued to remain a complicating factor in Nigerian-Israeli relations, the government was cautious, since the eventual shape of the Egyptian-Israeli negotiations was not yet predictable. Also, toward the end of the military regime the economy had started to be troubled by the uncertain course of the world oil market. The Obasanjo regime introduced stringent economic measures which were to become a precursor of what Nigerians euphemistically dub "austerity measures." Because of the critical role of oil in the country's economy, Nigeria became more active in OPEC, which was still in relatively good shape in the late 1970s.

Chief of Staff General Yar'Adua (the second-in-command) dashed any hope of a change in government policy in a declaration he made in Saudi Arabia: "In this conflict, our friends are the Arabs. We have always and shall always support the Arabs."[46] Lack of general Arab support for the Egyptian-Israeli peace treaty, and the corresponding domestic polarization at a time when the military was ready to hand over power to civilians, no doubt reinforced the government's attitude to leave things as they were.

TABLE 7.1

NIGERIA'S TRADE WITH ISRAEL,
1973–1984
(in $U.S. thousands)

Year	Imports	Exports
1973	5,631	10
1974	7,326	59
1975	13,350	35
1976	13,730	—
1977	18,613	3
1978	20,492	—
1979	19,453	58
1980	44,193	31
1981	61,777	91
1982	43,199	33
1983	32,300	1,000
1984*	21,200	200

Source: Central Bureau of Statistics, *Statistical Abstracts of Israel,* 1973–1982; *Foreign Trade Statistics Quarterly,* no. 3, 1984.
*Figures for January to September.

The accession of a democratically elected government in October 1979 led to a revival of pressure for a change of policy toward Israel. Once again Nigeria was gripped with "coalition politics." President Shagari's ruling National Party of Nigeria (NPN) worked out an accord with the Nigerian Peoples Party (NPP). The leadership of the NPP and of the Unity Party of Nigeria (UPN), the second largest party, were in favor of reestablishing ties with Israel.

The arrest and detention by Israel in May 1979 of a Nigerian officer serving in the UN Force in Lebanon (UNIFIL), Lt. Colonel Alfred Gom, on charges of gunrunning for the PLO ensured that the attention of the new government would be focused on relations with Israel.[47] All attempts by the military government to secure his release before it handed over power were futile.

On 25 November 1979 the Senate passed a motion calling on the government to secure his immediate release. Senator Ali, who sponsored the motion, claimed that Gom's detention was a calculated attempt by Israel to blackmail Nigeria into restoring diplomatic ties with her. And when Gom was tried, convicted, but deported rather than serving his jail term, army legislators pressured the government to reestablish ties with Israel.

The controversy over government policy toward Israel was becoming so heated that Shagari had to restate his policy at a press briefing in Lagos in late December 1979. He stressed that the country was not yet ready to establish ties with Israel. He argued: "Egypt has not consulted African and Arab countries on its decision to resume diplomatic relations with Israel. We, as members of the OAU, feel that we must be consulted, but this has not been so." He went on to appeal to the popular anti-apartheid sentiments of Nigerians. "Apart from that, Israel engages in business with our enemy—South Africa, thus complicating the whole issue." He warned that the government's review of the situation would have to be dependent on Israel's preparedness to review its own stand on South Africa. He concluded: "first and foremost we must think of what is best for Africa before embarking on anything."[48]

That did not, however, calm the political storm that was developing around the issue. The debates began to resemble the dangerous political polarization of the early 1960s. At the end of January 1980 Foreign Minister Ishaya Audu hinted that Nigeria might reopen ties with Israel, saying that "by and large it is desirable for Nigeria to do so." He also admitted that the Camp David agreements were enough reason to consider a review. "By the Camp David Accord and in resuming diplomatic exchanges with Israel," the minister said, "Egypt had relieved OAU member states of their commitment to her." He also believed that Nigerians were at a disadvantageous position in not having diplomatic representation in Israel. He argued that many Israeli citizens who lived and worked in Nigeria, as well as Israeli firms operating in the country, could well provide the services of a diplomatic mission for their country, while Nigeria lacked such a facility. He warned, however, that Israel was "too friendly with South Africa for Nigeria's comfort."[49]

In 1981 a group of 106 federal legislators tabled a motion in the House of Representatives calling on the government to reestablish diplomatic relations with Israel immediately. They cited the following considerations:

1. Egypt and Israel, the "principal belligerents" in the conflict, had established relations at ambassadorial level.

2. Nigeria had severed ties with Israel in sympathy with Egypt.
3. Further isolation of Israel now that it had withdrawn from African lands would be tantamount to partisanship in the conflict and a negation of Nigeria's policy of non-alignment.
4. The breaking of diplomatic relations was a "negative policy" which would not bring any solution.
5. Israel could contribute to Nigeria's agricultural, industrial, and social development.
6. With normal relations restored, Israel would remove "the present political impediments in the way of religious pilgrimages to the Holy Land."
7. Such a move would help further Nigeria's policy objectives in Southern Africa.
8. Nigeria had not severed diplomatic relations with Western countries which had more extensive links with South Africa.
9. The Palestinian question could only be settled by negotiations, which Israel had often advocated. "Israel is in a position of strength as a victor in a war it did not start. It is the Arab states that would opt for a peace settlement without preconditions."[50]

The motion generated very heated debate throughout the country and was later withdrawn before it could be formally debated in the House. Although no reason was given for the withdrawal, it was believed that such a debate could have caused serious damage to the fragile health of Nigeria's body politic. It is also possible that some understanding was reached between the government and the authors of the motion to the effect that the government's position was not immutable and that it would keep the issue under constant review. It was therefore not surprising that despite the Arab lobby and pressure from certain domestic quarters, the government did not hesitate to invite Israel to participate in the Inter-Parliamentary Union's conference in Lagos in April.

Nigeria's continuing economic difficulties also provided an additional reason for a change of policy. There was a widespread belief in the country that the oil glut, which was the major source of the country's economic pains, was caused by Saudi Arabia. The Saudi oil minister, Sheikh Yamani, was reported to have boasted in Vienna in 1981 that he occasioned the world oil glut.[51] Also, the Gulf Arab states often opposed Nigeria's position within OPEC.[52] All this led to calls on the government to withdraw Nigeria from OPEC. Such calls were sometimes linked with the whole issue of Nigeria's Middle East policy. The director of organization of the UPN, Chief Ebenezer Babatone, said: "If we were to be out of OPEC, certainly we would not be caught in the irreconcilable politics of the Arab members. We would also be able to negotiate for the price of our oil with any country in the world."[53]

However, the Israeli government's formal annexation of the Golan and Jerusalem and the bombing of the Iraqi nuclear reactor—events which the Arabs used to advantage in Nigeria—made it difficult for the government to reverse its policy. The invasion of Lebanon in June 1982 and the much-publicized massacres of Palestinian refugees at the Sabra and Shatila camps by pro-Israeli Lebanese militiamen provided strong reasons for putting the issue in the cooler.

These events also coincided with two unrelated domestic factors which worked against Israel. First, the alliance between the NPN and the NPP had gone asunder. A serious coalition of southern-dominated parties—the UPN, NPP, Peoples Redemption Party (PRP), and the Great Nigeria Peoples Party (GNPP)—was being built. Shagari, with an eye on the 1983 elections, was becoming more and more vulnerable to losing an important section of his northern homebase. It seems he decided to appeal to the Muslim sentiments of his northern compatriots in an attempt to foil the coalition. He even later warned the northern Muslims at Ilorin and Sokoto during the 1983 electoral campaign that if they voted for Chief Awolowo, his main rival, the Arabs would not allow them to make a pilgrimage to Mecca.[54]

And second, the economy was not showing any signs of improvement despite all the stringent measures applied by the government. In fact, the balance of payments situation was becoming critical. The country was lifting only about 840,000 barrels per day of crude oil out of OPEC's allocation of 1.3 million. A daily production of 1.8 million barrels was considered the minimum necessary to see the country out of the economic woods.[55] In early May 1982 Saudi Arabia and Kuwait showed keen interest in bailing the country out with a $1 billion aid package as an alternative to obtaining similar loans from the IMF, whose conditions were considered too harsh. In addition, Saudi Arabia threatened sanctions against oil companies that were boycotting Nigerian oil because of its uncompetitive (in obedience to OPEC's pricing rules) price.[56] Although it was later revealed that Saudi Arabia, acting under foreign pressure, blocked the $1 billion loan,[57] at the time the government believed the Arabs would help; it could therefore not afford to antagonize them by resuming ties with Israel.

There was an angry reaction in Nigeria to the events in Lebanon. The *Sunday Triumph* called on the government to break all forms of relations with Israel. At the UN the Nigerian permanent representative, Alhaj Yusuf Maitama Sule, said that "Israel must be made to pay dearly for its reckless and wanton aggression against Lebanon."[58] The government seized the opportunity to accede to the long-standing Arab request to allow the PLO to open an office in Lagos.

Economic and other non-formal ties with Israel have nonetheless continued uninterrupted. Israeli companies continue to enjoy both federal and state government patronage despite attempts by the *New Nigerian* and other pro-Arab lobbies to end such patronage.[59] The current reduction of the activities of Israeli companies reflects the general downward economic trend. Even so, they have done much better than many other companies, both local and foreign. In April 1984 it was reported that the Nigerian government owed Solel Boneh and Koortrade over $145 million. And during the runoff to the 1983 Nigerian elections, Israel supplied Nigeria with paramilitary equipment worth over $6 million, with an export credit of £4 million.[60]

The controversial reelection of Shagari in the 1983 general elections meant there were not going to be any immediate changes in the country's Middle East policy. Attempts were even made to create some anti-Israeli feelings in the country by alleging an Israeli invasion plot to which the UPN leader was linked. The allegation predictably brought a sharp reaction from the UPN. Its director of research and publicity, Chief M.C.K. Ajulu-Schuku retorted: "The people now shouting about a purported Israeli plot to invade Nigeria may be seeking to use the unseemingly event as an excuse for inviting Arab military presence into Nigeria. They may be doing this with the aim of converting our fatherland into an extended theatre of the Arab-Israeli conflict."[61]

However, the intervention of the military at the end of December 1983 froze the issue of relations with Israel, at least for a while, as the attention of both government and public opinion was directed to the dismal economic situation of the country. Moreover, the preponderance of northern and Muslim officers in the new military government did not suggest a possible change of policy. This became evident with the appointment of Ibrahim Gambari, known to be very critical of Israel and to be opposed to Nigeria's reestablishing ties with her, as foreign minister. In an article published in the *Daily Times* in June 1982, for instance, Gambari had argued that Nigeria's national interest and national security would be greatly "endangered if we were to consider reestablishing diplomatic relations with Israel."[62] The government's heated reaction to a visit by two of Nigeria's most important traditional rulers to Israel in August 1984, shortly after the Dikko affair,[63] is a reflection of the hard-line policy of the Buhari administration toward the Middle East.

The pattern of relations since the fall of the Shagari administration has remained largely unaltered. As in earlier times, there seems to be no national consensus on what the state of relations should be. Official political relations remain poor, with Nigeria taking pro-Arab stances on events in the Middle East. This was the case when it condemned Israel's raid on the PLO offices in Tunis in October 1985 without condemning the PLO's killing of Israeli civilians in Egypt and Cyprus that had provoked the attack.[64] But economic and other forms of nonformal relations continue to be unaffected by the poor state of political relations.

Nigerian-Israeli relations will no doubt remain controversial for as long as the Arab-Israeli conflict defies solution. However, the internalization of the conflict in Nigerian domestic politics will make the future course of relations between the two countries more dependent on Nigerian domestic political considerations than on what happens in the Middle East. The critical determining factor will no doubt be the personal inclinations of the head of state and his close foreign policy advisors, and their degree of determination to restore relations or not. However, the increasing importance of religious issues in Nigerian politics may cause the government to want to restore diplomatic relations with Israel, this in order to appear impartial between the Christians and the Muslims in the wake of Nigeria's short-lived but controversial membership in the Organization of Islamic States.[65]

NOTES

1. Ade Adefuye, "Nigeria and Israel," *International Studies*, vol. 15, no. 4 (October/December 1979), p. 631.

2. See Moshe Decter, *To Serve, To Teach, To Leave: The Story of Israel's Development Assistance Program in Black Africa* (New York: American Jewish Congress, 1977), p. 89.

3. Sir Ahmadu Bello, *My Life* (London: Cambridge University Press, 1962), p. 239.

4. Sir Abubakar Tafawa Balewa, *Nigeria Speaks* (Ikeja: Longmans, 1964), pp. 56–57.

5. See *Solel Boneh International* (Haifa: Haifa Press Ltd., n.d.).

6. Ibid.

7. *Nigerian Tribune*, 28 January 1963.

8. Leopold Laufer, *Israel and the Developing Countries: New Approaches to Cooperation* (New York: Twentieth Century Fund, 1967), pp. 144–145.

9. Adefuye, "Nigeria and Israel," p. 635; see also Olajide Aluko, "Israel and Nigeria: Continuity and Change in Their Relationship," *African Review*, vol. 4, no. 1 (1974), p. 47.

10. Ibid.

11. See A.B. Akinyemi, *Foreign Policy and Federalism: The Nigerian Experience* (Ibadan: University of Ibadan Press, 1974), p. 103.

12. See ibid.; Golda Meir, *My Life* (New York: Putnam, 1975), p. 337.

13. See Akinyemi, *Foreign Policy and Federalism*; see also Humphrey Assisi Asobie, "Domestic Political Structure and Foreign Policy: The Nigerian Experience 1960–1974" (unpublished Ph.D. thesis, University of London, 1977), pp. 282–379.

14. Ibid.

15. Adefuye, "Nigeria and Israel," p. 639.

16. *New Nigerian*, 20 December 1966.

17. Aluko, "Israel and Nigeria," p. 55.

18. Quoted in ibid.; see also *Sunday Sketch*, 25 January 1970.

19. Asobie, "Domestic Political Structure."

20. Adefuye, "Nigeria and Israel," p. 642.

21. *Nigeria Trade Summary*, 1966–70.

22. Aluko, "Israel and Nigeria," p. 55.

23. *Daily Nation* (Nairobi), 5 July 1967.

24. *New Nigerian*, 22 June 1967.

25. 1548th plenary meeting, 4 July 1967.

26. Ran Kochan, Susan A. Gitelson, and Ephraim Dubek, "Black African Voting Behaviour in the UN on the Middle East Conflict: 1967–72," in Michael Curtis and Susan A. Gitelson (eds.), *Israel and the Third World* (New Brunswick, N.J.: Transaction Books, 1976), pp. 289–317.

27. *Africa Research Bulletin* (hereafter *ARB*), May 1973, p. 2948.

28. Colin Legum (ed.), *Africa Contemporary Record 1973–74*, vol. 6 (London: Rex Collings, 1973), p. B742.

29. *West Africa*, 22 October 1973, p. 1508.

30. *Daily Express*, 14 October 1973.

31. *West Africa*, 15 October 1973, p. 1443.

32. Ibid., 29 October 1973, p. 1545.

33. Asobie, "Domestic Political Structure."

34. For details of government statements, see World Jewish Congress, *Africa and Asia Media Survey: African and Asian Attitudes on the Middle East Conflict,* January 1974, pp. 23–24.

35. *West Africa,* 26 November 1973, p. 1681–1682.

36. *West Africa,* 25 November 1974, p. 1446.

37. For details see Kunirun Osia, *Israel, South Africa and Black Africa: A Study of the Primacy of the Politics of Expediency* (Washington: UPA, 1981); see also Olusola Ojo, "Israeli-South African Connections and Afro-Israeli Relations," *International Studies,* vol. 21, no. 1 (1982), pp. 37–51.

38. *Daily Express,* 29 June 1978.

39. *Sunday Times,* 24 April 1977.

40. *Daily Times,* 10 May 1977.

41. *New Nigerian,* 1 June 1977; see also ibid., 13 June 1977; the *Nigerian Standard,* 29 June 1977; *Punch,* 28 December 1977.

42. See, for example, *Solel Boneh International;* see also Tahal Consulting Engineers Ltd., (a) *Qualifications in Water Supply;* (b) *Qualifications in Water Resource Development;* (c) *Qualifications in Agricultural Development, Irrigation Drainage* (Tel Aviv, n.d.).

43. Interviews and discussions in Israel, October 1984–February 1985.

44. Naomi Chazan, "Israel and Africa in the 1980s: The Dilemmas of Complexity and Ambiguity," paper presented at the International Conference on Africa and the Great Powers, University of Ife, June 1983, p. 7.

45. See, for example, *The Standard,* 17 January 1978; *Daily Times,* 14 October 1978; *Sunday Tribune,* 3 June 1979.

46. *Daily Times,* 12 October 1978.

47. On the "Gom affair," see *Daily Times,* 28 June 1979; *Sunday Punch,* 25 November 1979; *Sunday Times,* 20 January 1980.

48. *Punch,* 10 January 1980.

49. *Sunday Times,* 27 January 1980.

50. For details see "Israel," *Nigerian Forum,* July/August/September 1982, pp. 740–745.

51. Ibid., p. 698.

52. See, for example, *National Concord,* 4 February 1983.

53. *Punch,* 29 September 1981.

54. *National Concord,* 20 October 1983.

55. See *Financial Times* (London), 1 May 1982.

56. *Daily Sketch,* 4 May 1982.

57. *Nigerian Tribune,* 14 October 1982.

58. See *Sunday Triumph,* 29 August 1982: see also *National Concord,* 21 August 1982.

59. See, for instance, *Sunday New Nigerian,* 2 January 1983, p. 16.

60. On trade and debts see *Jerusalem Post*, 5, 29 June 1984.

61. *Daily Sketch*, 17 October 1983.

62. *Daily Times*, 30 June 1982.

63. Alhaj Umaru Dikko, a wanted Nigerian fugitive in London, was kidnapped and crated with the help of three Israeli citizens, and about to be flown to Lagos when he was rescued by the British police. Britain alleged Nigerian government involvement, which the latter denied, and relations between the two countries were severely strained. For details see *The Times* (London), 7, 13, 14 July 1984; on the Obas visit, see *Jerusalem Post*, 21 August 1984; *West Africa*, 27 August 1984, p. 1713.

64. *Guardian* (Lagos), 16 October 1985.

65. Nigeria was reportedly admitted as the forty-sixth member of the Organization of Islamic States in January 1986. Since then bitter controversies over the issue have been raging in the country. Following appeals to the government by religious organizations to examine the implications of the country's full membership in the organization, President Babangida had to set up a committee. See *West Africa*, 3 February 1986, pp. 230–231.

EIGHT

Conclusions

Africa's relations with Israel have undergone important changes since Israel's bold initiative to gain a foothold in Africa in the late 1950s. More than anything else, pragmatism has been a recurring theme of the relationship. Israel's initial motivation was its desire to break out of the isolation in the Third World that Arab diplomacy had created for it. Black Africa's positive response came from the African leaders' belief that they had much to learn from Israel's ability to "rapidly disengage itself from the shackles of the past, to construct a working proto-socialist economy, to combine economic pragmatism with a high level of services and to innovate agriculturally, socially and institutionally."[1] Israel soon developed a wide network of diplomatic and other ties with black African states. And her technical assistance programs, which brought hundreds of experts to Africa and took thousands of African trainees to Israel, became a dominant feature of Afro-Israeli relations.

However, the edifice of diplomatic relations which had developed in the 1960s collapsed in the wake of the October 1973 Arab-Israeli war, when national, continental, and international considerations led to Africa's severance of diplomatic ties with Israel. The bitterness felt in Israel, and the ensuing honeymoon between Africa and the Arabs, brought immediate postwar Afro-Israeli relations to a nadir of mutual political neglect. Although there were occasional contacts between Israeli and black African leaders, these remained isolated and sporadic and no appreciable change was discernible. This situation lasted until the signing of the Egyptian-Israeli peace treaty.

Meanwhile, Israel, out of pragmatic considerations and being no longer constrained by the necessities of Africa's friendship, intensified its links with South Africa. And unlike before, the ties became very demonstrative. It is even suggested that "Israel pursued its relationship

with South Africa with an element of vindictiveness."[2] Since 1974, when
Israel upgraded its diplomatic representation in Pretoria to ambassadorial level, Israel's links with South Africa have proliferated on virtually
every front. And by 1976, when the South African prime minister visited Israel, talk of an "Israeli-South African alliance" had become commonplace. However, the growing rapprochement between Israel and
black Africa following the Camp David accords and the Egyptian-Israeli
peace treaty, as well as the replacement of the Likud government by a
coalition of Labor and Likud after the 1984 Israeli elections, have led to
a significant change in Israel's relations with South Africa.

POLICY OPTIONS AND PROSPECTS

The more than two and a half decades of Africa's relations with Israel
have conclusively shown that Afro-Israeli links can hardly be divorced
from the resolution of the Middle East impasse. A resolution of the
conflict will no doubt accelerate the process of rapprochement with
Israel. In the interim, however, the need for a reassessment of Africa's
Middle East policy is long overdue. The choice before Africa is either to
maintain the status quo or to change it. A number of important factors,
however, need to be considered.

First, it is hardly contestable that Africa's break with Israel has not,
on the whole, worked in Africa's favor. The black African states' em-
ployment of the concept of the severance of diplomatic relations was
very unconventional, and it has not spoken well for their integrity. The
business of severing ties with other countries is a serious one in
diplomacy; indeed, it is an act short of war. If states were to resort to its
use against other members of the international system with whom they
have policy differences, there would be a total collapse of international
order, as very few states would be able to maintain ties. Despite the very
serious direct bilateral disputes between the United States and the Soviet
Union, even in the heyday of the Cold War, they did not sever diplomatic
ties. The importance of diplomatic communication as a means of fore-
stalling or resolving conflicts can hardly be overemphasized. That there
was not any African threat to take similar action against the Soviet Union when it invaded Afghanistan or against the U.S. for its invasion of
Grenada, or against Vietnam for its policy in Indochina, or against
Morocco and Libya for annexing Western Sahara and the northern part

of Chad, respectively, is suggestive of a mature appreciation of the severity of breaking diplomatic relations.

The breaking of ties with Israel over a dispute that poses no direct threat to the African states' core or secondary interests was, to say the least, indiscriminate. The history of diplomatic practice is replete with other, more effective, means by which the African states could have expressed their disapproval of Israel's policies. By breaking with Israel, Africa, among other things, inadvertently excluded itself from the diplomatic pressures and processes which could eventually help the Arabs to achieve their twin objectives of territorial reacquisition and Palestinian self-determination.

Second, the move seriously weakened Africa's diplomatic bargaining position with the Arabs. In the pre-1973 period potential African political support against Israel was valued, sought, and amply rewarded when given, by Arab states. However, having severed relations with Israel, there were no further practical initiatives which Africans could offer the Arab world. Although the African vote at the UN could ensure the passage of strident anti-Israeli resolutions, like the controversial November 1975 Zionism-racism resolution, the Arabs soon discovered that the political leverage to effect a settlement of the Arab-Israeli conflict lay not with the Africans, but with the United States and the other big powers. Arab states, despite the rhetoric of Afro-Arab cooperation, consequently felt a diminished obligation to reciprocate Africa's diplomatic support. A resumption of Africa's ties with Israel, even without the resolution of the Middle East conflict, would therefore strengthen international approval of Egypt's peace measures, reestablish Africa's independence in international affairs from the Arab League, and give it a measure of influence in moderating the Arab-Israeli conflict.

Third, there is a dire need for Africa's Middle East policy to be more in tune with the realities of the Middle Eastern system than at present. This is essential if Africa intends to make a positive contribution to the peace process in the region. The advocacy, for instance, of the concept of an immediate and comprehensive settlement via a Geneva-type UN-sponsored conference of all the parties to the conflict, with the participation of the superpowers, appears a sure recipe for an indefinite postponement of a settlement of the conflict. The application of this concept entails a frontal and simultaneous tackling of the entire complexity of the conflict, and of the political-ideological forces at work in the Arab-Israeli as well as inter-Arab spheres. It is important to note that, as on other issues, there is no inter-Arab common denominator on the Palestinian issue.

The idea is itself a negation of the very foundation of negotiation. Negotiations need not, for instance, collapse for lack of immediate agreement on all issues being discussed. Success at negotiations often involves the ability of participants to identify areas of mutual agreement and to isolate points of disagreement for future talks. The Egyptian-Israeli negotiations are an example of the importance of a gradualist approach, as opposed to the maximalist approach inherent in the concept of an immediate comprehensive settlement. The Egyptian and Israeli negotiators were able to deal with less complicated problems and defer the more controversial ones to future negotiations.

The concept of an immediate comprehensive settlement makes the solution of the less complicated problems dependent on the resolution of the more intractable ones. It radicalizes the negotiations by introducing all the elements of the conflict into the same forum, and it complicates negotiations by adding inter-Arab and inter-power conflicts which are not even tangentially relevant to the Arab-Israeli conflict.

Fourth, Africa should not make the attainment of peace in the Middle East a precondition for resumption of ties with Israel. Such a strategy seriously compromises Africa's sovereignty by making its policy a hostage to factors over which it has no control. The Africans have at the moment no leverage on any of the parties to the Middle East conflict, having compromised their neutrality by their automatic alignment, at all times on all issues, with one party to the conflict. In effect, what their policy has attained for them is "the gift of a collection of contentious and quarrelsome"[3] Arab states.

The critical problem in the Middle East is that there is no unanimity as to what sort of peace there should be, nor is there any consensus among Arab states, or within the PLO, on how to carry out the peace process. Every peace initiative or formula by one Arab state or a group of Arab states, or by a faction of the PLO (note the PLO-Jordanian initiative), is ruthlessly denounced by other Arab states or other PLO factions. Even following the Shultz initiative of spring 1988, the Arab world—including the PLO—as well as Israel appear so hopelessly divided that any expectations of an overall peace settlement in the region in the immediate future still seem overoptimistic. Egyptian Foreign Minister Boutros Ghali has fully recognized this fundamental fact. In an interview with Bahrain's *Akhabe Al-Haly* in August 1984, Ghali said that the prerequisite for the solution of the Palestinian problem was the settlement of regional inter-Arab conflicts.[4] The editor of the Saudi daily *Al-Ukhaz*, Muhamad Lari, asserted in July 1980 that the Arab League should be redubbed "Arab Revolt and Rebelliousness."[5]

It is still, even today, plausible to argue that most Arab leaders do not accord the resolution of the conflict any priority. Indeed, each leader seems to view its solution as a means for promoting his own standing. All of them, for example, call for the establishment of a Palestinian state, but Egypt seeks a link with Jordan (for fear of Syria taking over the "state"). Jordan prefers self-determination for the West Bank Palestinians (since that will ensure the return of the Hashemites to the region) while Syria too demands an independent state (but one, like Lebanon, under Syrian patronage).[6] It may even be possible that the very existence of the Arab-Israeli conflict prevents the eruption of other, even more dangerous, inter-Arab conflicts, since Israel constitutes a target for a certain portion of Arab radicalism which would otherwise be directed toward traditional inter-Arab targets. As such, it cannot be taken for granted that all the actors in the Middle East imbroglio desire an immediate and complete resolution of the conflict. It is no wonder then that Yassir Arafat, in assessing the true support of Arab states for the PLO, said in August 1982 that "the snow of Mount Hermon was warmer than the hearts of some of the Arab regimes."[7] Whatever form of "peace" is eventually established will have to be negotiated. And that process is not going to be an easy or short one. The need for Africa to grapple with this Middle East reality therefore becomes compelling.

Fifth, the present situation in which Arab states hold a veto over Africa's choice of friends not only reinforces the current asymmetrical relationship between the two but is also patently absurd. The overwhelming proportion of Arab investment and other financial flows since 1973 has been in the United States and Western European states. The black African share of Arab "aid" (investment) in the first decade of Africa's break with Israel in support of the Arab cause was less than six percent of the total Arab aid (about 7.8 percent of commitments of external financial assistance received by Africa during the same period).[8]

Yet the Arabs demand diplomatic isolation of Israel from black Africa as a condition for friendly ties with Arab states. No such preconditions are demanded of the Europeans or the Americans. The United States, Western Europe, and Japan maintain very fruitful relations with both Israel and the Arab states. In fact, the United States is the single most important ally, both economically and strategically, of both Israel and most of the key moderate Arab states. Leaders of Israel and the Arab states compete with each other to gain access to power elites in Washington, Paris, Rome, Bonn, and Bucharest. Even if only for reasons of self-pride, Africans need to change the humiliating unequal relationship between themselves and the Arab world.

Sixth, African opposition to the Israeli-South African ties is legitimate. However, by equating the problems in Southern Africa with those of the Middle East, the Africans have allowed their vital interest in the liberation of Namibia and the elimination of apartheid in South Africa to become a mere appendage of the Arab struggle. The insistence of the Arabs in 1975, despite black African objections, to inject the issue of Zionism into the UN-planned Decade of Action against racial discrimination (in Southern Africa) is proof of Arab insensitivity to African concerns.

Africa's break with Israel has worked against its interests in Southern Africa. The phenomenal growth of Israeli-South African ties in the 1970s was occasioned by Africa's isolation of Israel. Thomas Land sums it up:

> In theory, Black Africa was to enlist the support of the Arab World in unseating the white-minority administration of South Africa in exchange for the diplomatic isolation of Israel. In practice, South Africa gained by the process by strengthening its ties with an increasingly friendless Israel, while it went on trading with the Arabs as well as the rest of the world.[9]

There is no reason to doubt that with proper persuasion, Israel can be induced to scale down its South African connections and to end altogether the military component of that relationship, which is most offensive and damaging to African interests in the region. The increasing opposition to the Israeli-South African ties in Israel itself, even within the establishment, suggests that such a change of Israeli policy is possible. Africa will nonetheless recognize that because of the large Jewish community in South Africa and the sentimental attachment of Jews all over the world to the State of Israel, a call for a termination of all Israeli-South African links is unrealistic.

And, finally, Africa needs to weigh carefully the possibility of access to Israel's know-how in the field of arid zone agriculture at a time when the continent is afflicted with acute problems of famine and drought. This access is currently being hampered by the absence of formal ties. The universal recognition of Israel's expertise in this field is evidenced in the UN secretary-general's invitation to Israel to participate in a "conference on drought and starvation in Africa" held in Geneva in March 1985. Even if the Arabs were willing to assist, they lack the necessary skills. The Israeli offer to assist drought-stricken African countries[10] should be taken up. African leaders owe it to the helpless apolitical millions of their citizens to end the scourge of famine.

The future of Afro-Israeli relations is very difficult to predict, partly because of the fluidity and the ambivalence that pervade the current state of relations. Moreover, as Chapter 7 demonstrated, the Arab-Israeli conflict has become an internal political issue in many African states. Nigeria was not the only black African country in which the conflict became a contentious electoral issue; President Obote of Uganda also used it during the 1980 election campaign to influence Ugandan Muslims against voting for his opponents, who were favorably disposed toward a renewal of ties with Israel.[11] Thus, the state of political relations between Israel and some African states will depend more on how internal political games are played out than on the resolution (or non-resolution) of the Arab-Israeli conflict.

However, although Israel has been only too glad to renew relations with any African state, it is doubtful if it would go all-out to seek Africa's diplomatic relations as it did in the early 1960s. This may be due in part to economic limitations. Establishment or renewal of diplomatic relations between African states and Israel in the past often raised African expectations of substantial financial commitment by Israel for economic, technical, and even military assistance. Even when (and if) financial assistance was not a consideration for forming diplomatic ties, many states would probably still expect some form of quid pro quo that would, nevertheless, involve substantial financial outlay by Israel. And there is some question whether Israel would be able, or willing, to provide such assistance in view of its own economic situation—which, though improved, is still troubled. As a result, Israel is likely to be more active in soliciting diplomatic relations with a few select African states (as it has lately done successfully with Cameroun, Côte d'Ivoire, Liberia, Togo, and Zaire). In addition, it would probably be content with an improvement of political ties with the others, even if formal diplomatic ties are not immediately renewed.

It is also improbable that there would be a coordinated mass restoration of diplomatic relations by black African states as there was a mass severance of ties. Considerations of continental unity, which were partly responsible for Africa's break with Israel, would play no part in the restoration of such ties. Rather, pragmatic considerations of individual African states are likely to be the determining factor. It seems unlikely that some of the black African members of the Islamic Conference who receive the bulk of Arab aid would reestablish formal relations in the short run, assuming that to do so would deprive them of even the reduced level of Arab aid. And in any case, the growing importance of "Islamic solidarity" as distinct from "Afro-Arab solidarity" will continue to make many of the Islamic African states wary of reestablishing ties with Israel without a significant accommodation between Israel and most of its neighbors. Nevertheless, separate states' assessments of their own economic needs, security problems, and external alliances are likely to play a key role in Africa's relations with Israel in the near future.

NOTES

1. Naomi Chazan, "Israel and Africa in the 1980s: The Dilemmas of Complexity and Ambiguity," paper presented at the International Conference on Africa and the Great Powers, University of Ife, June 1983, p. 36.

2. Ethan A. Nadelman, "Israel and Black Africa: A Rapprochement?" *Journal of Modern African Studies,* vol. 19, no. 2 (1981), p. 212.

3. Opoku Agyeman, "Pan-Africanism Versus Pan-Arabism: A Dual-Asymmetrical Model of Political Relations," *Middle East Review,* vol. 16, no. 4 (Summer 1984).

4. *Akhaba Al-Haly,* 5 August 1984.

5. *Al-Ukhaz,* 27 July 1980, cited in *Contemporary Mideast Backgrounder,* no. 61, 8 October (1980), p. 3.

6. See ibid., p. 5.

7. *Newsday,* 31 August 1982, cited in *Contemporary Mideast Backgrounder,* no. 159, 8 May 1985.

8. Robert Anton Mertz and Pamela MacDonald Mertz, *Arab Aid to Sub-Saharan Africa* (Munchen: Kaiser, 1983), pp. 27, 48.

9. Thomas Land, "Black Africa Poised to Restore Relations with Israel," *New Outlook,* vol. 23, no. 2 (March 1980), p. 10.

10. *Jerusalem Post,* 11 March 1985.

11. Discussions with a Ugandan diplomat in New York, September 1982.

Index

Action Group (AG), 140, 144
Adjibade, Tiamiou, 67
African Development Bank, 60
African Heads of Missions meeting
  (1973), 48
African Intelligence Digest, 131
African National Congress (ANC),
  131, 132
African states
  and Arab states, 3, 15, 35–36,
    42–46, 50, 60–61, 92, 165, 167,
    168. *See also* Arab states
  and Camp David Accords, 86–91
  Christians in, 14
  and construction contracts, 103–
    104
  electronic imports of, 76–77(table)
  exports/imports of, 22–24, 36,
    37(table), 75, 79(table), 103,
    104(table)
  food crisis in, 91
  Middle East policies of, 164–170
  Muslims in, 15, 61, 156, 158
  and oil prices, 60
  press in, 87
  radicalization of, 45
  and severance of diplomatic ties
    with Israel, 3, 33, 35(table), 41,
    49, 50, 55–56, 164–165
  and socialism, 13
  and South Africa, 38, 168
  and superpowers, 92
  and United Nations, 26–27, 63,
    64(table), 70–71(tables)
  unity of, 48, 92, 170. *See also*
    Organization of African Unity
  and U.S. aid, 3
  and Zaire-Israeli relations, 96–97
  See also Afro-Israeli relations;
    individual states
Afrique Nouvelle, 66
Afro-Asian Conference, 8
Afro-Asian Institute, 78, 152
Afro-Israeli relations, 14
  and Arab aid, 3–4
  and capital assistance, 19–20,
    22(table), 169
  cooperation agreements, 19(table)
  and diplomatic representation, 16,
    17(table)
  and electronic equipment, 75, 76–
    77(table)
  and famine and drought, 168–169
  future of, 169–170
  and Israeli aid workers, 13–14
  and Israeli-Egyptian peace treaty,
    85
  and Israeli institutions, 12, 18
  and Israeli-South African
    relations, 4–5, 46, 67–68, 168.
    See also Israeli-South African
    relations
  and military assistance, 20–22, 73,
    74–75, 102

and Palestinian question, 3, 55–56
and Red Sea, 8
and severance of diplomatic ties, 3, 33, 35(table), 41, 49, 50, 55–56, 164–165
and state visits, 16, 18, 39, 98–99
and technical assistance, 10, 18, 20–21(tables), 34–35, 57, 75, 163
and trade, 9, 22–24, 23(table), 36, 37(table), 78, 79(table), 103
and United States, 3
See also African states; Israel; Israeli-Nigerian relations
AG. *See* Action Group
Agbro, 136(n54)
Agridev, 133
Ahdijo, President (Cameroun), 39, 41
Air Liberia, 101
Ajulu-Schuku, M.C.K., 157
Albania, 26
Alda, 79
Algeria, 44, 47, 62, 146
All-African Peoples Conference, 10
Allon, Yigal, 72
Al Madina, 95
Alves, Dos Santos, 88
Amcor, 103
American-Israel Public Affairs Committee, 94
American Jewish Committee, 91, 94
American Jewish Congress, 94
Amin, Idi, 36, 42, 52(n23), 62, 66–67
Amit, Meir, 125, 129
ANC. *See* African National Congress
Anderson, Jack, 132
Andu, Ishaya, 154
Angola, 88, 89, 115, 128, 129, 131
Anti-Defamation League, 94
Anya Nya rebellion, 47

Apartheid, 26, 65, 113–115, 120–121, 168
Aqaba, Gulf of, 8
Arab Bank for African Development (BADEA), 60, 95, 97
Arab League, 60, 61, 86, 95, 96–97, 109(n91), 165
Arab states
and Africa, 3, 15, 35–36, 42–46, 50, 60–61, 92, 165, 167, 168
boycott policy of, 9
and Camp David Accords, 86
and concessionary oil prices, 60
conflicts within, 166–167
and Egypt, 86
and OAU, 43. *See also* Organization of African Unity
oil embargo of, 50, 121
and Nigeria, 97, 143, 146–147, 155, 156
and 1967 war, 43–44. *See also* 1967 war
and PLO, 58, 166
slave trade of, 9
and South Africa, 46, 49, 62
and United Nations, 63
unity of, 43–44
visits to Africa, 44–45
and Zaire, 95–96
See also Organization of Petroleum Exporting Countries
Arafat, Yasser, 63, 167
Arava aircraft, 131
Arens, Moshe, 93
Aridor, Yoram, 126, 131, 133
Armscor, 120
Asamoah, Obed, 97
Association of South African Travel Agents, 128
Avriel, Ehud, 72
Ayari, Cheddi, 97
Aynor, Hanan, 72

Babatone, Ebenezer, 156

Bab el Mandeb straits, 74
BADEA. *See* Arab Bank for African Development
Balewa, Alhaji Tafawa, 140
Balton, 79
Banqui, Slyvan, 100
Bar-Lev, Baruch, 52(n23)
Barromi, Joel, 121
Bat-Dor Dance Company, 105, 128
Batsheva dance troupe, 128
Begin, Menachem, 74, 75, 118, 124
Belgrade Non-Aligned Conference, 24
Bello, Alhaji Ahmadu, 140
Ben-Gurion, David, 114, 115, 116, 118
Benin, 89
Ben-Zvi, Itzhak, 16
Biafra, 47, 144
Biko, Steve, 150
Blum, Leon, 14
Bongo, Omar, 62
Bophuthatswana, 132–133
Botha, Pieter Willem, 122, 124, 125
Botsio, Kojo, 14
Botswana, 45
Boumedienne, Houari, 46, 146
Broederbond, 111
Burundi, 41
Bush, George, 93

Cameroun, 3, 34, 77(table), 79, 89, 91, 169
Camp David Accords, 3, 85–91, 152
Canada, 132
CAR. *See* Central African Republic
Carter, Jimmy, 73
Casablanca Conference, 24, 25
Central African Republic (CAR), 13, 72, 75, 87, 100, 105
Centurion tanks, 130
Cervenka, Zdenek, 132
Chad, 15, 40, 42, 45, 92, 146
Chemavir-Nasok, 131
Christoffel Blindenmission, 105

Ciskei, 132–133, 134
Coker, G.B.A., 142
Comay, Michael, 113
Congo, 34, 37(table 3.3), 40, 46, 89
Cooper, Shimon, 115
Côte d'Ivoire, 3, 4, 6(n2), 24, 25, 34, 40, 50, 58, 169
    and Camp David Accords, 86–87
    exports/imports of, 37(table 3.3), 76(table), 105
Crocker, Chester A., 93
Cuba, 26

Dacko, David, 13, 14, 94
Daddah, Ould, 43
Dahomey, 25, 49
Daily Express, 151
Daily Nation, 97
Daily Star, 66
Daily Telegraph, 122
Dayan, Moshe, 72, 75, 129, 130–131
Decade for Action to Combat Racism and Racial Discrimination, 65–67, 168
Decalo, Samuel, 8
Degem Systems, 133
Die Burger, 117–118
Dikko, Alhaj Umaru, 158, 161(n63)
Diori, President (Niger), 45
Dipcharima, Zanna Bukar, 140
Doe, Samuel, 100
Doron, Aharon, 120
Drought, 3, 169

East Africa, 24
East Germany, 45
Eban, Abba, 48, 113, 145
ECA. *See* United Nations, Economic Commission for Africa
Economist, The, 130
EEC. *See* European Economic Community
Egar, Akiva, 78
Egypt, 3, 72, 85
    alliances of, 44

and Arab League, 86
diplomatic network of, 43
and Israel, 154. *See also* Camp
   David Accords
and Nigeria, 146–147
and October 1973 war, 49
and Palestinian state, 167
Egyptian Israeli peace treaty, 2, 3
Ehrlich, Simcha, 126
Ekangaki, Nzo, 62
El Al, 99, 100–101
Elbit, 131
Eliav, Arieh, 72
Enahoro, Anthony, 147
Entebbe, 72–73
Entente Council, 49
Eritreans, 43, 74, 146
Eshkol, Levi, 16, 114
Ethiopia, 10, 21, 34, 45, 50, 79,
   149
   and Arab states, 43
   Dergue in, 73
   exports/imports of, 37(table 3.3),
      76(table)
   and Israel, 73–74
   Jews in, 7, 46
   and Somalia, 146
European Common Market, 8
European Economic Community
   (EEC), 127
Eyadema, Etienne, 42, 101

Fahrbulleh, Boima, 100
Famine, 3, 168–169
FAO. *See* Food and Agriculture
   Organization
Feisal, King, 44–45
Fincham, Charles, 124
First Conference of Independent
   African States, 24
First Nigerian Trade Fair, 143
Food and Agriculture Organization
   (FAO), 18
Ford, Gerald, 124
Foreign Report, 74

Framework of Peace in the Middle
   East, 85–86
France, 14, 42, 48, 69, 93, 101,
   132, 146
Free State Choir, 128
FRELIMO. *See* Front for the
   Liberation of Mozambique
Friends of South Africa Society, 118
Frolinat rebels, 42–43
Front for the Liberation of
   Mozambique (FRELIMO), 115

Gabon, 24, 37(table 3.3), 48, 62,
   77(table)
Gabriel missiles, 129, 130
Gaddafi, Muammar, 41, 43, 44, 45,
   148
Gadna, 12, 13, 34
Gafny, Arnon, 125
Gambari, Ibrahim, 157–158
Gambia, 86
Generalized Preference System, 127
Ghali, Boutros, 90, 166–167
Ghana, 10, 21, 25, 37(table 3.3), 39,
   58, 60, 77(table), 79, 91, 94
Ghanian Times, 68
GNPP. *See* Great Nigeria Peoples
   Party
Golan, Joseph, 120
Golan, Tamar, 58
Golan Heights, 94, 107(n34), 156
Gom, Alfred, 153–154
Gowan, Yakubu, 39, 47, 49, 50,
   144, 145, 146, 148–149
Great Britain, 69, 132, 141, 161
Great Nigeria Peoples Party
   (GNPP), 156
Guinea, 25, 77(table), 101–102
Gumi, Alhaji Abubakar, 149
Gur Construction Company, 133

Ha'aretz, 9, 56, 131, 132
Hadassah-Hebrew University
   Medical School, 18
Hadera power plant, 126

Haig, Alexander, 93
Hapoel Games, 105
Harriman, Leslie O., 68
Hashemites, 167
Hassan, King, 43
Hatsofe, 56
Hausa/Falani tribes, 140, 145
Heftziba Company, 101
Herzl, Theodor, 27(n)
Herzliya flying school, 134
Herzog, Chaim, 99, 118, 120, 129
Histadrut, 91
Hod, Mordechai, 120
Holland, 105
Horwood, Owen, 126
Houphouët-Boigny, Felix, 11–12, 14, 49, 72, 99, 101

Ibos, 140, 145
ILO. *See* International Labor Organization
IMF. *See* International Monetary Fund
India, 114
Indian Ocean, 8
Inter-Faith Committee, 152
International Herald Tribune, 74
International Labor Organization (ILO), 18, 102
Internationai Monetary Fund (IMF), 156
International Telecommunications Union, 98
International Union of Local Authorities, 98
International Union of Socialist Youth, 13
Inter-Parliamentary Union (IPU), 95, 102, 155
IPU. *See* Inter-Parliamentary Union
Iran, 123
Iraq, 43
Iron and Steel Corporation (ISCOR), 127

ISCOR. *See* Iron and Steel Corporation
ISKOOR, 127–128
Islam, 15, 45. *See also* Arab states
Islamic Conference, 86, 170
Israel
  African visits of, 16, 18
  African visits to, 10, 16, 18
  aid projects of, 2, 11
  and apartheid, 26, 68–69 114–115, 120–121
  and arid zone agriculture, 168–169
  and Biafra, 145, 146
  construction companies of, 103–104
  creation of, 7
  diamond-cutting industry in, 119
  diplomatic initiatives of, 10
  Division of International Cooperation, 105
  electronic exports of, 76–77(table), 131
  and Ethiopia, 73–74, 103
  and Ethiopian Jews, 46, 103
  exports/imports of, 2, 22–24, 36, 37(tables), 75, 78, 79(table), 103, 104(table), 116–117, 119, 119(table), 127(table)
  and France, 48
  and Ibos, 145
  immigration policies of, 46
  inflation in, 123
  and Kenya, 72–73
  Labor Party in, 123
  and Lebanon, 97, 107(n34), 156
  Likud government in, 124–125, 134
  military assistance of, 12, 20–22, 73, 74–75, 102–103
  and OAU liberation funds, 46, 121
  and occupied territories, 36, 38
  and Sinai, 8, 95, 123
  South African lobby in, 115–116

technical assistance of, 10, 18,
    20–21(tables), 34–35, 57, 105
and Third World, 7, 8, 11,
    20(table), 93
tourists in, 78
trading companies in, 79
trading partners of, 103
as underdog, 33
and United Nations, 27, 66, 114–
    115, 116, 150
and United States, 93, 124, 167–
    168
and Zaire, 98–99, 105
See also Afro-Israeli relations;
    Israeli-Nigerian relations;
    Israeli-South African relations
Israel Discount Bank, 133
Israel-Ghana Association, 91
Israeli-Egyptian Peace Treaty, 85–91
Israeli Investment Authority, 125
Israeli-Nigerian relations
    and Camp David Accords, 154
    and construction projects, 141–
        142
    and Golda Meir visit, 143
    and Israeli loans, 143
    and Israeli-South African
        relations, 151, 154. *See also*
        Israeli-South African relations
    and Israeli Tunis raid, 158
    and joint companies, 141
    and Nigerian Civil War, 144, 145,
        147
    and Nigeria's leadership role, 148
    non-formal, 151–152, 157
    and October 1973 war, 148–149
    and paramilitary equipment, 157
    and reestablishment of ties, 154–
        155, 158
    and severance of ties, 149
    and technical assistance, 143, 147
    and trade, 152, 153(table)
    See also Israel; Nigeria
Israeli-South African relations, 46,
    67–69, 163–164

and apartheid, 114–115, 120–121
and arms trade, 120, 129–131
and coal, 123, 125
community of interests, 117–118,
    124
and cultural exchanges, 128
economic relations, 125–128
and exports/imports, 116–117,
    119, 119(table), 127(table)
and homelands, 132–134
and Israeli-Nigerian relations, 151
and military cooperation, 120,
    128–132
and 1967 war, 117–118
and nuclear development, 132
and October 1973 war, 121–122
and oil prices, 123
and tourism, 128
and trade, 126–128, 127(table)
and UN sanctions, 131
See also Israel; South Africa
Israeli-South Africa Trade
    Association, 119
Israel Philharmonic Orchestra, 128
Israel-South Africa Friendship
    Society, 124
ISRATEC '78, 126

Japan, 167
Jawara, Dauda, 86
Jerusalem, 16, 59, 156
Jerusalem Post, 56, 90, 104, 133
Jerusalem Song and Dance
    Ensemble, 128
Jewish Affairs, 118
Johannesburg Youth Ballet, 128
Jordan, 44, 167

Kaunda, Kenneth, 97
Keita, Modibo, 14
Kenya, 12, 19, 21, 37(table 3.3), 50,
    58, 61–62, 72–73, 76(table), 97,
    103, 105, 109(n91)
Kenyatta, Jomo, 12, 50
Kfir jets, 130

Kiano, J. G., 12
Kibbutz, 12, 13
Kimche, David, 92, 94, 95, 105
ki-Zerbo, Joseph, 101
Klibi, Chedli, 95
Koor, 79, 103, 127, 136(n54)
Koortrade, 157
Koran, 15, 149
Kuwait, 42, 102, 156

Land, Thomas, 168
Landau, David, 56–57
Lari, Muhamad, 167
Latin America, 93
Laufer, Leopold, 8
Lebanese War, 97–98, 156, 157
Lesotho, 34, 36, 49, 75, 87
Liberia, 3, 7, 10, 34, 45, 60, 87,
    100–101, 169
Libya, 42, 43, 44, 50, 100
Los Angeles Times, 74
Lurie, Arthur, 113

Ma'ariv, 133
Machel, Samora, 89
Madagascar, 25, 34, 45, 88, 89
Malan, Daniel Francois, 111, 115
Malawi, 19, 36, 49, 59, 75,
    77(table)
Mali, 41
Mariam, Mengistu Haile, 74
Mauritius, 49
Mazrui, Ali, 46, 50
Meir, Golda, 10, 11, 16, 114, 116,
    143
Memorandum of Understanding, 93,
    107(n34)
Mirage fighters, 120, 122
Mitterrand, François-Maurice, 93
Mobutu, Sese Seko, 39, 44, 94, 95–
    96, 99
Moda'i, Yitzhak, 126
Morocco, 96
Mossad, 73, 100, 103
Motorola, 103

Mount Carmel Center, 152
Moynihan, Daniel, 66–67
Mozambique, 89, 101
Mozambique National Airlines, 101

Nahal, 12, 34
Namibia, 115, 168
Nasser, Abdel, 14, 25, 43–44
National Council for Nigeria and
    the Camerouns (NCNC), 140,
    141, 144
National Party of Nigeria (NPN),
    153
NCNC. *See* National Council for
    Nigeria and the Camerouns
N'Diaya, Jean Pierre, 63
New Nigerian, 145, 149, 151, 157
New York Times, 120
Niger, 25, 41, 44–45, 97
Nigeria, 4, 16, 21, 47
    and Arab aid, 97, 156
    and Arab boycotts, 143
    and Arab diplomats, 15
    and Camp David Accords, 89
    civil war in, 47–48, 144–146
    coalition politics in, 153, 156
    coups in, 144, 150
    and Egypt, 146–147, 154–155
    exports/imports of, 37(table 3.3),
        76(table), 146–147, 153(table)
    Israeli companies in, 142–143
    and Israeli military assistance,
        102–103
    and Lebanese war, 157
    Muslims in, 156, 158
    National Development Plan, 141,
        143
    National Security Organization,
        103
    NPC in, 140, 141, 144
    and OAU, 148, 149
    and October 1973 war, 49, 148–
        149
    oil production in, 156
    and OPEC, 147, 152, 155–156

and PLO, 150, 157, 158
political crisis in, 142
political parties in, 153, 156
Radio-Television Kaduna, 62
religious diversity in, 140–141,
 158
and Solel Boneh, 104
southern press in, 143
tribes in, 140
and United Nations, 143–144,
 147, 148, 150, 157
UPGA in, 144
and Zionism-racism vote, 67
See also Israeli-Nigerian relations
Nigerian Construction Company,
 139, 141
Nigerian Federal Constitution, 139
Nigerian Peoples Party (NPP), 153,
 156
Nigerian Tribune, 142, 149
Nigerian Water Resources
 Development Company, 139,
 141, 142
Nigersol, 142
1973 war. *See* October 1973 war
1967 war, 25, 26, 33, 46, 48, 117–
 118
Njonjo, Charles, 62
Nkrumah, Kwame, 14, 25, 26
Non-aligned summit (1973), 41–42,
 148
Northern Peoples Congress (NPC),
 140, 141, 144
NPC. *See* Northern Peoples
 Congress
NPN. *See* National Party of Nigeria
NPP. *See* Nigerian Peoples Party
Nuclear Axis, The (Cervenka and
 Rogers), 132
Nyerere, Julius, 42, 68

OAU. *See* Organization of African
 Unity
Obote, Milton, 38, 42, 169

October 1973 war, 49, 121–122,
 148–149
Ogaden, 74, 146
OPEC. *See* Organization of
 Petroleum Exporting Countries
Ophthalmological Center, 13
Organization of African Unity
 (OAU), 2, 3, 25–26, 36, 150
and African unity, 48, 92
Arab states in, 43, 62
and Camp David Accords, 89
emergency session (1973), 55
and Golan Heights, 94
and Israeli aid, 46, 121
and Jarring Peace Mission, 39–40
and Lebanese invasion, 97
Middle East Mission, 47
and Nigerian Civil War, 146
and PLO, 59
and severance of diplomatic ties,
 55–56
and South Africa, 62, 68
summits of, 40, 48, 59, 63, 98,
 148
Organization of Islamic States, 158,
 161(n65)
Organization of Petroleum
 Exporting Countries (OPEC),
 61, 97, 147, 152, 155–156
Osago, James, 62

Padmore, George, 14
Palestine Liberation Organization
 (PLO), 42, 58, 59, 166
Palestinians, 3, 55–56, 88, 97, 167
Palindaba facility, 132
Peoples Redemption Party (PRP),
 156
Peres, Shimon, 72, 118, 125
PFLP. *See* Popular Front for the
 Liberation of Palestine
Pincus, Arye, 113
PLO. *See* Palestine Liberation
 Organization

Popular Front for the Liberation of Palestine (PFLP), 72
Portugal, 50
PRP. *See* Peoples Redemption Party

Rabin, Yitzhak, 72, 123–124
Racism, 65, 96
Rancy, John G., 100
Rand Daily Mail, 131
Raphael, Gideon, 72
Raviv, Ephraim, 127
Rawlings, Jerry, 94
Reagan, Ronald, 93
Red Sea, 8, 74
Reshef patrol boats, 130
Rhodesia, 128
Rhodesian Herald, 117
Rogers, Barbara, 132
Rogers, R.H.D., 129
Rosenne, Shabtai, 112
Rotoflight Helicopters, 131
Rubin, Leslie, 114
Rwanda, 35, 77(table)

Sabra and Shatila, 97, 156
Sadat, Anwar, 43, 45, 46, 89, 90–91, 152
Sankara, Thomas, 101
Saudi Arabia, 42, 44, 50, 155, 156
Schaar, Stuart, 14
Scorpion helicopter, 131
Scott, Jerkins, 101
Sebe, Lennox, 133
Second International Socialist Conference, 8
Selassie, Haile, 43, 73
Senegal, 44, 60, 77(table), 89
Senghor, Leopold, 14, 28(n11), 38, 39, 40, 50, 58, 72
Settlement Studies Center, 152
Shagari, President (Nigeria), 4, 153, 154, 156, 157
Shamir, Yitzhak, 92, 94, 98, 99, 102
Sharett, Moshe, 10, 11, 114

Sharon, Ariel, 92, 93, 94, 98, 99, 131
Shikuku, Martin, 62
Shimoni, Yaacov, 57, 58
Shlomo, Hillel, 99
Sierra Leone, 22, 60, 97
Sixth World Islamic Conference, 15
Smuts, Jan Christian, 111
Socialism, 13, 114
Solel Boneh, 36, 103–104, 151, 157
Somalia, 25, 73
South Africa, 4, 38, 46
   air force of, 130
   apartheid in, 26, 113–115, 120–121, 168
   and Arab states, 46, 49, 62
   Board of Deputies, 113, 114, 118
   exports/imports of, 119, 119(table)
   Israelis in, 113
   Jews in, 111, 112, 116, 117, 122, 168
   and Mozambique, 101
   and Namibia, 115
   Nationalist Party in, 111, 112–113
   nuclear development of, 132
   and OAU, 59
   and racism, 65
   and Suez Canal, 47
   and United States, 69, 132
   See also Israeli-South African relations
South African Foundation, 118
South African Railways, 125
South African Tourist Corporation, 128
South African Zionist Movement, 113
South Yemen, 43
Soviet Union, 26, 45
Soweto, 128, 150
Sudan, 42, 47, 146
Suez Canal, 39, 46–47
Sule, Alhaj Yusuf Maitama, 157
Sunday Nation, 61

Sunday Telegraph, 117
Sunday Times, 126
Sunday Triumph, 157
Swaziland, 36, 49, 59, 75
Swedish International Development
    Agency, 105
Syria, 43, 44, 102, 167

Tadiran, 75, 103, 131
Tahal, 151
Taiwan, 132
Tantur Institute of Advanced
    Ecumenical Studies, 78, 152
Tanzania, 21, 34, 35, 37(table 3.3),
    77(table)
Tekoah, Yosef, 121
Telli, Diallo, 36
Tettegah, John, 13
Teva Pharmaceuticals, 103
Third World, 7, 8, 11, 20(table), 48,
    93
Thompson, Adewale, 152
Times of Zambia, 62–63, 87
Tiran, Straits of, 7, 39
Togo, 3, 25, 34, 41–42, 49, 169
Tolbert, William, 89, 91
Tombalbaye, President (Chad), 15,
    42
Toure, Sekou, 99
Transkei, 132
Transvaal Coal Owners' Association,
    126
Traore, Drara, 101
Tubman, William, 7
Tunisia, 41

Uganda, 21, 22, 34, 37(table 3.3),
    40, 42, 73, 97, 169
UN. See United Nations
UNDP. See United Nations
    Development Program
UNESCO. See United Nations
    Educational, Scientific, and
    Cultural Organization

Union for the Total Liberation of
    Angola (UNITA), 131
UNITA. See Union for the Total
    Liberation of Angola
United Nations
    Anti-Apartheid Committee, 68,
        117
    Charter, 16
    Decolonization Committee, 102
    Economic Commission for Africa
        (ECA), 27
    General Assembly sessions, 41, 59,
        63, 64(table), 69, 70–71(tables)
    Jarring Peace Mission, 39
    and Lebanese invasion, 98
    and 1967 war, 26–27
    resolutions, 26, 36, 39, 59, 85,
        89
    sanctions against Israel, 116
    sanctions against South Africa,
        130–131
    Zionism-racism vote, 67, 124, 150,
        168
United Nations Development
    Program (UNDP), 18
United Nations Educational,
    Scientific, and Cultural
    Organization (UNESCO), 18,
    59
United Progressive Grand Alliance
    (UPGA), 144
United States
    Agency for International
        Development, 105
    aid to Israel, 124
    and Arab states, 167–168
    and Ethiopia, 73
    House Foreign Affairs Committee,
        95
    and Israel, 93, 124, 167–168
    -Israel Cooperative Development
        Research Program, 105
    and Israeli assistance programs,
        105
    Jews in, 3, 91, 98

and October 1973 war, 50
and South Africa, 69, 132
and Zaire, 95
Unity Party of Nigeria (UPN), 153,
  156, 157
University of Ife, 142
Unna, Yitzhak, 122
UPGA. *See* United Progressive
  Grand Alliance
UPN. *See* Unity Party of Nigeria
Upper Volta, 20, 25, 49, 97–98,
  101
Uzi submachine gun, 120

Vered, 36
Viljoen, Coustard, 131–132
Vorster, John, 68, 111, 124, 125,
  129–130

Warnke, Jurgen, 105
Washington Post, 132
Weiler, M. C., 113
Weinstein, Julius, 122
Weizmann, Chaim, 111
West Africa, 40

Western Sahara, 146
West Germany, 69, 105, 132
WHO. *See* World Health
  Organization
World Health Organization (WHO),
  18, 27
World Jewish Congress, 99

Yaacov, Ben, 145
Yakhil, Haim, 116
Yamani, Sheikh, 155
Yameogo, Maurice, 9, 115
Yoruba, 140
Young, Andrew, 9
Youtar, Perce, 115
Yugoslavia, 26
Yusuf, Tanko, 152

Zaire, 3, 4, 24, 34, 37(table 3.3),
  41, 91, 95–96, 98, 105, 169
Zaire Trade Union, 91
Zambia, 34, 50, 60, 77(table), 97
Zanzibar, 9
Zimbabwe, 59
Zionism, 14, 15, 41, 65, 67, 90,
  102, 112